FITTING IN, STANDING OUT

In American high schools, teenagers must navigate complex youth cultures that often prize being "real" while punishing difference. Adults may view such social turbulence as a timeless, ultimately harmless rite of passage, but changes in American society are intensifying this rite and allowing its effects to cascade into adulthood. Integrating national statistics with interviews and observations from a single school, this book explores this phenomenon. It makes the case that recent macrolevel trends, such as economic restructuring and technological change, mean that the social dynamics of high school can disrupt educational trajectories after high school; it looks at teenagers who do not fit in socially at school – including many who are obese or gay – to illustrate this phenomenon; and it crafts recommendations for parents, teachers, and policy makers about how to protect teenagers in trouble. The end result is a story of adolescence that hits home with anyone who remembers high school.

Robert Crosnoe is a professor in the Department of Sociology and (by courtesy) the Department of Psychology as well as a faculty research associate at the Population Research Center at the University of Texas at Austin. His research focuses on the ways in which the educational pathways of children and adolescents are connected to their general health, development, and personal relationships and how these connections can be leveraged to explain demographic inequalities in educational and socioeconomic attainment. This research has been funded by the National Institute of Child Health and Human Development and by young scholar awards from the William T. Grant Foundation and the Foundation for Child Development. Dr. Crosnoe has published more than 70 books and articles in journals such as *Developmental Psychology*, *Child Development*, *American Educational Research Journal*, and *American Sociological Review*. He has also won awards for early career research contributions from the Society for Research in Child Development, the Society for the Study of Human Development, and the Children and Youth Section of the American Sociological Association.

Fitting In, Standing Out

NAVIGATING THE SOCIAL CHALLENGES OF
HIGH SCHOOL TO GET AN EDUCATION

Robert Crosnoe

University of Texas at Austin

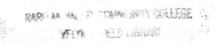

CAMBRIDGE
UNIVERSITY PRESS

CAMBRIDGE UNIVERSITY PRESS
Cambridge, New York, Melbourne, Madrid, Cape Town, Singapore,
São Paulo, Delhi, Dubai, Tokyo, Mexico City

Cambridge University Press
32 Avenue of the Americas, New York, NY 10013-2473, USA

www.cambridge.org
Information on this title: www.cambridge.org/9780521182034

First published 2011

Printed in the United States of America

A catalog record for this publication is available from the British Library.

Library of Congress Cataloging in Publication data
Crosnoe, Robert.
    Fitting in, standing out : navigating the social challenges of high
    school to get an education / Robert Crosnoe.
        p. cm.
    Includes bibliographical references and index.
    ISBN 978-1-107-00502-0 – ISBN 978-0-521-18203-4 (pbk.)
    1. High school student orientation.   2. Teenagers – Life skills
    guides.   3. Teenagers – Education.   4. Adolescence.   5. Social influence.
    6. High school students – Social life and customs – 21st century.   I. Title.
    HQ796.C87   2011
    305.2350973'090511–dc22   2010030587

ISBN 978-1-107-00502-0 Hardback
ISBN 978-0-521-18203-4 Paperback

To high school students past, present, and future,
especially Joseph and Caroline

To my teachers, especially Merrill, Sandy, and Glen

To the members of the Old High Class of 1990, especially
the one who is now my sister

CONTENTS

Acknowledgments   *page* ix

PART I   HIGH SCHOOLS AS
CONTEXTS OF DEVELOPMENT

1 Pressures on Teenagers and Their Schools   3
2 A Day in the Life   22
3 The Two Sides of High School   37
4 Updating and Expanding Our Perspective   63

PART II   A CASE STUDY OF SOCIAL AND
ACADEMIC EXPERIENCES IN HIGH SCHOOL

5 The Stakes of Social Marginalization   83
6 Teenagers at Particular Risk   114
7 How Teenagers Know What They Know
   and Why It Matters   130
8 Sources of Resilience   174

PART III   HELPING TEENAGERS
NAVIGATE HIGH SCHOOL

9 Solutions within Schools   203
10 Looking to Parents and Other Adults   230
11 In Search of Theory and Action   241

Works Cited   247
Index   265

ACKNOWLEDGMENTS

When I started this project, I did not really know what I was getting into or how long it would take. In fact, I did not even know I was starting it, as it grew out of a series of seemingly unrelated activities in which I slowly began to see a pattern that needed more focused attention. I eventually worked on the data collection and analysis and then the writing for years, facing a great number of challenges and disappointments along the way. It became the endeavor that defined the early part of my career, how I figured out just what I wanted to do, and I am glad that I kept going. Over the course of this project, I also grew up a great deal, settled into a very happy marriage, and became a father twice over. There was a lot going on, and I do not think that I could have put all of this together without a lot of support.

The work that went into this book was generously funded by grants from the National Institute of Child Health and Human Development and the William T. Grant Foundation. Practically speaking, I could not have done anything without the financial resources these grants afforded me, but all of the money in the world would not have made any difference if not for the amazing intellectual support I received at the same time. First, Chris Bachrach at NICHD helped me flesh out the ideas for my study in an early grant proposal and then allowed me to change course in the middle of the funded project when I decided that I needed to move beyond statistics and go back to high school. Second, the William T. Grant Scholars program funded the rest of the project as I saw it to the end. Being a part of this program was, without a doubt, the most important experience of my professional career and, more generally, my intellectual development. The insights and wisdom of the people at the foundation, my fellow scholars, and our advisors/ consultants are all over this book. I could not feel any more love and gratitude. Third, I wrote the bulk of this book while in residence at the Center for Advanced Study in the Behavioral Sciences, back at my old stomping grounds on the Farm at Stanford University. It was an amazing year that gave me time to think and the stimulation and camaraderie to think more deeply and richly than I would have otherwise.

Of course, the intellectual support for this book also came from my home base at the University of Texas at Austin, including my great colleagues on the 23rd floor of the Tower, as well as the mentors I have been lucky to have at the Population Research Center and the Department of Sociology. Over the last several years, I have also expanded my networks well beyond Austin, and I think that shows. Of those both near and far, I want to thank, especially, Jane Brown, Ken Frank, Aletha Huston, Tama Leventhal, Chandra Muller, Barbara Schneider, and the members of the NICHD Early Child Care Network, as well as my great team of graduate students past and present who worked with me on this project, including Jennifer March Augustine, Carey Cooper, Kurt Gore, and Belinda Needham.

Perhaps most important of all is the emotional support, of which I have a surplus in all I do thanks to wonderful parents who, no matter what, always seemed so proud of me; smart, funny, and interesting siblings who married and procreated very well; and a new set of parents, siblings, and children that proved to be among the best rewards of marriage. And, naturally, there is my son and my daughter, who remind me where my heart is all the time.

And, always, all of these different kinds of support come together every day in a single person, Shannon Cavanagh, for whom I will never be able to give thanks enough.

PART I

HIGH SCHOOLS AS CONTEXTS
OF DEVELOPMENT

1

Pressures on Teenagers and Their Schools

These are definitely not the glory days of the American educational system. Schools have been stung by a steady stream of testing data showing a large achievement gap between American students and teenagers in other countries. Demographic changes have led to the proliferation of overcrowded classrooms and increased demand for special services for many new and expanding segments of the student population. No Child Left Behind and other educational policies have ratcheted up accountability standards and imposed a series of increasingly harsh sanctions all the way up to school closing. Simultaneously, funding has been cut to the point that many school districts face major budget shortfalls. Against this backdrop, bemoaning the state of American education and, in particular, criticizing teachers have become major discussion points in electoral politics and media debates. Such challenges have placed enormous pressures on schools and fueled a sense of pessimism – some of it warranted, some of it not – in the public at large.[1]

In the face of these major financial, curricular, and organizational pressures on the educational system as a whole, the everyday pressures

[1] For more in-depth discussions of the challenges facing American education and the debates surrounding these challenges, see the landmark 1983 report *A Nation at Risk* by the National Commission on Excellence in Education, a more recent report, *Rising Above the Gathering Storm* (2007), by the National Academy of Sciences, the results of the Trends in International Mathematics and Science Study (Schmidt et al., 2001), or a 2008 edited volume by Hess.

that teenagers encounter as they navigate the social worlds of American high schools seem far less important. Indeed, in the minds of many, helping teenagers cope with the social ups and downs of high school life does not rise to the level of pressing task when compared to the larger-scale challenges of raising school performance and effectively educating a new generation for entry into the global economy. This is often true even among those who readily acknowledge how much such social experiences matter to any one teenager.

Over the last decade, I came to accept this conventional wisdom, that the problems teenagers have on the social side of high school pale in comparison to the systemic academic problems faced by high schools across the board. Early in my dual career as a social demographer and developmental psychologist, I devoted much attention to the ways in which the adjustment and functioning of American teenagers are both served and undermined by friendships, dating, and other peer dynamics in their high schools. My work was often met by criticism that it had no policy relevance. Peer dynamics, the criticism went, cannot be manipulated by policy intervention on a large scale and, therefore, do not represent a useful or practical venue for improving schools.[2] Eventually, this criticism – coupled with my sincere interest in policy solutions to educational crises – turned me away from the social experiences of teenagers in high schools. Instead, I focused on more established levers of policy action, such as coursework offerings, teacher credentials, school structure and composition, and other institutional factors that are already connected to extant policy initiatives aimed at raising school performance levels or reducing major group disparities in academic performance within and across schools.

Recently, however, spending a year in a large public high school (I call it Lamar) as part of a mixed-methods study on pathways to college made me change my mind on this issue once again. Looking

---

[2] James Coleman discussed the debate about the policy utility of social dynamics in schools in his 1990 book *Foundations of Social Theory*.

into national patterns of educational attainment and then seeing how these patterns played out in Lamar, I realized that, because social experiences in high school have such demonstrable effects on academic progress and college going, the *social* concerns of teenagers are *educational* concerns for schools in ways that cannot be so easily dismissed. Figuring out how to translate this knowledge into action is a challenge, but it is a worthwhile one.

As my time at Lamar made me reconsider what I thought I knew as a social scientist, I was reminded of a lesson that I and many other adults learned when we were teenagers, the same lesson that many teenagers are learning right now. High school can put you in your place.

THE MOTIVATION FOR THE BOOK

An Argument about Teenagers and Their High Schools

This book is concerned with the interplay of the academic and social sides of secondary education in the United States, how this interplay factors into the educational challenges and goals of today, and how it can be practically leveraged to meet those challenges and advance those goals. On the individual level, this interplay involves the intertwining of teenagers' social development with their scholastic pathways within schools. On the institutional level, it involves the feedback loop between schools' peer cultures and their curricular structures.

On both levels, this interplay between the academic and social sides of high school has been the subject of much attention from social and behavioral scientists for quite a long time. As some prominent examples, the sociologist James Coleman detailed the inversion of high school peer values relative to "conventional" adult norms, the psychiatrist Michael Rutter and his colleagues (Maughan, Mortimer, and Ouston) revealed how not taking a full accounting of the social processes of education led to an underestimation of school effectiveness, developmental psychologists such as Barber and Eccles and economists such as Akerlof and Kranton have mapped out the identity-based norms of major peer crowds within schools, and multidisciplinary teams (e.g., Steinberg, Dornbusch, and Brown) have systematically analyzed how schools and larger social structures organize peer groups by race/ethnicity and social class that come with different kinds of messages and influences (Akerlof & Kranton, 2002; Eccles & Barber, 1999; Steinberg, Dornbusch, & Brown, 1992; Rutter, Maughan, Mortimer, & Ouston, 1979; Coleman, 1961). Such work is part of a larger body of accumulated evidence that peer norms and values about academic achievement, risky behavior, and sexual activity both promote and disrupt academic progress.

Within this general consensus, however, are some areas left open for debate. First, to what extent has recent societal change, both local and global, altered the consequences of and mechanisms underlying the link between peer dynamics and academic considerations identified by past research? Second, does the experience of navigating school-based value systems and normative structures have academic consequences regardless of the actual substance of those values and norms? Third, how can the link between the academic and social sides of secondary schooling be made more amenable to policy intervention?

In this book, I extend an already rich body of scientific knowledge by directly addressing each of these three areas of debate. My argument is that

- Dramatic changes in the demography of the U.S. youth population, the reorganization of the American educational system, the revolution in communication/information technology, and the restructuring of the national and global economy have intensified the long-standing consequences of the social side of schooling for teenagers' futures.
- The process of adapting to the systems of norms and values within a school can disrupt teenagers' long-term educational pathways, *regardless* of whether those values and norms are proacademic,

antiacademic, or neutral, if such adaptation becomes a time-consuming enterprise or if a lack of adaptation exerts a generalized spoiling effect on teenagers' orientation to their schools.

- The future consequences of teenagers' adaptation (or maladaptation) to high school peer cultures can be addressed through policies that expand the stated mission of high schools beyond instructional and vocational services, extend the notion of academically "at-risk" groups beyond demographic terms, and target the specific curricular points at which nonacademic experiences affect academic decision making.

A False Dichotomy

As context for this argument, consider some of the major national debates about high schools in recent years. At the top of the list is No Child Left Behind,[3] with its twin pillars of standardized testing and school accountability. Also important are a series of court decisions curtailing the scope of school desegregation, efforts to create small learning communities in schools, dueling strategies for the classroom instruction of English language learners, calls to increase investment in preschool education, and initiatives to reduce "leakage" from the math/science pipeline (Gamoran, 2007; Schneider, 2007; Heckman, 2006; Genesee, Lindholm-Leary, Saunders, & Christian, 2006; Kahlenberg, 2001). Implicit in these debates and policy activities is the notion that the academically measurable outputs of education – test scores, grades, graduation and college-going rates – set the true benchmarks of student and school success and that alterations to the institutional organization and pedagogical arrangements of schools provide the best means for meeting such benchmarks.

[3] The actual No Child Left Behind legislation (the Elementary and Secondary Education Act as reauthorized by the No Child Left Behind Act of 2001) can be found at http://www.ed.gov/policy/elsec/leg/esea02/index.html.

To a certain extent, I agree with this characterization of education. The problem is that this characterization prioritizes one role of
high schools in the United States – the high school as a formal organization that delivers instruction and curricula to students in order
to increase the economic productivity of the nation. Even if this role
serves as the primary standard of evaluation for the educational system, it de-emphasizes another role of high schools that is important
in its own right and that also contributes to and subtracts from the
organizational role.

That *other* role of high schools concerns what Coleman long ago
referred to as adolescent society.[4] As romanticized and demonized in
movies (*Fast Times at Ridgemont High, Heathers, Mean Girls*), television shows (*21 Jump Street, 90210, Glee*), and books (*Sweet Valley
High, Gossip Girl*) across generations, adolescent society refers to the
rules, rituals, and customs that arise organically when large numbers
of young people come together within high schools for long periods
of time nearly every day of the week over a number of years. In this
way, the hallways, classrooms, lunch rooms, and playing fields of high
schools become fertile ground for the emergence and evolution of a
youth culture that both is influenced by and contributes to the larger
popular culture. Of course, high schools contain many adolescent
societies, not just one, and these adolescent societies differ markedly
from school to school and from community to community. Still, adolescent society, in all its forms, has been an undeniable product of the
American educational system for some time.

As two young women at Lamar who came from different family
backgrounds and were members of different peer crowds explained
to me when I asked them to describe what going to high school was
all about:

> Like when you go to school, it is not like oh let me get this paper
> done that is due tomorrow. It is like, well how can I change myself

---

[4] The name of Coleman's book is *The Adolescent Society: The Social Life of the
Teenager and Its Impact on Education* (1961).

to be accepted by others. Because adults can sit here and say that school is important and that is what you are *supposed* to go to school for, but you are affected by these teenagers daily. And that is who you spend your day with.

It is just a struggle for popularity and strength ... that is it, it is everything school is not *supposed* to be.

Here, the key distinction is between what high school is supposed to be in theory and what actually goes on in high school in reality. In other words, high school is, in theory, about attaining an education but, in reality, is often far more about navigating a social terrain that may or may not place value on education and academic achievement. These two contemporary high school students are voicing the same sentiment expressed by the Midwestern teenagers that Coleman surveyed back in the 1950s. They claimed that being popular was more important than being a good student.

Both then and now, long-term academic considerations certainly matter to young people, but they are often obscured by more immediate social considerations. The main output of this side of high schools is more developmental than educational – it concerns social well-being, emotional and psychological health, engagement in risky or conventional behaviors – and, as such, is often viewed as external to the narrowly defined official educational mission of schools and outside the purview of educational policy. Consequently, although its significance is easily recognized in discussions of nonacademic problems facing high schools, such as in the national debate over school violence in the wake of the 1999 Columbine massacre, it is far less likely to be highlighted in discussions of how to address the academic problems of high schools.

Yet, the official mission of the American educational system is not so narrow, and the separation between the social side of high school and teenagers' development on one hand and the academic side of high school and students' scholastic progress on the other is not so clear. Along these same lines, the scope of educational policy is not confined to coursework, curriculum, and funding. In fact, a long-standing aim of public education has been to promote social stability and produce an educated, healthy civic populace. At the same time, the social side of high school can affect academic benchmarks just as it affects the health and well-being of students. Indeed, educational policies that target the academic functions of high school without attention to the potentially undercutting role of the social dynamics of high school will never realize their full returns (Steinberg, Brown, & Dornbusch, 1996; Cremin, 1957). Going back to those major contemporary debates about education mentioned in the first paragraph of this section, each one touches on social dynamics – girls and minority students feeling frozen out of high-level math and science classes so valuable in the new economy being just one example (Riegle-Crumb, 2006; Hyde & Kling, 2001) – and, therefore, calls for responses that address the phenomena's social underpinnings as well as their academic consequences.

Beyond issues of school performance and educational policy, recognizing the significance of the social side of high school and its implications for the academic side is also an issue for individual teenagers and the adults in their lives. Far removed from the daily rhythm of high school, adults may be understandably tempted to dismiss or downplay the social challenges of high school as a rite of passage, growing pains, or something that teenagers will live through and eventually forget. From the perspective of adulthood, they may consider the social lives of teenagers as *secondary* distractions to their *primary* academic responsibilities. Yet, the social problems that many teenagers face in their high schools are implicated in depression, suicide, substance use, sexual behavior, eating disorders, and other behaviors and conditions that affect mental health and general well-being in the present and that have consequences for adjustment and functioning well into the future (Crosnoe, Frank, & Mueller, 2008; Crosnoe & Needham, 2004; Harris, Duncan, & Boisjoly, 2002; Bearman & Bruckner, 2001). At the same time, by affecting academic decisions and actions in the present, social problems can disrupt trajectories into higher education that have major ramifications for socioeconomic attainment in the long run. Thus, parents, teachers, counselors, coaches, mentors, and other adults need to be cognizant of how current social problems can pose risks to short-term and long-term trajectories across domains of development and be attendant to these risks as they guide teenagers through high school and demand service and support from high schools.

THE GOALS OF THE BOOK

My goal in conducting this research and writing this book, therefore, is to demonstrate how teenagers' navigation of the stratified, digitized peer cultures of today's high schools affects their navigation of the curricular structures of these schools, how the connection between these pathways now differentiates their future life chances in the modern era, and how families, school personnel, and policy makers can use this information to promote the success of teenagers and their high schools. To advance this goal, I have focused on a subset of students at risk for poor (or poorer than expected) post–high school educational outcomes, not because of their intelligence, skill levels, family backgrounds, or demographic profiles but instead because of their positions in the social structures of their high schools.

Specifically, teenagers who do not fit in socially in their high schools are who interest me. To be more exact, I am interested in teenagers who *believe* that they do not fit in socially. I set out to determine the extent to which such feelings of social marginalization within a high school could engender short-term coping mechanisms that, by interfering with the accrual of valued academic credentials in high school, could reduce their chances of attending college after high school. In other words, I began looking to specify a pathway by which a high school social position unrelated to academic status or academic values could have long-lasting effects on the life course after high school is over by disrupting academic progress during a critical period. Although studying all teenagers who perceive themselves to be socially marginalized, I pay special attention to two subsets of the teenage population

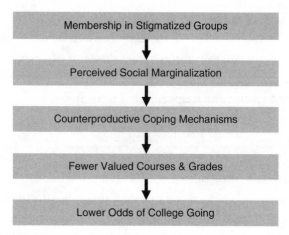

Figure 1.1. Not Fitting In: A Social Psychological Pathway with Academic Consequences.

who are at heightened risk, as a group, for social marginalization and, partly because of this risk, have generated a great deal of public concern in recent years: teenagers who are overweight and teenagers who are lesbian or gay. Figure 1.1 depicts the basic pathway being considered in this book.

This focus on perceived social marginalization means that some teenagers who, by outward appearances or common sentiment, are not actually marginalized will be counted as marginalized. I argue that this blurring of the lines between objective and subjective social marginalization is acceptable because, to paraphrase a classic social psychological theorem by W. I. Thomas, something is true if the consequences are true.[5] Applying the theorem to this specific case means that some teenagers' coping responses that set into motion a chain of events that lead to truncated trajectories of educational attainment result not from an objective social standing. Instead, they emerge from what teenagers believe their social standing to be.

[5] See Thomas's 1928 book (with Thomas) *The Child in America* for more on the theorem and its development.

I view such teenagers as a useful case study for updating the knowledge base on the link between the academic and social sides of high school for five interrelated reasons. First, their self-perceptions are likely formed within peer cultures that cross actual and virtual planes of social interaction. Second, these self-perceptions can occur within many diverse segments of the increasingly heterogeneous U.S. high school population. Third, the consequences of feeling socially marginalized can play out independently of whether peer values are in opposition to or support of the educational mission of the school. Fourth, the cumulative course sequences that are now so strongly linked to college going are especially vulnerable to short-term socioemotional disruptions. And, fifth, the historically high current returns to higher education mean that even short-lived social problems that disrupt college going can have lifelong consequences for the individual that may aggregate to the societal level.

To look into this potentially valuable case study of teenagers who feel socially marginalized in high school, I conducted several years of empirical research on the social cultures of American high schools. This work takes two forms: 1) statistical analysis of quantitative data from high schools across the United States and 2) qualitative analysis of data culled from an ethnography of Lamar.

National Numbers and Local Voices

Statistics from a nationwide data collection effort called the National Longitudinal Study of Adolescent Health (Add Health)[6] give the

---

[6] Add Health is a nationally representative sample of 7th to 12th graders, organized and run by investigators at the Carolina Population Center at the University of North Carolina at Chapel Hill with major funding from the National Institute of Child Health and Human Development (www.cpc.unc.edu/addhealth; Harris, 2008). Sample schools were selected with a stratified design, based on region, urbanicity, sector, racial composition, and size. Most contained the 9th to 12th grades, with the remainder containing 7th and/or 8th grades too. All schools not containing 7th and 8th grades were then randomly matched to one middle

big-picture view of the ways in which the social side of high school influences contemporary teenagers' educational trajectories. In the late 1990s and early 2000s, thousands of adolescents from across the United States – as well as their parents, friends, and principals – filled out surveys about their lives, families, and schools. Importantly, the rich information on social contexts and teenagers' behavior was supplemented by the collection of teenagers' high school transcripts. I focused on the portion of the Add Health sample enrolled in high school at the onset of the study, examining how social experiences *during* high school predict the odds of teenagers enrolling in college *after* high school while taking into account other important factors, such as race, social class, immigration status, IQ, family background, and school location, that are related to both social and academic status. As I mentioned above when laying out the goals of the book, my primary interest was in the Add Health teenagers who reported that they felt socially marginalized in their high schools, and I paid particularly close attention to those who were overweight and/or lesbian/gay. My analyses of Add Health involved advanced statistical procedures.

school that fed into them, with the probability of the feeder school being selected proportional to its student contribution to the high school. The final sample included 132 middle and high schools. During the 1994–5 academic year, nearly all students in the sample schools completed the In-School Survey, a short questionnaire designed to create a sampling frame for later, more intensive rounds of data collection. Of these 90,118 students, a subgroup selected evenly across high school–feeder school pairs participated in the In-Home Interview between April and December 1995 (Wave I; $N = 20,745$). Attempts were then made to follow up all Wave I respondents, except for those who had been seniors in high school, between April and September 1996 (Wave II, $N = 14,738$). Finally, attempts were made to follow up all Wave I respondents, this time including the Wave I seniors, between August 2001 and April 2002 (Wave III, $N = 15,197$), when they were aged 18–26. Approximately 77% of the original Wave I sample participated in Wave III. To supplement these adolescent-reported data, Add Health also collected data from one school administrator, a parent, and the U.S. census at Wave I. High school transcripts were collected as part of Wave III as part of the Adolescent Health and Academic Achievement project headed by Chandra Muller (www.prc.utexas.edu/ahaa/). Over 90% of Wave III respondents consented to have their transcripts collected.

I have tried to accessibly summarize the results of such analyses in the text, leaving the mechanical details to the footnotes.

These national numbers quantify the link between the social side of high school and teenagers' long-term educational attainment in the contemporary United States and assess how this link varies across diverse races and social classes and differs by gender. As such, they demonstrate the extent to which this focal link is a national issue of some quantifiable magnitude.

Of course, as much valuable information as surveys and statistics provide, they often lack nuance and detail, and their power to identify mechanisms is limited. To dig deeper, I spent the better part of a year at Lamar, a large and diverse public high school serving over 2,200 students in Austin, Texas.[7] One of the first high schools in the city, it is set on prime real estate in the middle of town, has excellent facilities, attracts students from some of the most socioeconomically advantaged neighborhoods, and has other students bused in from some of the most disadvantaged neighborhoods. As a result, it is an economically, racially, and linguistically diverse melting pot.[8]

Over the course of the year, I spent many hours as an anonymous observer – watching social interactions in the classrooms, in the hallways, during lunch periods, and on the grounds of Lamar

[7] Lamar High School is a pseudonym. I submitted this study to the Austin Independent School District and requested permission to recruit students from a local high school, preferably one that was large and demographically diverse. After approving my proposal, district personnel assigned me to a specific high school in the city and granted me full access to its classrooms and building. Neither the district nor the school provided me records or any other information on the students or the school.

[8] According to the official statistics compiled by the Texas Education Agency, Lamar has 2,209 students. Of these, 57% are white, 36% are Latino/a, 6% are African American, and 1% are another race/ethnicity. One-fourth are identified by the district as economically disadvantaged, and 6% have been labeled Limited English Proficiency students. Roughly two-thirds of 9th graders and three-fourths of 11th graders pass the state-mandated Texas Assessment of Knowledge and Skills standardized tests, and the state gives the school an accountability rating of "academically acceptable."

talking to many students, teachers, and parents while taking copious notes. Within this larger study, I also spent more concentrated time with 32 specific teenagers in the school. Recruited from 9th and 10th grade general curriculum classes,[9] they covered the full demographic spectrum and were split evenly by gender. They were mostly white or Latino/a with a few African American and Middle Eastern teenagers too. Several, not all of them Latino/as, were immigrants or the children of immigrants. The majority lived with both parents, but a sizeable portion lived with only one. Their parents ranged from high school dropouts to professionals with Ph.D.s.[10] Moreover, these teenagers came to Lamar from all sides of the city – from the affluent neighborhoods along the lake line in West Austin, from newly created middle-class suburbs spreading out on the plains of South Austin, and from the poor and working-class neighborhoods east of the interstate that has historically divided the haves and have-nots of the city.

Recall that I was interested in teenagers who were socially marginalized *and* those who were the agents of marginalization and that I also wanted to know about teenagers who were subjectively marginalized but not objectively marginalized, vice versa, neither, or both. Following these interests, I chose to sample teenagers at Lamar without knowing anything, at least at the onset, about their social situations in the school. As I interviewed these teenagers and their peers, perused yearbooks and school newspapers, and generally followed school events,

[9] The two classes represent the only two nontracked classes that all students are required to take. Most students in the school take them in their first or second years. The classrooms were assigned by the school district. My four research assistants and I attended the classes, told the students about the study, and then passed around a sign-up sheet. We intended to enroll the first 30 students who contacted us but ended up enrolling 32.

[10] The gender breakdown was actually 55% male and 45% female. As for race/ethnicity, the sample composition was 45% white, 33% Latino/a, 15% African American, and 7% Asian American. The average level of parent education (maximum of all parents in the house) was 3.3, which represented some college.

I came to see that the 32 teenagers with whom I spent the most time at Lamar occupied all parts of the social hierarchy of the school:

- One was a finalist for homecoming court and several were student council officers, but at least one reported having no friends at all.
- More than a few boys and girls were successful athletes, with a three-sport letterman included as well as members of the soccer, lacrosse, softball, swim, football, and track teams. School clubs were well represented too. Over half of the teenagers, however, were not involved in a single school activity of any kind.
- Many were stellar students taking high-level classes and holding perfect or near-perfect grades. Some were struggling, with 10 reporting a C-range grade point average and at least 5 having failed a class in the past year.
- Many loved Lamar and viewed it as a major part of their lives. A nonnegligible minority, however, reported that they hated it and just about everyone in it.

When focusing on these teenagers at Lamar, I and my graduate students – Jennifer March Augustine, Carey Cooper, Kurt Gore, Belinda Needham – went to their classes and met with them at the school. They filled out a survey giving us information about their family backgrounds and academic histories. With art supplies, magazines, and disposable cameras, they made collages in which they tried to tell us who they "really" were.[11] These "Who I Am" projects provided information on identity development, social functioning, and mental health that proved to be valuable when understanding why some teenagers felt socially marginalized and how they coped with it the ways they

---

[11] The students were given complete anonymity, covered by a certificate of confidentiality from the National Institute of Child Health and Human Development. Their parents signed consent forms for their participation. In addition, the students themselves signed assent forms at the close of the study, granting permission for the use of their interviews and collages.

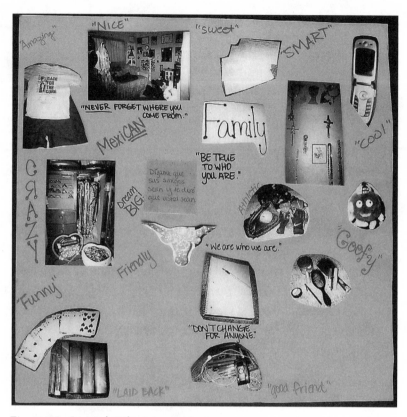

Figure 1.2. Juanita's Who I Am Project.

did. Figure 1.2 captures one of these collages, made by an academically successful, athletically involved Latina named Juanita.

While discussing this collage, I came to see how Juanita's ethnic heritage, strong family ties, and tightly knit group of girlfriends she had known since childhood gave her a foundation of emotional and interpersonal strength. This foundation, in turn, helped her to rise above many of the social distractions of high school and stay on track academically.

If the national numbers from Add Health provide the outlining frame and structure of this book, then the local voices of Juanita and the other Lamar students offer the finer-grained level of substance and insight that allow those broad parameters to be unpacked and contextualized. Essentially, I started with the Add Health analyses, worked down into the Lamar data to identify underlying mechanisms, and then, based on what I found at Lamar, worked my way back up to Add Health to pursue newly formed questions. Although not without its challenges and problems, this two-pronged strategy proved to be rewarding for this line of inquiry.

Up front, I should explain that although I conducted the Lamar ethnography to address specific questions, I often draw on the stories, insights, and thoughts of the Lamar teenagers when trying to make larger points. In other words, I use what I saw and heard at Lamar to illustrate important themes or ideas from the general literature on the academic and social sides of high school or when I think that something from Lamar will help to capture what is going on in the Add Health analyses.

A Preview of Findings

The results of this study generally support the pathway depicted in Figure 1.1. Yet, the story is far more complex than this simple figure suggests. To forecast some of this complexity,

- Feelings of social marginalization appeared to reduce college going through the link between counterproductive coping mechanisms (e.g., skipping school) and disrupted accumulation of course credits and grades. This sequence was independent of the academic values of peers at the school level or within peer groups in the school and also held even when more objective social statuses (e.g., network positions) were taken into account.
- Boys and girls did not differ markedly in this general sequence, but the degree to which being overweight and/or lesbian/gay set into motion this sequence was much greater for girls than for otherwise similar boys.

- How this not-fitting-in phenomenon played out was similar across various races, social classes, and immigration statuses.
- Social interactions providing somewhat ambiguous and potentially misreadable clues about social value explained how teenagers came to believe that they did or did not fit in at school.
- Counterproductive coping mechanisms (e.g., disengaging from school) largely represented teenagers' attempts to correct or reduce identity discrepancies and crises resulting from feelings of social marginalization in school.
- Social networking online and other forms of "new" communication factored into self-perceptions of social position and into identity work in both positive and negative ways.
- School-based factors (e.g., sports teams) and positive family processes promoted resilience among boys who felt socially marginalized, while more school-based factors and interpersonal support from peers promoted resilience among girls who felt socially marginalized.

Thus, the risks to teenagers' future prospects and to academic performance posed by social problems in high school appear to be significant, independent of the actual valence of peer values vis-à-vis academics, facilitated by teenagers' interpretations of subtle or covert social feedback rather than by direct peer pressure, and somewhat reactive to protection by social supports and arenas for the enactment of positive identities. Moreover, the risks posed by social problems in high school tap into a cumulative process and, therefore, cannot be considered short-term issues that teenagers will grow out of by the end of high school.

THE ORGANIZATION OF THE BOOK

The details behind these general results and the rationale for these conclusions will be made clear in the subsequent chapters of this book.

In the next chapter (Chapter 2), I follow two teenage boys from Lamar through a typical day in their lives. The purposes of this chapter are to illustrate the multifaceted nature of everyday high school life and to demonstrate to older readers how many of the details of this everyday life have evolved in some subtle and some striking ways. In Chapters 3 and 4, I summarize the basic lessons and conclusions from past research on the link between the academic and social sides of high school before discussing ways in which this important line of research needs to be updated to a contemporary setting and expanded to equally cover many different processes besides positive/negative peer influences.

The next four chapters (Chapters 5–8) focus on a specific example of the high stakes involved in this larger phenomenon of the link between the academic and social sides of high school. This example concerns the obstacles to going to college faced by teenagers who feel socially marginalized in their high schools (especially those who feel thusly because of their body size and/or sexuality) and how personal, school, family, and community resources can help some of them break down these obstacles.

Finally, I close the book (Chapters 9–11) with theoretically and empirically grounded recommendations for how parents, school personnel, policy makers, and other adults can act to ensure that the social side of high school supports, rather than undermines, the academic side of high school. In doing so, I focus on *all* teenagers who may be at risk for educational problems tomorrow because of what is happening to them socially in high school today.

2

A Day in the Life

The basic premise of this book, building on a long line of developmental and educational research, is that American high schools house two intertwined and occasionally competing arenas of activity – the social activity of peer culture and the scholastic activity of the academic curriculum. The interplay between these two arenas of activity is not a new phenomenon nor a newly studied one. Still, it does get obscured, for a variety of reasons, in policy-oriented discussions of education and can sometimes be dismissed by parents and other adults who are more focused on the significance of academic progress and credentials to teenagers' long-term trajectories into adulthood. Moreover, the very nature of this interplay is evolving in qualitative ways against the backdrop of major macrolevel social change.

As a starting point, then, I want to take readers through a typical day in the life of two teenagers. I chose two Lamar High students who come from different parts of town. Both are teenage boys, although I could have easily picked two teenage girls and achieved the same effect. These boys' days are, superficially at least, quite different from each other. Beneath the surface, however, they share some basic commonalities, commonalities that provide a valuable window into both the historical continuities and recent developments of modern high school life.

FROM THE WEST SIDE

Chris is at the end of his sophomore year at Lamar.[1] He lives with his white, upper middle-class parents and brother in a hilly neighborhood that abuts one of Austin's green ribbonlike lakes.

Morning

Getting up at eight o'clock, Chris pulls himself out of bed and heads to the bathroom, stopping by his desk on the way to check the late baseball scores from the night before on his computer and to look for pokes on Facebook. According to his IM window, his people are not up yet, or at least no one is logged on.

By the time his teeth are brushed and his pants are on, that has changed. One buddy asks for a copy of Chris's English assignment. Chris shoots the assignment along as an attachment with a stern command to change enough stuff so that they do not get caught. The other tells him to check out the MySpace page of a popular (and wealthy) senior girl. When Chris does, he sees a new gallery of party pictures from Circus, an unofficial but major Lamar social event to which he had finally gained entry this spring thanks to his senior brother. In the pictures are 100 or so people he knows from school in various poses, some with beers in hands, others not. They are all white. The propulsive, angry beats from Panic at the Disco that the senior girl has as her signature song come out of the computer so loud that it stirs his mom to yell up the stairs that he needs to get moving. He does, after all, have

---

[1] The day descriptions in this chapter are primarily based on interviews with two boys at Lamar. Some of the details have been changed to protect their identities. Moreover, in a few instances, some information was incorporated into these descriptions from interviews with other similar students as a means of fleshing out the full day.

to make the rest of the flyers for the 10th grade fund-raiser and take another stab at finishing *Invisible Man*.

His brother drives them both down from the hills. They stop and pick up his brother's girlfriend along the way. Cigarettes light up immediately (only tobacco in the morning). The two seniors pick up the conversation that they have been running continuously – verbally, via text, via IM – for months now: who is going to college where. His brother is sure about Colorado, the girlfriend long ago decided on Vanderbilt. Both schools have sizable populations of recent Lamar alumni and, as a result, strong Austin-based social networks. This year's senior class has been attending parties at both of these schools and many others for so long now the campuses no longer feel like distant or unknown territory. Given that the remaining days of the school year are dwindling fast, the college talk focuses mostly on the few undecideds in their crowd; not undecided about going to college, just undecided about where. Chris always likes listening to this conversation, even if it can get repetitive. He knows that he will be one of the ones doing the deciding in a year or two. He also knows that he can visit his brother and his brother's friends starting next year – go to football games, go to parties, meet girls, stay out all night if he wants, and get drunk without having to worry about getting caught.

As Lamar looms into view, its gray Soviet-style architecture at odds with the plush rolling hills surrounding it, they head instinctively to the west side parking lot, the one filled with Tahoes and Explorers and the occasional BMW, the one where every face is a familiar one. Just walking from the car to the side door of the school takes a while because the three of them keep getting engaged in conversations with friends.

This morning, they are 15 minutes ahead of schedule. That gives them more time to hang out with their friends before all the real school stuff begins. Chris follows his brother and his brother's girlfriend up the stairs and into the atrium on the second floor. That is where the teenagers like them – the upper-middle-class kids, various athletes, and the like – hang out in the off times of the school day. This area looks out over the cafeteria and bottom floor of the school. In between the administrative offices and the library, it functions as the epicenter of the school. It is lined with glass display cases full of trophies and banners and decorated with recruiting posters from colleges and universities across the country as well as digital pictures from various students who have taken trips to these campuses in the past year. Chris sits down in the sophomore corner. There is unusual activity today because the yearbooks have been distributed and because the second big *private* social event of the year for this crowd – Shootout, with its band, kegs, armbands, and out-of-town location – is coming soon. What discussion isn't devoted to that event is spent complaining about finals. The bell finally rings at 9:15 (because someone finally listened to all of that research on the circadian rhythms and brainwaves of teenagers and moved back the start time of school). Everyone in the atrium scatters into the densely packed hallways filled with a sea of white, black, and brown faces. The cacophony is overwhelming.

The morning is a grind for Chris, with all of his pre-AP classes lined up in a row. He is pulling As, but it is tough work. Most of his closest friends – a group of nine guys and five girls he has known since elementary school – take the same classes. Because they all need to be on (or their parents keep them on) the AP track and because there are only so many pre-AP and AP classes at Lamar, they typically get to move from class to class more or less en masse. This is a good thing because they help each other get by – talking to each other about homework, translating what teachers say for each other. Perhaps more importantly, they harass each other when one of them gets a bad grade, their taunts of being ACC bound (short for Austin Community College) providing enough motivation to ensure that the next grade will be better.

Algebra II is Chris's best class and his worst class. On one hand, Algebra is pretty boring for anyone. On the other hand, Chris knows that this is one of those high school classes that is a must on the long, step-by-step road to college. He also really likes his teacher, a relatively young, attractive woman who graduated from Lamar 10 years before. He feels like she understands him and his friends, thinks that they are the easy part of her job, although she definitely seems to enjoy occasionally poking holes in their egos.

Afternoon

When lunch period arrives, Chris passes three female friends who are heading off campus, and he tags along. Although Lamar is technically a closed campus, no one ever questions students like them when they come and go. Within a few minutes, the group is sitting in a bagel place down the road. The conversation is devoted to various stories about their classmates as well as their peers – the ones who look like they do – in other Austin schools. There is the junior girl from Westlake who outed herself on Facebook, the ongoing investigation of a sophomore who downloaded thousands of songs before people got serious about imposing all of those copyright laws, the senior guy who is staying in Austin next year for UT to be near his younger girlfriend, the sophomore girl who sometimes is one of the girls' best friends and sometimes (including now) is one of their worst enemies. They also discuss plans for who will be included in their gang (no individual dates allowed) for Shootout, debate whether it is acceptable to attend a French Club trip to Europe in June, and review the latest tally of who is bailing out of or jumping into Young Life Wilderness camp in July. By the end of lunch, Chris realizes that maybe his time would have been better spent finishing the last two chapters of *Invisible Man*.

Afternoon classes are much easier. Health, which everyone has to take to graduate, is a joke. Even as the semester draws to a close, he knows none of the students in the class. It is the one time of his life, at Lamar or otherwise, when he is part of a racial or class minority. His teacher is a football coach – the school has to put coaches somewhere. Coach simply presses play on the VCR for another inspirational video about not having sex or not drinking or some other "not." This would be a good time to dive back into *Invisible Man*, but instead Chris uses his cell phone to text another friend who is down the hall in speech class. They use that modern version of shorthand that has developed through IM and texting. Its baffling to his parents and teachers, but Chris and his friends can type it out without thinking. Chris texts at school only in between classes or in this particular class, although he often finds messages waiting for him as he changes from class to class. There are details that need to be ironed out now about their Saturday hunting trip in the Hill Country. Health, and Ralph Ellison, can wait.

School officially lets out at 4:15, but Chris's school day is not over. He and the other lacrosse players gather down on the practice field. They will be there for two more hours, and it is a hard workout, especially under a Texas sun that is particularly unforgiving this time of year. His team, JV now, is what Chris considers "his" guys. Most of them, including Chris, are moving up to varsity next year, and he cannot wait. For now, the team plays matches against schools that are, to say the least, privileged, tony private schools and elite suburban schools. Those are the people who tend to play lacrosse. Lacrosse is a cool social status for white, middle-class guys like Chris. It gives him the edge over the other sophomore guys trying to land girls or get invited to parties. More seriously, he also knows that it can be a trump card over all those other guys like him who want to eventually go to the same East Coast colleges or southern universities. Chris is beat up and sore by the time that practice is over and then has to sit down to hear a lecture from the coaches about studying to avoid the sanctions of the no pass/no play rules. This is a silly lecture to give considering how well they all do in school. When he is on his way home with his brother, he gets a text from his buddy complaining about the lecture – "OMFG – we rnt the bball team."

Evening

Their dad pulls in from work right behind them, and dinner is waiting by the time they get inside. No matter how late Chris gets home from practice or other school activities, no matter how much homework he has to do, his mother insists that they sit down and eat dinner together. His parents are not the most talkative people, but they always try to keep the conversation going at dinner. His brother suspects that they read somewhere that conversation-filled dinners are a sign of good parenting and, ever the good students, follow the rules.

During dinner, they talk about what they did in class that day, whether he likes *Invisible Man* as much as his mother did when she first read it, whether his Chemistry teacher has gotten to organics yet, whether anyone else in health class has gotten pregnant. There is some casual interest in the cheerleading tryouts, more in the recently released lacrosse schedule for next year, and even more in whether four of his brother's undecided friends have gotten closer to deciding about college. His parents do not say anything, but they are relieved that Chris's brother is going to Colorado, even if the out-of-state tuition will kill them. They were afraid that he might want to stay in Texas somewhere, which is not thinking big enough. Chris absorbs a lot during these conversations. Having listened to his parents and brother banter about school for the last 4 or 5 years, he has never really had to ask any questions for himself. The road has always been very clear to him.

Two hours of homework follow dinner, interrupted by one reality show, a few forays onto the Web, an unintentionally long engagement with his new Wii (it's like crack, his brother says), and a few text messages. He can do all of this while IMing. Chris hates homework, but he does not complain. Like his brother told him years ago, school is your job for the next few years. Math and science are just what you do to make your living until you go to the real world. He finally settles down in bed around 11 and polishes off the last of *Invisible Man*. It goes totally over his head, but he thinks that he gets enough to be able to BS his way through the test. When he turns out the light, his cell phone lights up, a text from his buddy about a UT fraternity party coming up. Chris is tired, so he will respond first thing in the morning before he goes back to school once again.

FROM THE EAST SIDE

Carlos is a classmate of Chris, but the two do not know each other. Carlos lives in East Austin with his mother, father, and three siblings. It is a densely populated, rundown neighborhood in the shadow of Austin's downtown skyline.

Morning

Carlos gets up early. For one thing, his parents and oldest brother all go to work by eight o'clock, and so the small house begins bustling before the sun rises. For another, he rides the bus to Lamar, and that means he cannot just wait until the last minute to take off for school. His bedroom is wallpapered with posters of cars, pictures of his mom, Tejano rock CD covers, and, on one wall, the newspaper clippings about the shooting death of a cousin. Not an inch of wall space is left bare. His little brother is sitting on the floor of the bedroom playing *Grand Theft Auto: San Andreas*. After so many after-school marathon sessions with his friends, Carlos can beat that game fast, and he is working on getting the money to buy the new version for himself. He knows that making a few As this period would probably do the trick for his mom. That is all she cares about – making good grades. Ten minutes of GTA turns into 45 minutes, and Carlos realizes that he is going to be late if he does not get going. He throws on a shirt, runs his fingers through is close-cropped hair, and motors. His mom will not let him leave without a full breakfast, but, by the time he sits down, his cell buzzes. One of his boys down at the bus stop wants to know where he is.

The bus stop is home territory – his neighborhood, his people. Everybody here has lived on these surrounding blocks for years. There used to be a few black kids around, but now they are all Mexicans. Some speak in Spanish, some only in English, most in a mixture of the two. This is their social scene before they go to school and almost immediately get dispersed in the madding crowd of Lamar. All of his boys are there. He calls them his crew. They stick together and remind each other that they are so much better than those sorry-ass punks at Lamar in their SUVs and college T-shirts.

When they load on the bus and take off, he looks out the window as his street passes. His house is on the corner, a wood-framed bungalow type that is starting to look more than a little neglected. A hundred yards or so beyond that is the duplex where his sister lives with her husband and new baby. He can just barely catch a glimpse of the red roof of his brother's crib. After high school, when they all have good jobs, he and his crew will move out of their parents' houses and get an apartment or maybe a house together right on this same street. He does not want to leave. This is home, these guys are his family – brothers from another mother, that is what they call themselves.

Pretty soon, the bus crosses under the interstate that separates Austin's poor and brown to the east from the rich and white to the west. In an instant, they are downtown, the bodegas and Spanish-language billboards replaced by shiny new towers and bustling cafes. They pass through the bar district, 6th Street, where thousands of UT students gather every week from Thursday night through Saturday night, soaking up the music, drinking, socializing, hooking up, and drinking some more. This part of the bus ride gives Carlos and all of the other kids from his hood a glimpse of what college life is like. Soon, the bars fade and are replaced by the string of law offices, advertising agencies, and high-tech firms, busy people walking with purpose. Carlos stares at them through the bus windows.

The buses line up in scores in front of Lamar so that getting to the drop-off point takes a while. By this time, the bus has settled down into a calm but somewhat dispirited quiet. School's on again. Most people are on their cell phones or gaming. Carlos has his DS out. He and his best friend sit side by side, punching away at the keys. As soon as the bus lurches to its final stop, the kids start streaming out onto the front walk of Lamar. Along with the others from his block, Carlos flows down the front walk, past the Performing Arts Center where the band kids are already camped out in small groups, through the main doors where the coaches keep a careful watch on any nonsense, past the pit where the goth kids are clustered. He does not stop. He does not know any of these people. He is in Lamar, but he is not in *his* school yet.

Finally, Carlos reaches the back hallway of the first floor, underneath the atrium where Chris and his friends hang out in the short interval before the first bell rings. This is where the Mexican kids convene every morning. Here, he catches up with his boys who were not on his bus, the ones from different neighborhoods, the ones who drive. Armed Forces recruitment posters line the walls around the vending machines. Be All That You Can Be. Some of the younger boys are trying to tip the drink machine, shake out some Cokes, as a gaggle of girls laugh and roll their eyes simultaneously. One of the security guards turns the corner and sharply barks at them to cut it out. Carlos sees one of his brother's friends. They have plans to go to the car show on Friday, and they talk this through detail by detail. Carlos loves vintage cars. They are his favorite thing in the world. Getting an old car and fixing it up for show is his big dream right now. He knows that he will do it.

Carlos likes his teachers. They are mostly nice to him and seem to want him to do well. They also get mad at him when he does not try. When the bell rings and he walks to class, he passes one teacher after another. "Hello Carlos," they all say. "Good morning Carlos." They know his name, and that makes him feel good. The cliques on the second floor do not know his name, but those people do not matter to him at all. They are scared of him, or at least scared of his friends, and that is what he likes.

His first few classes are blowoffs. He feels like he is too smart for the dumbed-down stuff they teach, and his crew is scattered out across the school in classrooms just like this one. So, most days he bends over his desk and draws, usually cars but occasionally horses. He also likes to re-create the covers of his favorite CDs and then pass them out to his boys. Everyone thinks that he is a good artist, including his favorite teacher. She encourages him to sign up for art at Lamar or to take one of the art classes at his boy's club, but he never has. Art is fun, not part of school, and making it homework would kill the buzz. As his history teacher drones on about the New Deal, he wishes that he could call his older brother or sister. They are out of school now and often do not have much to do in the morning, so he could blow off some time with them. He has been busted at least a dozen times for cell phone use this semester, however, and is getting tired of the lecture. Drawing is a better way to spend the time.

For lunch, Carlos is back in the downstairs hallway with his people again. Instead of lunch, they just get chips from the machines. They do not sit down to eat like dorks in the cafeteria or the cliques in the atrium. They mill about. He and a few of his friends decide to wander outside, but they immediately get herded back in by an assistant principal. The APs are always on him and his crew. Whenever they see them coming, they immediately prepare for trouble. No freedom at all. Instead, they go upstairs, sit down by the library doors to watch people pass by. Lots of older girls, the popular ones, move back and forth. They always seem busy, always have so much to do. Carlos and his friends make comments about each one, but not too loud. They could really get in trouble if one of *these* girls complains, and none of them needs that kind of hassle. Every once in a while, an older boy or boys will walk by. They seem far less comfortable than the girls. No matter what they say, the white guys are scared of the Mexican guys. They steer clear of them. Carlos knows they have no reason to fear him, but he also does nothing to disabuse them of this fear. He simply tilts his chin up in the barest of greeting. Another AP comes by, tells them to stop loitering and go eat lunch. He tells his boys that he will catch them later and dips into the library.

The library is one place that Carlos can regularly access a computer, and he likes to log on every couple of days. He has an e-mail account now, and he trades e-mails with his cousins down in the valley. That is how they stay connected to each other. He does not know that many other people with e-mail accounts, so most of the e-mails he gets are junk, advertisements for porn and things. Some of the e-mails that he sent to his favorite band, a Mexican rock group who played in Austin in the winter, have gotten brief replies, and that is cool. He wants to start a Facebook page, or wherever it is that the kids in his classes set up their Web sites, but he never has time in these stolen minutes in the library to figure this out. So, in the end, he spends the rest of his lunch period looking at car pages, putting together his dream car in his mind.

Afternoon

After lunch comes IPC, which is the amalgam of science subjects that many students at Lamar take after Biology but before (or in lieu of) Chemistry. Now that Carlos knows how easy the class is, he cannot help but wonder sometimes if maybe he should have taken Chemistry instead. All of his boys were taking IPC, his older siblings took IPC, and so it seemed like what he was supposed to do at the time. If he had only known then what he knows now. His cell buzzes with a text. He sees it is from his brother but ignores it for now.

After IPC, he goes to Algebra I. It is the one class in which he really tries hard. The teacher pushes him, and he likes that. She is not so nice to his boys, which bothers him, but she pays special attention to him and encourages him. She has even talked to him about going to college, what he needs to do to get there – taking the PSATs in the fall, going on into Chemistry and Algebra II next year even though, technically, he does not have to keep taking math and science. Carlos is intrigued, but, at the same time, it all seems a little confusing to him. No one in his family has ever gone to college, he does not want to leave Austin, and UT probably costs a ton of money. It is in the back of his mind though. He thinks about it sometimes. Maybe he will catch up with the teacher before the year ends and talk to her about his schedule for next year. His mom would like that, and his mom is the most important person in his life.

Unlike Chris and his buddies, Carlos and his crew do not linger at Lamar once school lets out. They do not do sports or school activities, which are for West Austin kids or the real jocks, and buses leave within minutes of the final bell. So, while some students gather in clusters in the PAC, on the playing fields, or in the parking lots, Carlos has to run to the bus. The same trip ensues in reverse, through downtown, across the interstate, onto his turf. No one is at home. He likes the alone time because it is one of the few times that the house is quiet. He turns on the TV and falls back on the couch with a Coke in hand. He knows that he should do his IPC worksheets and finish writing that book report on *Lord of the Flies* for English, but instead he winds up wandering back to his bedroom and tackles the PlayStation again. Every once in a while, he glances up at the faces of his boys looking down on him from the pictures on the wall.

Evening

After a couple of hours, his little brother comes back from their aunt's house, where he spends the afternoons after school. His mom comes in from work a bit later, then his dad. Just as the house is filling up again, he gets a text from one of his boys. They are all hanging out by the convenience store down the road. This is what they do, mobbing 10 or 20 deep until dark. Carlos jumps on his bike and heads out to meet them. There are about a dozen or so guys already there, mostly middle school and early high school guys. They race their bikes around together, have wrestling matches, smoke, kill the time. There is a fight every once in a while, but not today. They usually involve this group and another one from a different school. Carlos does not fight. He is small and not in great shape. His friends do, but he always lets them know he has their backs. True To the End is the Lamar school motto, but Carlos and his crew think that they are the only ones at Lamar who really know what that means and live by it. They are true to each other, those bonds built and carried on during endless afternoons and evenings just like this one.

Carlos finally comes home when the sun goes down. There are no streetlamps on most of the streets in his neighborhood, so he pedals back in the dark with some of his boys. He should be scared, but he is not. His parents have already eaten, but there is food for him. His mom is a great cook, and he sits down to eat by her as she watches TV. They talk about school. She really wants him to do well. He finally tells her about his conversation about college with his Algebra teacher. This delights his mom. She wants nothing more than for one of her kids to go to UT, and Carlos has always been the best student. They talk about what he might need to do, and he tells her what his teacher told him. She urges him to figure out all of the steps that he needs to take, and when, including the PSAT. She wonders where he can find out this information. She is a little concerned about the teacher's advice about classes. If Carlos takes hard classes like Chemistry, won't that make his grades go down? Won't that hurt his chances of going to college? That seems risky to her. Carlos agrees and promises to ask around about this. Talking with his mom always helps. She makes him feel good. Instead of watching TV with her, he decides to go back to his room and do that IPC and English homework for tomorrow.

WEST MEETS EAST

Chris and Carlos attend the same high school, yet not. One could say they are in different worlds, even though their neighborhoods are only 15 minutes apart. As a result, these two boys are following divergent paths through this stage of their lives that will, in all likelihood, lead to quite distinct circumstances as they move through their 20s and beyond.

Although the details of their days are quite distinct, however, the general spirit of their days is largely the same. That general spirit is that high school organizes and dominates their lives. It does so in the form of classes, homework, and other educational pursuits that have become more systematically organized, internally differentiated, and cumulatively connected than in the past. The school also dominates their lives in the form of social demands and activities that link teenagers together both inside and outside the school. As in the past, these social demands take the form of face-to-face interactions with schoolmates before, during, and after school; group socializing in classes, clubs, and teams and on designated crowd-specific turfs in every hallway, corner, and room. In a more contemporary way, they also take the form of IMing, texting, and e-mailing between teenagers and their larger social crowds at all hours of the day; the constant barrage of youth-focused media (including social networking sites like MySpace and Facebook) that help to dictate what high school life is about; and the virtual universality of cell phone use that ensures that no one is ever too far out of reach.

The common point to take from these snapshots of the lives of two boys from opposite ends of town is this: high school does not begin or end with the ringing of bells but, instead, is the pervasive context in which teenagers live their lives. It is so pervasive that its official credentialing and instructional components cannot be separated from its unofficial interpersonal and developmental components.

3

The Two Sides of High School

The work that I have done on teenagers and high schools, including the study that is the focus of this book, is grounded in a rich interdisciplinary field of research. That field goes by many different names, but I like a phrase that Sanford Dornbusch used in a review essay in two decades ago: *the social structure of schools* (Dornbusch, Glasgow, & Lin, 1996). In short, high schools have a social organization that is just as well defined as their academic curricula. As social and behavioral scientists have looked into this social organization and its links to schools' academic structures, they have uncovered useful insights into adolescent development, secondary education, and how the two relate to each other. In this chapter, I try to synthesize this vast literature as a way of laying out what is known, what is insufficiently known, what is unknown, and how the work that I have done on socially marginalized teenagers in high school grows out of and extends this literature.

MAPPING THE SOCIAL STRUCTURES OF HIGH SCHOOLS

If we deconstruct the high school into its most basic elements, we are left with two general sets of processes. The *formal processes* of schooling refer to the inputs and outputs of education – e.g., staffing, curricula, teaching materials, course offerings, grades, test scores, graduation rates – that are most concretely linked to the official mission of the educational system, which is to shape children and adolescents into skilled, well-informed adults who can take their places in and contribute to the labor market and the larger polity.[1] The *informal processes* of schooling, on the other hand, refer to the social and psychological underpinnings of the system, how people come together within schools and divide and subdivide into groups. Informal processes are about relationships, about the interpersonal contexts of development. Less tangible than formal processes, they are not organized by a clear and public mission.

Long since removed from their own high school experiences and now immersed in or connected to the labor market and its accompanying stratification systems, adults tend to think about schools through the prism of formal processes, about the concrete credentials and skills that young people can derive from school to get ahead in life in the "real world" of adulthood. When I talked to the teenagers at Lamar, however, and asked them to explain to me what high school was all about, what the essence of going to high school really was, their responses universally focused on informal processes.

For example, a white 10th grader named Cooper said that the most important thing about high school was "the people I meet. *Definitely.*" He went on to say that he saw high school as "just a big building with people in it."

As another example, Katina, a young European immigrant also in the 10th grade, responded that, on the most basic level, school was simply the place "where I go to meet all my friends and hang out and stuff."

As a final example, a classmate of Cooper and Katina took a picture that he thought best captured what going to high school was really like for teenagers:

> It was a picture of Friday after school after the bell rang and just down that long hallway that leads to the theatre. It's just always

---

[1] Cremin's 1957 biography of Horace Mann and his 1980 book, *American Education*, both provide an excellent history of the early years of the American educational system, including its founding principles and formal goals. Another useful historical text is Labaree's 1988 book about the history of Central High School in Philadelphia.

packed with people. I think that's kind of – like, that's just it. There's not really one – like small groups of people. It's just one big thing. That's what kids kind of have to do. They have to be able to flow through everyone.

These feelings expressed by Cooper, Katina, and Christian were echoed by all the teenagers at Lamar to whom I talked, no matter their race, family background, immigration status, or academic standing. For them, going to high school was all about the people. It was about that *flow*.

This dichotomy between the terms adults and teenagers use to understand and discuss the role of high school in teenagers' lives is reflected, to a lesser extent, in the social and behavioral science literature on secondary education. For the most part, the formal processes of education have been the focal point of this literature for decades. Indeed, many major programs of educational policy – from school integration to curricular restructuring to class size reductions (Wells, Holme, Revilla, & Atanda, 2008; Lee, Smith, & Croninger, 1997; Mosteller, 1995; Schofield, 1995) – have been directly based on or informed by well-documented empirical patterns of the formal processes of education. Still, even though the informal processes of education have not received equal amounts of attention from social and behavioral scientists, they have certainly not gone unstudied. In fact, integrating insights from research across many different disciplines produces a fairly detailed, cohesive picture of informal processes in American high schools. The centerpiece of this smaller, but still rich, literature is the concept of culture.

High School Culture

If culture refers to the shared customs, rituals, and values that make some society, organization, or group what it is, then clearly American high schools develop and cultivate their own cultures. As reflected in the title of a groundbreaking book on education, *Fifteen Thousand*

Hours (Rutter, Maughan, Mortimer, & Ouston, 1979), young people spend a great deal of time at school. The natural end product of thousands of relationships playing out, in concert with each other, inside schools for such long periods of time is a unique, organic culture that gives each school its own "personality" distinct from other high schools, even from those high schools that look quite similar from the outside (Lightfoot, 1983).

As noted in the opening chapter of this book, the 1961 publication of *The Adolescent Society* was a seminal point in the study of high school culture. This book was based on a study that James Coleman conducted in a set of Midwestern high schools, which led him to conclude that the American high school is not merely a subset of American society but, instead, its very own society with its own rules, customs, rituals, practices, and language. According to Coleman, high school is a place in which athletics are the apex of the status hierarchy, value systems are constructed in direct opposition to the conventional values espoused by parents, teachers, ministers, and other adults, and the things that help to set up successful transitions to adulthood (e.g., academic achievement, good behavior) are devalued and even scorned. Based on this research, Coleman concluded that improving the academic progress and prospects of American teenagers involves, as a first step, explicitly recognizing that *this* high school culture is the setting in which teenagers are being educated.

In subsequent years, *The Adolescent Society* has been criticized for generalizing too broadly from a pool of racially/ethnically and socioeconomically homogenous high schools to an increasingly diverse population of American youth and for emphasizing a monolithic youth culture crossing schools over the cultures (and subcultures) of individual schools. Furthermore, his boldest claim – that high school cultures are in direct opposition to adult culture – is now largely dismissed. Teenagers do create their own culture, but it is more of a reimagining of adult culture than a subversion or perversion of it. Except in the most extreme corners of adolescent society, young people tend to espouse values that are in line with their parents' values and to engage in behaviors that, while not always smart, are generally harmless (Furstenberg, 2000).

Despite these criticisms, the general truths of *The Adolescent Society* – that the high school is its own culture, one in which education occurs – still stand. In recent decades, this understanding of high school culture has been expanded and deepened in important ways.

One valuable tradition in research on high school peer culture has shed light on the reciprocal, even symbiotic relations between the peer cultures of high schools and the larger youth culture. This oft-used term, youth culture, refers to a subculture of the American culture as a whole, one encompassing many general trends and practices among American teenagers across high schools in different cities and states that is fed by mass media and more subtle forms of diffusion.[2] As illustrated by numerous ethnographies, such as *Peer Power* by Patricia Adler, *Freaks, Geeks, and Cool Kids* by Murray Milner, and *Keepin' It Real* by Prudence Carter, the high school is the proximal setting in which tangible aspects of youth culture – images from MTV and other television programs, music (especially, today, rap music and hip-hop), youth-oriented magazines, messages and lessons from adults – are ingested, reconstituted, and then sent back up to that more distal level of "society" in the form of slang, styles of dress, ritualistic behavior, fads, and stereotypes. In a process that encapsulates the interpretivist perspective on cultural production,[3] this endless top-down/bottom-up cycle begets a vibrant youth culture within each school that is similar to what might be found in other schools but is ultimately unique. Echoing *The Adolescent Society*, Milner's book explicitly argues that such cultural production going on in high schools reflects teenagers'

---

[2] The 1992 edited volume by Greenberg, Brown, and Buerkel-Rothfuss gives an excellent window into youth culture in the United States.

[3] Most works in the interpretivist tradition focus on cultural production among young children (e.g., Corsaro, 1992; Fine, 1987), but that is not always the case. Eder's work on adolescents, for example, clearly comes from this tradition.

agentic efforts to exert control over a setting (i.e., the school) in which they feel so little personal control.

School Talk, which was written by Donna Eder, Catherine Evans, and Stephen Parker in 1995, captures the macro-micro link at the heart of this line of research on school peer culture. Although focused on middle school, its insights easily translate to high school. Eder and her colleagues document how views about gender and sexuality are socially constructed in school cafeterias, hallways, bathrooms, playing fields, and so on. Essentially, young people pick up ideas about what it means to be a girl and a boy from adults, from their own media consumption, and from viewing the world outside school. Collectively, they work with these ideas in social interactions at school, which are weighted by and conflated with the unequal status positions of individual youth at different levels of the social hierarchy in the school. What results is an explicit system of rules about how boys and girls should talk, dress, and act as well as with whom they should associate. These rules then *enforce* hyper-traditional sex roles in the student body that *reinforce* larger systems of gender inequality in society as young people grow up.

Another valuable tradition in research on high school peer culture has illuminated the ways in which such cultures are organized by and around "caste systems" (to borrow a metaphor from Milner's book) that position individual students in social roles, sometimes arbitrarily, in ways that can become self-fulfilling. Across disciplines, social and behavioral scientists have done a great deal of work mapping out the peer crowds found in American high schools. These peer crowds are on a smaller level than the student body as a whole but on a larger level than friendship groups. As described by Peggy Giordano, Kenneth Frank, and others, peer crowds are aggregates of cliques capturing large bands of peers within schools who occupy the same social space and share some collective identity.[4]

---

[4] Giordano wrote an informative review article on adolescent social relations in the 2003 volume of *Annual Review of Sociology.* Frank published a study in *American*

What is interesting is how much continuity there is in peer crowds across high schools, how the same kinds of peer crowds pop up in school after school. Indeed, the pioneering studies of the psychologist Brad Brown, in collaboration with Laurence Steinberg, Sanford Dornbusch, and others, revealed a striking degree of similarity in the presence and naming of peer crowds across a set of high schools that were geographically, racially, and socioeconomically diverse (Brown & Klute, 2003; Steinberg, Brown, & Dornbusch, 1996; Brown, Eicher, & Petrie, 1986). Such peer crowds – jocks, populars, burnouts, geeks, and the like – have been identified repeatedly in ethnographies (see the work of the sociologist David Kinney and the linguist Penny Eckert) and in larger-scale quantitative analyses (see the work of the psychologists Mitchell Prinstein and Annette La Greca and of the sociologist Daniel McFarland).[5] This similarity probably reflects the embeddedness of individual high schools in the larger cultural and stratification systems of American society, as highlighted by Eder, Milner, and other social and behavioral scientists noted above. These crowds organize friendships and dating, compete for power and status, and shape arenas of socialization for youth who identify with them but also for youth who are identified with them by others.

The work of Jacquelynne Eccles, Bonnie Barber, and Margaret Stone, which builds on the seminal work of Brown, offers a good illustration of this aspect of high school peer culture. They drew on the archetypes put forward in the iconic teen movie of the 1980s, *The Breakfast Club*, which covered a day of detention at a suburban Chicago high school with five teenagers who each represented a particular stereotypical aspect of high school peer culture: the jock (played by Emilio Estevez), the princess (Molly Ringwald), the nerd (Anthony

Journal of Sociology (Frank et al., 2008), based on Add Health data, that revealed different ways to think about peer crowds.

[5] See Eckert's 1989 book, *Jocks and Burnouts: Social Identity in the High School*, or articles by the other researchers mentioned: McFarland and Pals (2005), Prinstein and La Greca (2002), McFarland (2001), Kinney (1999).

Michael Hall), the basket case (Ally Sheedy), and the criminal (Judd Nelson) (Stone, Barber, & Eccles, 2008; Barber, Eccles, & Stone, 2001). Eccles, Barber, and colleagues asked teenagers in a large sample of high school students to think about the groups associated with each of these archetypes in their high schools and then to locate themselves in one. Essentially, these groups can be viewed as existing at the meeting point of the two major dimensions of school-sanctioned achievement and compliance: academics and sports. For example, the brains are high on academic achievement but low on sports achievement, while the princesses tend to be low on both and the jocks tends to be high on both. This mapping also applies to other, perhaps less archetypal, peer crowds that constitute subcultures of the high school peer world, suggesting that what seems to be such a complex social system to adults is actually far simpler in reality. What matters is that groups develop an identity that then subsumes individual members of the group, regardless of whether the identity is self-generated or imposed from the outside, regardless of whether individual teenagers view themselves as part of the group or are labeled by others as such.

For me, the takeaway message of this research tradition is about transactions among different levels of society: 1) the peer culture that arises in any given American high school is, at once, the consumer *and* wellspring of the larger youth culture in the United States, and 2) the subcultures that arise within high school peer cultures are made up of individual teenagers but, once formed, are larger than the sum of their parts.

Linking High School Culture to Teenagers' Developmental Pathways

The work on high school peer culture discussed so far is important in its own right as a window into understanding the social systems of American adolescents in general and American high schools in particular. Just knowing how groups form in high schools and what they represent is valuable in that it provides a far better understanding of what high schools are like.

Yet, such understanding does not usually motivate or inspire educational policy or school reform, the flurry of interventionist activity centered on school culture and bullying generated by Columbine and the longstanding interest of schools as sites of substance use education (e.g., DARE) notwithstanding. Perhaps this occurs because informal processes are easier to dismiss as outside the realm of what "real" education is supposed to be. Harkening back to a quote from a Lamar student in Chapter 1, the formal processes capture what schools are "supposed to be," and so the attention of policy makers and other adults in charge of running high schools, or of the youth attending them, is focused on what high schools are supposed to be and not always what they are. Thus, No Child Left Behind, the most massive federal push for school reform in modern history, says next to nothing about school peer culture. Along those same lines, annual rankings of the best and worst high schools in the United States – in *Newsweek*, for example – are based entirely on the formal processes of education with no regard for the kind of peer cultures to which students may be exposed in any given school.

Although I agree that the formal processes of education legitimately provide the standards by which students and schools are evaluated, I also argue, like Coleman, Rutter, and others, that our ability to assist young people pursuing higher education and/or entering the labor force in ways that help to support a stable and successful adult life and contribute to the American economy and society requires a careful consideration of informal processes as well. The simple reason is that the informal processes of secondary education matter to teenagers' lives in both the present and the future.

Much of the research on the developmental significance of high school peer culture is concerned with the health and well-being of teenagers – their psychological functioning, self-perceptions, engagement in risky behavior, and social competence (Kreager, 2008; Crosnoe, Muller, & Frank, 2004; Watt, 2003; Harris, Duncan, & Boisjoly, 2002;

Bearman & Bruckner, 2001). All of these aspects of development are vitally important, and studying them drives home the reality that high schools are contexts of development and not just institutions of academic instruction and learning. Yet, to the extent that educational policy and school reform are motivated by risks to and supports for the formal processes of education, these clear links between high school peer culture and teenagers' development might not be so effective at motivating change in the educational system. Given this, one way to use this knowledge base to motivate educational policy and reform is to demonstrate how high school peer culture and its developmental consequences – the very essence of the informal processes of education – affect the formal processes of education. In other words, to what extent do the informal processes of education impair schools' abilities to achieve their formal goals, such as raising overall academic performance rates and reducing demographic disparities in these rates?

Certainly, social and behavioral scientists have established strong connections between aspects of high school peer culture and teenagers' academic performance and identified the developmental mediators of these connections. The prevailing values and normative behaviors of students on the school level and the peer crowd level are both associated with teenagers' grades, test scores, and course-taking patterns in expected ways. Importantly, these associations do not seem to be merely a function of the factors selecting teenagers into different kinds of schools and, within schools, into different kinds of crowds. For example, Eccles, Barber, and Stone tracked their *Breakfast Club* teenagers over time and found that crowd identification in high school was one of the most powerful predictors of the teenagers' short- and long-term academic progress. This finding has been echoed in other studies of high school peer crowds and academic outcomes taking rigorous steps to address selection effects, including one conducted by the Nobel Prize–winning economist George Akerlof (see Akerlof & Kranton, 2002; also see Frank, Muller, et al., 2008). On a related note, peer dynamics – particularly mismatches between peer cultures and personnel/administration in high schools – have been implicated in socioeconomic and racial achievement gaps (Carter, 2006; Tyson, Darity, & Castellino, 2005; Ainsworth-Darnell & Downey, 1998; Steinberg, Dornbusch, & Brown, 1992; Ogbu, 1991).

Certainly, dismissing the social ups and downs of high school as a "rite of passage" or a "phase that we all go through" can be easy for adults to do. What they are doing is seeing past the pressures and demands of high school peer culture *today* toward the social and economic rewards of high school academic success *tomorrow*. To the extent that this rite of passage has effects today that can be felt tomorrow, however, this viewpoint can undermine efforts to improve schools in ways that better serve the future prospects of young people and of society. If teenagers' negative experiences on the informal side of schooling engender depression that disrupts achievement that leads to truncated rates of educational attainment, and so on, then the informal processes are an obstacle to the successful functioning of the educational system. If, on the other hand, teenagers' positive experiences on the informal side of schooling promote self-confidence in ways that increase persistence in advanced coursework that promote the educational trajectories that have profound consequences for long-term development, then the informal processes are a tool for fulfilling the educational mission of the system.

Connecting the Sides

The point that can be taken from the preceding discussion is that educational policy and reform need to better recognize how the intense social dynamics and pressures of high school life, both positive and negative, have long factored into the academic successes and failures of American teenagers. What matters is why. Over the years, various answers to this "why?" question have been put forward. Synthesizing this rich literature, I came up with a very general model of how the informal education that goes on in high school affects the formal education.

The bolded arrows marked A and B in Figure 3.1 represent the core of this integrative model. Basically, an important link connects social experiences in high school to academic progress, and that link is personal and interpersonal development. In short, the peer culture of a high school serves as the social arena in which teenagers individuate from their parents and develop their own identities (Path A), a process that can both support and interfere with the academic behaviors and efforts necessary to make the transition from high school into college (Path B). For the remainder of this chapter, I deconstruct this integrative model, using the insights and experiences of Lamar teenagers and findings from past analyses of Add Health to illustrate each piece.

THREE ROLES OF HIGH SCHOOL PEER CULTURE (PATH A)

Path A captures the informal education that goes on in schools. It is an education, led by peers and not adults, in which young people learn about themselves, their places in the world, and how to maintain or change their positions. Integral to this process is a major developmental task of adolescence – teenagers establishing their own lives separate from their parents in preparation for adulthood. For the most part, the informal education that they receive in the peer cultures of their high schools helps them meet this challenge. Yet, teenagers' relative emotional immaturity, insecure identities, and developing neurological makeup coupled with a tendency toward risk taking and antiadult attitudes in their peer groups mean that, *sometimes*, what is ultimately a healthy process is manifested in some troubling and potentially dangerous ways. Whether this process is positive or negative is rooted in three roles the school peer culture (and, of course, its various subcultures) serves in the lives of teenagers.[6] These three roles are listed in the

---

[6] For more thorough descriptions of the role of peers in adolescent development, including the concepts of socialization, opportunity structure, and

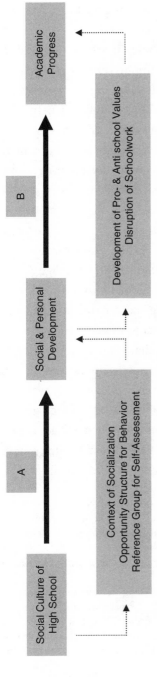

Figure 3.1. An Integrative Model Linking the Social and Academic Sides of Education.

box under Path A, representing the linkage between high school peer culture and teenagers' social and personal development.

Before discussing these three roles, I should stipulate three things: First, stressing the importance of high school peers in teenagers' lives is not equivalent to claiming that parents and other adults have little or no influence over young people. This claim has been made explicitly by some, most notably by Harris in *The Nurture Assumption*,[7] and it has been less intentionally implied by many social and behavioral scientists writing about adolescent development. Yet, as argued by Steinberg and others, the bulk of the evidence confirms that parents are primary figures in the lives of teenagers and maintain a great deal of power to intervene in what goes on among peers.[8] Even though parents clearly do matter, however, the relative balance of power between parents and peers does shift during the teenage years in meaningful ways. Importantly, high schools are ground zero for this phenomenon.

Second, the language used in this line of research, from Coleman on, often suggests (perhaps unintentionally) that there is a single, uniform peer culture that characterizes any one high school and encompasses all high schools. Clearly, this is not true. One need only spend a single day in one high school to see its myriad social subsets and how unique they all are. One need only to then go across town to another high school to see how much its general climate and all of its particular subsets differ from what was seen in the first school. While recognizing this truth, there are also many commonalities that cut across schools.

identity development, see reviews on adolescence by Steinberg and Morris (2001), Furstenberg (2000), and Dornbusch (1989). For more on adolescent brain development in particular, see articles by Dahl and Spear (2004) and Steinberg (2008).

[7] *The Nurture Assumption* came out in 1998 and was featured on the cover of *Newsweek*.

[8] The many works of Steinberg on teenagers in Wisconsin and California offer numerous examples of how parents retain power in teenagers' lives even as teenagers become more peer focused. His presidential address at the Society for Research on Adolescence (published in *Journal of Research on Adolescence* in 2001) summarizes a good deal of this work. Also see Parke and O'Neil (1999).

Third, as in all developmental phenomena, high school peer cultures and their links to teenagers' adjustment and functioning differ in incredibly meaningful ways by race/ethnicity, immigration, social class, and gender. These differences cannot be ignored, not from a standpoint of just trying to understand high schools and not from a standpoint of trying to improve them. I have spent an enormous amount of time elucidating and deconstructing those differences. Still, I also think that there is value in assessing very general patterns, of figuring out what the big picture is, as long as the important details do not get lost in the process.

High School Peer Culture as a Context of Socialization

What goes on in high school peer cultures teaches teenagers about the "right," or at least preferred, way to live. Despite how so many adults view the social worlds of teenagers, this school-based peer socialization has little to do with overt peer pressures. Instead, it occurs when teenagers observe what is valued in their school and internalize these messages into their own worldviews because they admire, respect, or fear the people giving them. It is a subtle process, much in the same way that parents' and teachers' socialization of young people is subtle, occurring in a million different, often unnoticed, unconscious instances over the course of any given day. Clearly, high schools – and their peer cultures and various subcultures – differ wildly in this regard. Where teenagers attend high school, therefore, affects the odds that they will encounter socializing messages from peers in line with or contradicting the kinds of socializing messages that they have probably long received from parents at home.

This logic connects to a prominent theory of crime. Sutherland's Differential Association Theory asserts that young people learn how to behave by assessing the ratio of positive and negative messages about behavior in their social groups and that these groups are, in turn, organized by larger community and institutional structures. In other words, the way society is set up helps to determine the types of socialization messages that someone will be exposed to in his or her primary and secondary relationships.[9] In Path A of Figure 3.1, the high school is the element of social organization that helps to determine the peer culture in which teenagers are immersed during a developmental period when peers are a major force of socialization.

To illustrate this role of high school peer culture, consider some of the prevailing peer values in the Lamar student body. Lamar falls in the middle on the spectrum of peer values about the "coolness quotient" of academic achievement. Like many high schools in the United States, peer norms in most social groups there tend to equate motivated, effortful achievement with geekiness. As one white 10th grader explained,

> Then there's just the so-called losers and nerds and stuff, who just get As in all their classes and stuff. People somehow see that as a weakness.

And, as one of his female classmates explained about what she viewed as her success at hanging with one hip crowd while studying seriously on the side,

> [The other students] think that I just kind of blow off my schoolwork and maybe copy off other people. So that's kind of lame, but it's also kind of cool, because then I've got this cool reputation, but I also get good grades, you know.

Not surprisingly, then, many high-achieving students at Lamar felt conflicted about success and their pursuit of it. At the same time, Lamar is like many other high schools in that the kinds of adult outcomes that are predicated on academic achievement in high school (e.g., going to college, getting a job that brings in money) are also valued across

---

[9] Sutherland's original formulation of Differential Association Theory was published in 1947.

a wide variety of peer crowds. As one working-class Latina remarked while describing students who go off to prestigious colleges,

> Those people were renowned at school and everyone looks up to them, just knowing that they have done a lot.

These two countervailing forces merge into a clear, consistent message for teenagers, one that appeared to cross almost all of the subgroups of the peer culture at Lamar. That message is do well, but do not do too well, and be sure that it seems like you were not even trying. Most students coming into Lamar, regardless of their backgrounds or their peer crowds, will be exposed to this socializing message simply because of their enrollment at Lamar. They might not all be equally susceptible or immune to this socializing message, but they are more or less equally exposed to it.

High School Peer Culture as an Opportunity Structure for Behavior

When trying to understand why some teenagers act one way and others act another way, opportunity is a crucial consideration. In short, the kinds of behaviors that are prevalent in high school peer networks allow some teenagers to act on their proclivities and desires, block others from doing so, and lead still others to act against their proclivities and desires.

Opportunity is more practical than socializing messages about right and wrong. Regardless of whether teenagers have internalized social norms about some behavior, who they know at school affects the odds that they can realistically engage in that behavior on a regular basis. A girl may want to smoke pot, but if no one at her school is into that scene, how will she figure out how to get pot and how will she know what to do with it if she does manage to get it? Will she smoke it alone, and will this limit the amount of time she can spend with

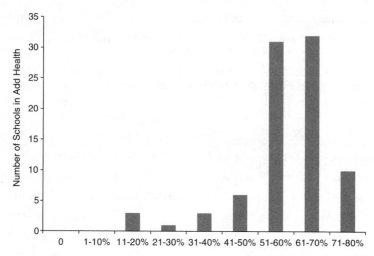

Figure 3.2. Drinkers as a Proportion of High School Student Body in Add Health

friends? Alternatively, a boy may have no desire to enroll in college-preparatory courses, but if AP courses are plentiful in his high school and are popular in his and other peer crowds, he might wind up in one almost by chance. Again, where a teenager attends school matters. School assignment helps to determine the opportunity structure that teenagers will enter.

As an example, the 80-plus American high schools in Add Health can be categorized according to the proportion of drinkers in the student body (see Figure 3.2). Not surprisingly, given what is known about teen drinking in the United States, there is no high school in this representative sample in which no teenager has avoided drinking alcohol in the prior year. Indeed, no high school even comes close to this benchmark. Fortunately, no high school is composed entirely of students who report alcohol consumption in the last year either. Every high school has at least a pocket of nondrinkers in the student body. Between these two extremes, however, the distribution of high schools in terms of their rates of drinking is somewhat even, approaching the expected bell curve shape.

What is worth noting is that although private urban schools tend to cluster on the left side of this distribution and suburban public schools on the right, high schools on either end of the distribution differ only minimally in terms of socioeconomic composition, racial/ethnic representation, and enrollment size. What differentiates them is not so much which teenagers attend the school but rather what they do once there. In this way, the high schools at different points along this distribution offer different opportunity structures for *any one teenager* to engage in drinking. He or she will have fewer opportunities in terms of parties and availability and know-how on the left side, more on the right side.

My colleagues Ken Frank and Chandra Muller and I matched teenagers in Add Health who were similar in just about every way (e.g., race, social class, achievement, family background, parental drinking, etc.) and attended schools that were highly similar (e.g., demographic makeup, size, sector). They differed primarily in where their high schools fell on the drinking distribution in Figure 3.2. What we found was that a teenager who attended a "teetotaler" school had much lower odds of drinking than her or his otherwise very similar counterpart in a "party" school.[10]

For teenagers in the teetotaler high school, it was simply hard to drink, no matter their desires or genetic predispositions or what their close friends were doing. Consider the difficulty of obtaining alcohol without the insider information about where minors can purchase alcohol without ID that likely flows more freely through a party school or the very low likelihood of being offered drinks in a highly social group situation that might entail either real or perceived pressure to accept. For teenagers in the party high school, however, drinking was something more likely to just happen as a matter of circumstance, regardless of who they were or whom their close friends were. Alcohol is there, and peers know how to get it without being caught, which

[10] See our 2004 article in *Social Problems*.

makes drinking much easier for a teenager with even the slightest inclination to do so.

The takeaway message from this discussion is that engagement in some behavior – whether it be healthy or risky, conventional or pro-scribed – is a function of both personal choice *and* the opportunities provided by larger social and institutional settings, like the high school. Sometimes personal choice matters more, sometimes it matters less, depending on who and what is around. Again, therefore, where students attend high school matters.

High School Peer Culture as a Reference Group for Self-Assessment

High school peers also serve as a looking glass for teenagers trying to figure out who they are and where they fit in the world. This image is a reference to a classic theory of social psychology – the Looking Glass Self – that contends that humans rely on messages they receive in social interaction to evaluate their own worth.[11] In other words, the people we encounter every day serve as the mirror in which we see ourselves. They reflect what we look like back to ourselves. In high school, peers, whether individually, in groups, or en masse, provide feedback about how teenagers are doing that shapes how they feel about themselves.

Returning to an earlier example, consider a boy who does not drink (or want to drink) but attends one of those party schools from Figure 3.2. Conceivably, his failure to go along with the crowd or his standing apart from a highly valued and normalized social activity could generate extensive negative feedback from peers about his social inadequacy

---

[11] See Charles Horton Cooley's 1902 book, *Human Nature and the Social Order* (republished in 1983) for the original articulation of the Looking Glass Self. Elaborations and extensions can be found in pieces by Yeung and Martin (2003) and Cast, Stets, and Burke (1999).

or his general "differentness." If internalized, this feedback could, over time, cripple his sense of himself as a likeable, socially competent person. In the end, what seems like a developmentally positive thing – not drinking – could have some negative consequences. As a result, some of the advantages of not drinking could be chipped away by the negatives of social marginalization. Indeed, my aforementioned work with Frank and Muller showed just that, with the link between abstaining and mental health significantly weaker among teenagers attending high schools characterized by high rates of drinking. Determining the tipping point between these two processes is difficult.

Drawing on Lamar for another illustration of this role of high school peer culture, consider the experiences of a white sophomore named Ray. Because Ray was occasionally a goofy and absentminded young man, his friends called him Kelso, a nickname that eventually spread through the high school. This nickname is a reference to the handsome yet dim-witted teenage character on the long-running television show *That '70s Show*, played by Ashton Kutcher. For a long time, this Kelso designation really bothered Ray, who was well aware that it was applied to him because of his behavior and personality far more than because of his looks. Ray would vent, "I really hate it because I am not Kelso though. I am not. I am my own person. It really makes me angry." Yet, he also realized that, at times, he fell into the role of Kelso at school because that was easy. Over time, he began to doubt himself. So, the reflection in the looking glass was unappealing to Ray, but he was having trouble escaping it. It was seeping inside of him.

In sum, the peer cultures and subcultures of high schools expose teenagers to various socializing messages, present opportunities to engage in certain behaviors, and provide a standard for self-evaluation. Consequently, where teenagers attend school is not just about the *formal* education that they will receive there but also about the *informal* education – about the world, about the self – that they will receive.

TWO REASONS WHY WITHIN-SCHOOL DEVELOPMENT
MATTERS ACADEMICALLY (PATH B)

The second major part of Figure 3.1 (Path B) captures the connection between formal and informal learning in American high schools. The social and personal development that occurs within high school peer cultures (the informal education of high school) has short- and long-term consequences for the accumulation of academic credentials (the formal education of high school). This linkage plays out primarily through two mechanisms. Both are listed in the box under Path B in the figure, representing the linkage between teenagers' social and personal development and their academic progress.

Development of Pro- and Antischool Attitudes

Following the tenets of Differential Association Theory described in the section on High School Peer Culture as a Context of Socialization, as well as several developmental perspectives, exposure to social messages about the value of some behavior is important because of how such messages are internalized by individuals. Whether a high school peer culture has pro- or antischool attitudes, therefore, is one factor influencing whether a teenager develops a pro- or antischool mind-set. Whether a teenager develops a pro- or antischool mind-set, in turn, factors into her or his academic behavior. In short, teenagers who like school and value education exert more academic effort, especially in the face of challenges and obstacles. Consequently, those with proschool attitudes tend to achieve more and progress further than students who are more apathetic about or dismissive of the importance of schooling, even when actual aptitude is taken into account (Carter, 2006; Weinstein, 2002; Johnson, Crosnoe, & Elder, 2001; Steinberg, Brown, & Dornbusch, 1996).

In a conversation I had with a young woman at Lamar, Lizzie discussed the difficulty of being caught between peer groups with different values. She meandered around a bit but eventually came to a thoughtful and insightful conclusion that illustrates this very phenomenon.

> Yeah, I think that's true, for the most part. Because if I know these people who don't care about anything, they are really just [like], "Let's just skip school and go hang out at Barton Springs and stuff. That sounds really fun. Better than school." You know, if I hang out with them and that's all the influence, you know, anything I hear is, "Let's do things that aren't beneficial for us, but we think are beneficial, because we have fun for a minute," then that's all you will hear. Like, OK, I'm going to insert something I learned from school this year. Like when Hitler came to power and he was telling everybody that Jews are bad, and then if all you hear is that Jews are bad, you're going to start thinking Jews are bad. If you hear that the sky is green, and you're like, "No, I'm pretty sure it's blue." You look up in the sky. It's blue. But then people are like, "No. No, it's green." You might start believing it. So it depends on what the influence is from other people [and] what they are telling you.

Instead of the color of the sky, consider what might happen if the standard of "achievement" in high school is what is being debated. If a teenager attends a high school in which he or she is bombarded with peer messages that academic success does not matter or that it is somehow secondary to social success and internalizes these messages into his or her own view of school, then he or she will be more likely than some similar student immersed in a different high school peer culture to disengage from his or her academic pursuits. Something similar might happen if he or she attends a school in which behavioral opportunities (e.g., plentiful partying) provide a social context that waters down proschool values and fuels the kinds of social feedback that can cause even a good student to rethink the role of high school academic success in his or her life.

Of course, some teenagers will maintain their own – or their parents' – mind-set about school, either positive or negative, regardless of what is going on among their peers. We also know that behaviors affect attitudes as much as attitudes translate into behavior.[12] Still, many teenagers who are malleable, socially oriented, and unsure about what they should be doing will be sensitive, in terms of the academic mindset and accompanying behaviors, to school location.

Disruption of Schoolwork

Social and emotional disruptions to and distractions from conventional academic pursuits are going to be more plentiful in some high school cultures and subcultures than in others. The rate and degree of such disruptions and distractions are significant because high school requires a good deal of focus that is quite vulnerable to interference.

For example, one reason that excessive drinking outside of high school is strongly associated with academic problems in high school is because it interferes with teenagers' concentration on and completion of required scholastic activities, such as homework.[13] As another example, high school comes with a lot of challenging work, full of ups and downs, that requires a certain level of drive and self-confidence to keep going (Marsh, Trautwein, Ludtke, Koller, & Baumert, 2005; Weinstein, 2002). Teenagers who are struggling with their sense of self-worth because of the feedback received day in and day out from peers or who are merely overwhelmed and unsure about all of the "rules" they have to follow are less likely to have that confidence. Moreover, they are more likely than other teenagers to be preoccupied with that very immediate social situation at school at the expense of their long-term academic prospects.

As two boys at Lamar explained to me separately when talking about people they knew at their school whose academic problems had nothing to do with intelligence or ability,

---

[12] See the chapter, "Attitudes, Beliefs, and Behaviors," by Schuman in *Sociological Perspectives on Social Psychology* (1995).

[13] See my 2006 article in *Sociology of Education* for more on the connection between adolescent drinking and academic performance in secondary school.

With a lot of kids, I think it brings down their grades sometimes. Because they are always just like ... they are not so much thinking about school as they are, "Oh, I hate all those people. They suck. They ruined my life or whatever." So they just stop caring about school and stuff and stop doing work in class and just fall behind and fail their classes.

Yeah, I guess it's just like you stop worrying about the more important stuff in your life and you start worrying about little things, like, is this person going to hang out with me? Is this person going to reject me? Blah, blah, blah. All that sort of stuff.

In other words, sometimes the first priority of high school is taking care of yourself, not homework. Sometimes, all that matters is what happens today. Again, this is a probabilistic phenomenon – some teenagers are immune or semiimmune to it, but many are not.

In sum, the social and personal development that occurs in the context of high school peer cultures can affect academic progress by altering or reinforcing teenagers' existing orientation to scholastic success and/or by interfering with the pursuit of such success regardless of what that orientation might be. The first mechanism is dependent on the prevailing academic values in a high school, but the second is not.

SCHOOL CULTURE, DEVELOPMENT, AND ACADEMIC PROGRESS

Linking together the two main paths (A, B) in Figure 3.1, we can see how even capable teenagers with supportive parents may face academic problems if they are immersed in high school peer cultures and subcultures that are not supportive of academic success and/or are not conducive to healthy development. The flip side is that even at-risk teenagers may exceed their academic potential if their high school cultures provide them a safer, more encouraging space to come of age and pursue their education.

This phenomenon is not new. The consequences of the search for oneself amid the contradictory messages of youth culture in general, and high school peer cultures and subcultures in particular, has played out for some time among American teenagers, as evidenced by *The Adolescent Society* as well as by social histories of adolescence in the United States, such as John Modell's *Into One's Own* and Joan Jacob Brumberg's *The Body Project*. The latter two books demonstrate that this story is at least a century or two old.

Even an old story, however, can use fresh perspective. In the next chapter, I describe two new, fresh ways to think about the link between informal and formal education in American high schools.

4

Updating and Expanding Our Perspective

What goes on in the informal processes of education filters into what goes on in the formal processes of education. This statement summarizes an already well-documented pattern in interdisciplinary research, but one that we can take further. I argue that there are two significant ways to push this line of research forward. The first is by contextualizing high school peer cultures in the larger historical moment, which will provide new insight into how the connection between informal and formal education plays out and why it matters. The second is by focusing less on the dichotomy between "good" and "bad" peer cultures and more on how the process of adaptation to peer cultures itself can transcend the "valence" of values and norms being promulgated in a school. My goal in delving into both is to set up high school peer culture as a *current* issue of educational policy that social and behavioral scientists can *continue* to inform in meaningful ways.

THINKING ABOUT SOCIAL CHANGE

Even though the connection between the informal and formal processes of education in American high schools has clear elements of timelessness, it does vary in ways that add a timely component to that timelessness. Indeed, we are now in a historical moment in which this connection is reshaping itself and, in the process, is likely becoming more intense. In particular, four historical, societal trends need to be incorporated into the integrative model depicted in the past chapter. In short, dramatic changes in the demography of the U.S. youth population, the reorganization of the American educational system, the revolution in communication/information technology, and the restructuring of the national and global economy are changing the implications of the social side of schooling for how teenagers' lives turn out.

Changing Demography

The size and composition of the teen population of the United States has changed dramatically over time. The most recent data from the Census Bureau indicate that more than 17 million teenagers are enrolled in high schools across the nation, an all-time high. As seen in Figure 4.1, this high school enrollment rate exceeds even the previous peak that occurred in the 1970s when the biggest part of the baby boom generation was transitioning into and through the high school years.[1] This very demographic trend is why the high school graduating classes of 2008, 2009, and 2010 were the biggest ones in history.

The size of this cohort is a mixture of three things. First, today's teenagers are part of what is often referred to as the echo boom, which means that they represent the collective product of baby boomers becoming parents themselves – one massive bulge in fertility producing another a few decades later. Second, we have done a great deal to reduce drop-out rates in the American educational system, keeping larger portions of teenage cohorts in secondary school for longer periods of time. Third, the United States has experienced a surge in immigration in recent decades after a period of relative dormancy. This contemporary uptick in immigration is a direct result of the reform

---

[1] See the report "School Enrollment: Social and Economic Characteristics of Students: October, 2003" from the U.S. Census Bureau (www.census.gov) for statistics on the teen population in the United States.

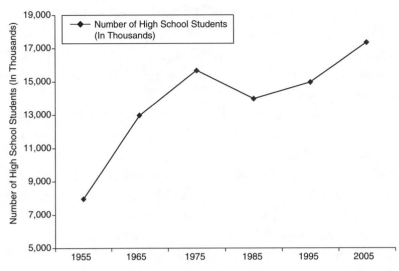

Figure 4.1. High School Enrollments in the United States.

of immigration laws in the 1960s, which eased many long-standing restrictions on immigration, including national and regional quota systems. Now, Latin America and Asia – not Europe – are the primary sending regions in U.S. immigration.[2] This racial/ethnic diversification of the immigrant pool, coupled with higher fertility rates among many racial/ethnic minority groups relative to whites in general, has greatly increased the heterogeneity of today's large teen population. Whereas when I was born in the early 1970s four out of five children were white, whites now make up just more than half of today's teen population in the United States and far less than that in many states, including Texas.[3]

As incoming high school cohorts grow and diversify, competition among students (and families) within schools intensifies. Of course, academic positions in a high school's formal curriculum (e.g., A grades,

---

[2] See Zhou's 1997 article in the *Annual Review of Sociology* for more on immigration laws and their effects.

[3] See the aforementioned Census Bureau report.

slots in a specific class, National Honor Society election, being valedictorian) are a source of competition, but so too are activity positions in its extracurriculum (e.g., making a sports team, joining a club) and social positions in its peer hierarchy (e.g., finding a group of like-minded peers, dating).

Along these lines, the work that I have done with my colleagues Monica Johnson and Glen H. Elder, Jr. using Add Health over the last decade highlights the potential implications of these dramatic demographic trends for young Americans and, more generally, for the American educational system. Specifically, our work has demonstrated that teenagers are more likely to feel that they belong at school, to feel connected to school personnel, and to be competitive for finite slots in school clubs, groups, and activities and on school athletic teams when they attend a *small* high school in which a *large* proportion of the student body is of the same race/ethnicity and/ or immigration status as themselves.[4] Because all of these different dimensions of socioemotional connectedness in high school foster academic engagement and attachment to the educational system, the growing size and diversity of American high schools represent important challenges to educators.

The bottom line of this changing demography, therefore, is that the cohort of American teenagers now enrolled in high school is enormous and diverse. The end result is bigger, more heterogeneous high schools with lower adult-teenage ratios, segregated peer networks, and far more competition for grades, class placements, activity placements, and the social dynamics related to all three.[5]

---

[4] This statement summarizes general themes from the Add Health analyses reported in our 2001 and 2004 articles in *Sociology of Education* as well as our 2004 article in *Social Science Quarterly* (Crosnoe, Johnson, & Elder, 2004; Johnson, Crosnoe, & Elder, 2001).

[5] The National Center for Education Statistics provides an overview of school size and other characteristics in "Overview of Public Elementary and Secondary Schools and Districts" on its Web site (http://nces.ed.gov/).

School Reorganization

Recent decades have witnessed a massive reorganization of American high schools as well as an overhaul of the aims of educational policy, much of it to answer criticisms of the educational system for its unfavorable international comparisons in math and science (see the *Nation at Risk* [National Commission on Excellence in Education, 1983] and *Rising Above the Gathering Storm* [National Academy of Sciences, 2007] reports). The result has been an increasing emphasis on choice and options in American education, as described in *The Shopping Mall High School* in the 1980s and illustrated by subsequent studies from numerous scholars, such as Valerie Lee, Adam Gamoran, and Barbara Schneider (Attewell & Domina, 2008; Morgan, 2005; Gamoran & Hannigan, 2000; Schneider, Swanson, & Riegle-Crumb, 1999; Lee, Smith, & Croninger, 1997).[6] This increased choice means that today's high school is incredibly differentiated and cumulative in terms of its academic curriculum.

A high school student today is charged with navigating a curriculum that has hundreds (even thousands) of options, in terms of elective courses versus required courses, different sections within each course category, and different levels within these different sections of course categories. This expansion and differentiation of the curriculum in most high schools has created a near infinity of pathways from 9th grade through 12th grade. Each of these pathways comes with a probabilistic, if not necessarily intended, outcome varying in terms of long-term payoff and future prospects. Some outcomes are highly valued and sought after, such as getting into an elite college. Other outcomes, such as dropping out of high school, are dead ends that severely diminish chances for social mobility. Because of the cumulative nature of learning, the self-propagation of teacher, parent, and self-expectations and the complex chains of prerequisites and requirements, curricular

---

[6] Powell, Farrar, and Cohen published *The Shopping Mall High School* in 1985.

pathways through high school are quite difficult – and occasionally impossible – to change once set in motion at the start of high school or even before entry into high school. On top of all of this curricular diversification, No Child Left Behind (NCLB) mandates and performance benchmarks generate pressure at the school administration and staff levels that trickles down to teenagers and dramatically increases the implications of any one curricular pathway through the system.[7]

Worth stressing is that choice is a loaded term in the American educational system. Choice about classes to take or curricula to enter are often fully available to well-informed families with empowered social positions (e.g., college-educated, professional parents, especially those who are white and native born), but they often exist only or mostly in theory for other families – especially socioeconomically disadvantaged and/or racial/ethnic minority teenagers and their parents (Schneider, 2007; Plank & Jordan, 2001). Importantly, large-scale studies by Morgan, Stanton-Salazar, Lucas, and others have documented how teenagers from such groups, cut off from valuable informational channels and lacking social standing in high schools, can be pushed through the curricular maze of high school on low-level, dead-end pathways without even knowing what has happened to them until it is too late (Morgan, 2005; Stanton-Salazar, 2001; Lucas, 1999).

As an example, my colleague Chandra Muller and I have demonstrated that parents' involvement in schooling as well as their own educational backgrounds make the biggest difference in the high-end, college-preparatory course enrollment patterns of Add Health teenagers during the first two years of high school. After teenagers have moved past this point of high school, their coursework patterns are so set and so self-perpetuating that virtually the only thing determining where in the curriculum a teenager enrolls in one year is where he or she was enrolled the year before. Thus, a "choice" about

---

[7] The Winter 2006 issue of the *Harvard Educational Review* provides an excellent discussion of the different facets of No Child Left Behind.

course enrollment at the *start* of high school ultimately ends up being a "choice" about the number and level of credentials that a teenager will have accumulated at the *end* of high school. This national pattern was writ small in Lamar, a school struggling to meet NCLB's Adequate Yearly Progress goals. There, teenagers' math course placement in 10th grade, the first year in which choice in which math course to take is widely available, is closely tied to their social class background. That 10th grade placement then appears to be just about the sole criterion determining how far teenagers eventually progress in math by the end of high school.[8]

The bottom line of school reorganization, therefore, is that today's high school curriculum is diversified, cumulative, and tied to national standards, with an appearance of student choice and agency that, in reality, is heavily dependent on the social status of families. The end result is a high-stakes game in which seemingly simple course-taking decisions and actions eventually accumulate into self-propelling, highly constricted academic trajectories that are make or break for both teenager and school.

IT Revolution

Information technology has exploded over the last decade as today's teenagers have come of age. This explosion includes the development, production, and mass marketing of Internet and wireless communications (e.g., cell phones, handhelds) as well as the proliferation of different ways to use such communications to connect with others.

Today's teenagers live connected.[9] With much less socioeconomic and racial variation than might be expected, they communicate with

---

[8] This research was presented at the 2006 meeting of the American Sociological Association and is currently under second invited review at an academic journal.

[9] Brown, Green, and Harper (2002) provide a good description of the transformation of the information technology landscape in the last decade.

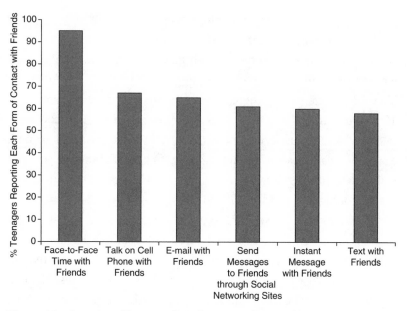

Figure 4.2. American Teenagers' Media Use with Friends.

teachers, do their homework, and study online. Moreover, they also conduct their social lives on a virtual plane through cell phones (including texting), Web pages, and e-mail in school, at home, and almost everywhere in between. Indeed, as depicted in Figure 4.2, data from the Pew Internet and American Life Project show that although the modal type of teenagers' interactions with friends is still face to face, most teenagers now utilize a variety of electronic forms of contact to supplement this face-to-face time. These technologies have become such a taken-for-granted part of teenagers' lives that they make the everyday operations of high school, both academic and social, occasionally appear unrecognizable to many adults.

The increasingly wired nature of American high schools is offering many young people social connections outside of high school and allowing them to find people out there who are just like they are. In this sense, it is creating communities for young people that maybe they never would have had before. At the same time, however, this dramatic trend in communication is also strengthening youth culture in general and the peer cultures within high schools in particular.

For example, the wired world is concentrating and strengthening the self-consciously rebellious and independent messages – don't mess with me, never compromise, be real – that have long been a dominant theme in popular culture geared toward youth. Consider what I observed on popular social networking sites (e.g., MySpace, Facebook). Just about every girl at Lamar had an account on one of these sites. Their pages differed widely, but, to a third party, each represents something very similar: a near-daily effort to try on and present different personalities to the world as a means for eliciting positive feedback from others. I saw this clearly in a young woman named Katina. She was shy, polite, and bookish at school. After school, she and a group of classmates became smoking, drinking, cursing, fighting "badass bitches" online. The language and images were offensive and startling. According to the comments posted, however, this self-presentation also brought her and her friends a certain amount of respect, respect that she clearly craved.

More locally, social networking sites also allowed the kinds of negative social dynamics occurring in the hallways at school to follow some teenagers home. Many of the girls, for example, described how they would monitor the pages of other Lamar teenagers, and several had vivid stories of online attacks from others at school. Everyone was keeping a watchful eye on everyone else. The home page for MySpace proclaims it to be *A Place for Friends*. Likewise, Facebook's home page declares that *Facebook Helps You Connect and Share with the People in Your Life*. What these sites really represent, however, is a place for teenagers to figure out who their public self is, both apart from and within their high school social worlds.

The bottom line of the IT revolution, therefore, is that much of the day-to-day academic operations of high school have been transferred to the realm of computers and other electronic devices, and wireless communication has become a primary arena for social interaction.

The end result is a connection between teenagers and their high schools that never ends, merging in-school and out-of-school life to a whole new degree.

Economic Change

Three recent books by various teams of economists and demographers – *Century of Difference* by Claude Fischer and Michael Hout, *The Race between Education and Technology* by Claudia Goldin and Lawrence Katz, and *Divergent Paths* by Annette Bernhardt, Martina Morris, Mark Handcock, and Marc Scott – describe in exhaustive detail how, since the early 1970s, the American (and global) economy has slowly transitioned from its long industrial phase dominated by heavy manufacturing into a postindustrial phase dominated by the information and service sectors. One result of this macrolevel economic restructuring is that the labor market has taken on an increasingly hourglass shape, in which broad strata of secure, valued, mostly professional jobs sit at the top, even broader strata of unstable, low-paying, mostly service-type jobs lie at the bottom, and very little exists between the two. This hourglass is inequality crystallized, separating the haves from the have-nots and reducing the chances that the latter can transition into the former.

All of this economic restructuring has transformed the role of educational attainment in society in general and, in particular, as a mechanism of inequality. A college education – especially in high-value fields like science, business, and technology – has become absolutely crucial to pushing through the labor market bottleneck. Indeed, the long-term returns to getting a college or postcollegiate degree have now reached historic levels. Consider the historical trends evident in statistics compiled from the U.S. census by the College Board (see Figure 4.3). They demonstrate that earnings premiums – how much more college graduates earn than high school graduates – have increased steadily for men. For women, who have long enjoyed even

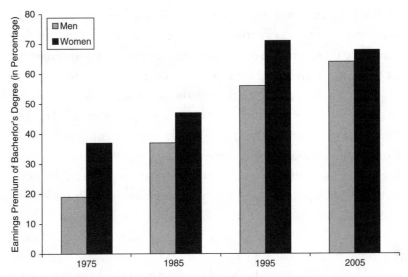

Figure 4.3. Earnings Premium for Bachelor's Degree versus High School Diploma, by Gender.

bigger premiums than men, this increase has plateaued in recent years, but the clear upward historical trajectory is still striking.

Statistics like these illustrate why Fischer and Hout call higher education the "dividing line" in society.[10] At the same time as the benefits of higher education are increasing almost exponentially, the real costs of higher education have also skyrocketed as a result of tuition increases, decreased funding, wage stagnation, and population growth. The result is a supply-demand, risk-reward crunch in which today's youth are caught. Not just a problem for individuals, this crunch is seriously undermining the flow of highly skilled workers into the upper-level, professional strata of the labor market that have become absolutely crucial to maintaining economic competitiveness in a global economy that requires innovation just as much as, if not more than, productivity (Goldin & Katz, 2008; Turner & Bound, 2006, Hoxby, 2004).

[10] From *Century of Difference: How America Changed in the Last One Hundred Years.*

This modern educational dilemma is seen most vividly in the experiences of teenagers from economically disadvantaged families, especially those who are racial/ethnic minorities and/or immigrants. In the past, a high school diploma was an effective route for climbing out of the low-wage labor market into more stable, financially rewarding jobs. The unionized jobs in the automobile plants and steel mills of yesteryear are good examples of this once common, now largely foreclosed path to mobility. Today, these young people need to gain post–high school credentials to have the same chances for social mobility, but, on a practical level, their opportunities to enter this realm of education are also narrowing (Schneider, 2007; Fischer & Hout, 2006; Hirschman, 2001; Katz & Autor, 1999). Given the role of education in noneconomic outcomes, including family formation, marital stability, and physical and mental health, the implications of these changes for certain segments of today's youth cohort go far beyond money.[11]

As an illustration that this phenomenon is not solely about what sociologists refer to as the status attainment process, consider different sets of studies conducted in the 1960s. One set revealed that obese teenagers were less likely to attend college than nonobese teenagers, primarily because the stigma associated with obesity disadvantaged them during the application and interview process. Another seemingly unrelated set documented that college enrollment in young adulthood was closely linked to lifelong earnings (Blau & Dudley, 1967; Canning & Mayer, 1966). Contemporary studies, including work I have done with Add Health, have replicated that link between obesity and college enrollment, and another set of recent studies already mentioned has reported that the earnings payoff of college enrollment has increased.[12]

---

[11] My colleagues John Mirowsky and Catherine Ross have written extensively on the link between educational attainment and the health, well-being, and behavior of adults. See their 2003 book as a starting point. For more on the nonincome effects of educational attainment, see Fischer and Hout's 2006 book.

[12] See my 2007 article in *Sociology of Education* as well as a study conducted by the economists Guldi, Page, and Stevens for the MacArthur Network on Transitions to Adulthood.

Putting together all of these different pieces of information reveals that the persistent social stigma of obesity among teenagers is now more consequential in the long term than it used to be.

The bottom line of economic change, therefore, is that the restructuring of the American economy has reduced the ultimate social and economic returns to high school graduation and increased those returns for college education. The end result is a link between high school experiences and college enrollment that constitutes a make-or-break period in the long-term social, psychological, and economic prospects of young people.

The Convergence of Macrolevel Trends

Together, these four macrolevel trends have made American high schools larger, more impersonal, more academically and socially competitive, less bounded, and far more consequential for the rest of life. As a result, the socializing contexts, opportunity structures, and looking glasses provided by a high school likely matter more to the kind of adult a teenager will turn out to be today than in the past. Thus, the potential importance of studying the connection between informal and formal education in high school is now quite high, and new mechanisms for this connection needed to be looked into more closely.

LOOKING FOR DIFFERENT ANGLES

The potential for the informal education that goes on in high school to disrupt and/or support the formal education is a reality of American education, especially, as I have just argued, today. This reality cannot be ignored if educational policy and school reform are to work. Again, this is not a new or particularly groundbreaking statement. After all, this was one of the main points Coleman tried to make when writing *The Adolescent Society* in 1961. It was also the motivating spirit of a more recent (1996) book, *Beyond the Classroom: Why School Reform Has*

Failed and What Parents Need to Do, by the interdisciplinary team of Steinberg, Brown, and Dornbusch. Carrying on the Coleman tradition, they argued that modern school reform in the United States had not delivered what was promised because the social dynamics of education have been largely ignored in educational policy and management.

Reflecting the general thrust of the literature, these influential works focused primarily on one very important mechanism by which informal and formal education go together – the tendency for high school peer cultures to foster antiacademic and generally antiadult attitudes that then shape teenagers' own orientations to academic effort and achievement. In other words, most of the attention among social and behavioral scientists studying this connection has been on the challenges schools face getting young people to learn and achieve when the general interpersonal cultures of school peers do not prize learning and achievement. The problem, these voices argue, is that people in the high school do not value education. Fix that, the theory goes, and the "real" school reforms (e.g., new curricula or pedagogical styles, an infusion or redirection of funds, reorganization of classroom arrangements) can fulfill their potential.

Let me reiterate that this basic argument is a very important one that is integral to improving educational policy. It is captured by one major piece of the integrative model I presented in Chapter 3: high school peer culture (context of socialization) → social and personal development (the development of anti- or proschool values) → academic outcomes. Yet, recall that this integrative model had other pieces and paths, and they need to be studied intensively in addition to the work being conducted on that one important part of the model. One of these alternate foci is, in my reading of the literature, especially understudied relative to its potential value to both theory and action: high school peer culture (reference group for self-assessment) → social and personal development (disruption of schoolwork) → academic outcomes.

In short, informal processes can undermine formal processes even in high schools with strongly proacademic, conventional peer cultures and few oppositional subcultures if these processes engender a highly personal struggle to manage social pressures, find one's place, and maintain a positive sense of self. In this scenario, the informal barriers to producing academic gains in the high school can persist even if the culture of the school is somehow changed to be strongly academic in orientation. In other words, the policy stance suggested by research on that first piece of the model would go only so far if uninformed by research on the alternate piece.

As an illustration, two very smart girls at Lamar had run into academic difficulties despite being in peer groups that, to adult eyes at least, seemed good. An articulate and literate 9th grader named Ava who was one of the self-professed "band nerds" crowd had trouble with the so-called mean girls at school. Because she did not like going to Lamar as a result of these problems, she often found herself not doing the things that Lamar required of her, despite her primary exposure to academically oriented peers. For Olivia, a high-achieving working-class African American classmate, the post–high school journeys that were taken for granted by her friends and peers made her very uneasy because they were so far from what her life was like now. Even going to college in San Marcos, which is less than an hour away from her home, filled her (and her parents) with anxiety that proved to be a big distraction. These girls faced academic risks *despite* a good deal of academic benefits in their own peer groups, in Lamar as a whole, and in their families. Such unrecognized risks may be a fatal flaw in our efforts to improve the prospects of high schools and their students.

Thus, even if we can change the value structure of a high school peer culture, or its subcultures, that might not be enough to address the real vulnerabilities of educational policy that Coleman, Steinberg, and others have elucidated over the years. To demonstrate this potential problem of not taking social understanding of high school far enough, consider two major policy interventions charged with improving the performance of American schools.

The first policy intervention is NCLB, which was formulated by the Bush administration and passed by Congress in 2001. Perhaps the largest federal policy on schools in history, it is also one of the most politically contested. Although I am not as sanguine about the faults of NCLB as some educational scholars, I do take issue with its almost exclusive focus on the formal processes of education. The idea that the formal goals of this sweeping legislation can be achieved without any attention to the informal dynamics of high schools is scientifically uninformed. Although much of this disconnect concerns the general tone of values in high school peer cultures (first, focal piece of the integrative model), part of it also concerns the risks posed by the social psychological struggles of teenagers in high schools with even the most achievement-oriented peer cultures (second, alternate piece of the integrative model). As just one example, two of the most well-known priorities of NCLB are its strong emphasis on accountability and its strong emphasis on testing. These emphases may be motivating and productive for many students, thereby allowing schools to meet their performance benchmarks. Yet, some students find this kind of pressure socially and psychologically painful, a situation that, if widespread enough, can chip away at some of those school gains.[13]

The second policy intervention is the racial integration of schools, which has a long history in the United States since the *Brown* decision and has been one of the most important social justice actions ever taken by the state. Overall, racial integration on the school and classroom levels seems to have improved the academic prospects of minority students, mostly by improving (although certainly not

---

[13] See essays by Karen, Dworkin, Ingersoll, and Epstein in the Perspectives on Critical Issues section of the April 2005 issue of *Sociology of Education* for a good discussion of the pros and cons of No Child Left Behind.

eliminating) the unequal distribution of resources (e.g., funds, well-trained teachers, learning materials) to the schools that students from different racial/ethnic groups attend. At the same time, racial integration has also introduced some negative side effects, mostly having to do with what happens when members of different groups mix in the same schools. For example, African American youth often face real threats to their self-concepts and self-esteem in integrated schools and have more trouble achieving social stature. These problems on the informal side of school can chip away at gains on the formal side of school.[14] Again, all of this can occur completely independently of the academic value system of schools, although the value system does likely factor into the equation.

In both cases, formal policies produce results. I am *not* arguing otherwise. What I *am* arguing is that the full potential of these policies, and others like them, has not been realized. Progress can be made toward reaching performance goals on the school or student level, but these goals cannot be reached until that last remaining impediment – which has nothing to do with teaching styles or textbooks or with whether teenagers value school or not – is addressed.

If we have to choose between focusing on the informal or formal processes of education, then we should focus on the latter in order to have the *biggest* impact, but policies do not necessarily have to focus on one or the other. Furthermore, they do not have to focus on only one dimension of informal processes at a time. This same logic extends beyond policy and intervention to the everyday actions that parents, teachers, coaches, and mentors take to help teenagers do well. In this current historical moment, our help will go only so far if we do not consider all of what is happening in high schools.

[14] See Goldsmith (2004), Mickelson (2001), Cohen and Lotan (1997), and Schofield (1995). Also, Richard Kahlenberg's 2001 book, *All Together Now*, is about socio-economic integration but provides a discussion of these same issues.

WHY ALL OF THIS MATTERS

In this chapter, I have tried to explain why the rich interdisciplinary body of research on the connection between informal and formal education in high school is still a work in progress. Just because we know a great deal about this connection does not mean that we know everything, or that our scientific grasp cannot still evolve as circumstances change. Consequently, updating our perspectives and thinking about multiple mechanisms leading to the same endpoint helps us to cultivate a more current, multidimensional understanding of a seemingly timeless issue of education. In turn, that understanding can point to specific ways to help teenagers from all demographic segments of society manage the intense social demands in and around their high schools while they accrue the kinds of educational credentials that are increasingly crucial to doing well and to contributing to society in the 21st century.

In the next section of the book, I take a very *specific* approach to the connection between informal and formal education as a means of adding to our *general* understanding of it. As noted in Chapter 1, this specific take centers on a consideration of what happens academically to young people when they do not fit in socially at high school.

PART II

A CASE STUDY OF SOCIAL
AND ACADEMIC EXPERIENCES
IN HIGH SCHOOL

5

The Stakes of Social Marginalization

Based on the integrative model put forward in Chapter 3 and its elaboration in Chapter 4, we have a general picture from past research about how teenagers' social experiences in high school can filter into their academic experiences. This general picture, in turn, can be mined for various action/intervention strategies by looking at it in different ways.

First, this general picture can be approached by contextualizing it within major macrolevel trends that converge in the current historical moment. Doing so emphasizes the need to understand 1) how social problems in high school are intensified by the new media and by the increasingly impersonal, institutional qualities of schools, 2) how the academic consequences of such social problems extend beyond traditional indicators of academic performance, like grades, to encompass the pathways that young people take through complex, differentiated curricula, and 3) how these academic problems during high school forecast post–high school prospects, thereby allowing the risks of high school social experiences to filter across the life course.

Second, this general picture can be approached by shifting attention away from the "good crowd versus bad crowd" dichotomy and toward the process of social adaptation to high school peer cultures more generally. Much has been written about this crowd dichotomy and its relation to teenagers' academic performance, and it is well understood. What is less understood are the academic risks associated with teenagers' social struggles to be accepted by their peers in high school, struggles that occur no matter how academically rigorous or lax a school is, no matter how scholastically focused or dismissive its student body is or its various subcultures are. In other words, all high school peer cultures and subcultures, no matter their academic orientation, require some work from teenagers, and that work may interfere with schoolwork.

Putting all of this together, teenagers who have trouble adapting to the increasingly diffuse and digitized social worlds of their high schools may be distracted from their academic pursuits through high school that, more and more, are part of a highly stratified and cumulative process of educational and socioeconomic attainment in the long run. This specific link between the informal and formal processes of education is a potential trouble spot for high school academic reforms, one that can impede improvements in underperforming or at-risk high schools and keep even the "best" high schools from reaching their full potential. One clear way to see this link in action and understand why it is important is to look closely at something that adults often view as a natural outgrowth of high school: teenagers feeling like they do not fit in.

NOT FITTING IN

In educational research, a great deal of attention has been paid to what happens to young people who feel like they do not measure up academically in their schools. As exemplified by the work of Herbert Marsh, Jacquelynne Eccles, and many other educational psychologists, this literature suggests that teenagers who view themselves as lacking academic prowess will have lower rates of achievement over time. Of course, part of this association might simply reflect reality.[1]

---

[1] Marsh's work on the frog pond effect can be reviewed in a 2003 piece in *American Psychologist* with Kit Tai Hau. A good summary of Eccles's expectancy model and related work can be found in her 2002 piece in *Annual Review of Psychology* with Alan Wigfield.

In other words, they are correctly gauging their lower academic skills that then translate into lower performance. Yet, this phenomenon also occurs among young people matched on academic skills and past performance. When they differ in self-assessments of academic worth, they tend to differ in subsequent performance. Importantly, because schoolmates serve as the frame of reference, the skill and performance level of the school as a whole matters. Young people with objectively strong academic and cognitive skills may see themselves as lacking such skills if they attend schools in which the overall skill level of students – the standard of comparison – is high. In other words, what matters is how teenagers *perceive* themselves in the *context* of the student body of their schools. The reason this matters, both theory and empirical evidence suggest, is that teenagers who view themselves as not up to the academic challenges of school downgrade their aspirations, devalue such success, and lower their effort.

This academic phenomenon has a corollary, I argue, in the social arena; specifically, when teenagers feel like they do not measure up socially in their high schools. These feelings could take the form of perceived isolation or rejection. They could also tap into self-perceptions that one simply does not belong regardless of social position. As demonstrated shortly, most teenagers have such feelings at one point or another in high school. As a result, these feelings are easy to minimize as something that is normal, a part of a rite of passage that will soon pass without ultimate harm. At the same time, these feelings are often viewed as socioemotional issues that are disconnected from the academic experience.

These views of teenagers' feelings of not fitting in may be too dismissive for several reasons. First, although many teenagers may have these feelings from time to time, some experience much more severe and persistent states of perceived social marginalization. Second, the same mechanisms that link problematic academic comparisons to teenagers' academic outcomes could also link perceived social marginalization to these academic outcomes. In other words, teenagers who feel like they do not fit in might also get off track academically for many of the same reasons. To the extent that academic experiences during high school can disrupt educational trajectories after high school, the consequences of feelings of not fitting in socially would then have potential to persist long after those feelings have faded. Thus, teenagers who feel like they do not fit in socially at high school might have truncated rates of educational attainment after high school, regardless of their own academic capabilities or the academic values of their schoolmates.

A National Picture of Not Fitting In

To explore these issues, I looked at the slightly fewer than 8,000 teenagers in Add Health who were in high school at the start of data collection in the mid-1990s and were subsequently followed to 2001.[2] In Wave I, the Add Health interviewers asked teenagers a series of questions about their social experiences in high school and their general social psychological orientation to their schools. To look at a full range of feelings of not fitting in, I identified teenagers who reported that they felt rejected, felt unwanted, had trouble with other students, did not feel close to others at school, and/or did not feel part of things at school. Giving teenagers a point for each one of these five feelings that they reported as having had in the past year and then summing, I was

---

[2] The core Add Health sample originally contained 20,745 students in 7th to 12th grades in 1995, but all of the analyses presented in this chapter were based on a subset of this sample containing 7,876 members of the original sample. First, to be included in my sample, Add Health respondents had to be enrolled in a high school at Wave I. This selection filter did not affect the representativeness of the sample but instead shifted it from the 7th–12th grade segment of the population to the 9th–12th grade segment. Second, Add Health high school respondents had to remain in the sample from Wave I through Wave III, regardless of school enrollment status over time. Most variables were measured at Wave I, the socioemotional response variables were measured at Waves I and II, and the college outcome was measured at Wave III.

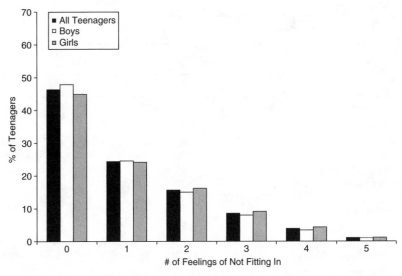

Figure 5.1. Number of Feelings of Not Fitting In at School Experienced by Teenagers.

able to capture a population distribution of perceptions of not fitting in at high school in a nationally representative sample of American teenagers.

Figure 5.1 captures this distribution. Table 5.1 provides the basic characteristics of teenagers at each point along the distribution.

The average teenager only had one feeling of not fitting in, which, most often, was the feeling of not being close to others at school or the feeling of not being part of things at school.[3] In general, therefore, the teenagers in Add Health felt at least OK about their social situations in high school. Yet, fully 30% of the teenagers had two or more feelings of not fitting in, and one teenager in 20 reported four or five such feelings.

---

[3] The mean score on the not-fitting-in scale was 1.03 with a standard deviation of 1.22. Looking at individual items, 17% of teenagers reported feeling rejected, 12% reported feeling unwanted, 15% reported having trouble with other students, 33% reported not feeling close to others at school, and 27% reported not feeling a part of things at school.

Table 5.1. *Characteristics of Teenagers with Different Numbers of Feelings about Not Fitting In at School*

	Number of Feelings of Not Fitting In					
	0	1	2	3	4	5
BOYS						
% white	53.97	50.38	49.12	54.79	57.25	48.72
% African American	18.81	18.47	14.96	13.20	8.40	5.13
% Latino/a	15.67	18.26	21.83	19.80	19.08	30.77
% Asian American	9.05	9.67	11.09	10.23	9.16	10.25
% other race/ethnicity	2.37	3.22	2.99	1.98	6.11	5.13
% with college-educated parents	33.05	27.28	24.82	27.06	32.82	23.08
% living with both parents	61.36	54.46	52.11	53.13	49.62	48.72
% in private school	9.82	7.63	7.04	6.27	8.40	7.69
Average % minority students in teenager's school	45.81	49.34	56.64	48.62	47.92	62.16
Average % students with college-educated parents in school	35.07	32.94	33.45	32.91	32.30	33.71
n	1,812	931	568	303	131	39
GIRLS						
% white	56.37	46.46	46.15	48.79	48.04	69.39
% African American	19.37	25.45	24.28	21.44	18.99	10.20
% Latino/a	13.76	17.58	17.65	20.38	17.32	14.29
% Asian American	8.16	7.37	9.35	7.23	10.06	4.08
% other race/ethnicity	2.29	3.03	24.13	2.14	5.59	2.04
% with college-educated parents	32.64	27.88	23.38	26.54	21.22	22.45
% living with both parents	58.22	54.24	51.58	46.65	49.16	46.94
% in private school	10.39	8.18	5.73	8.58	5.03	2.04
Average % minority students in teenager's school	46.98	52.66	52.02	49.49	49.07	44.27
Average % students with college-educated parents in school	34.74	33.95	32.89	33.88	32.32	32.04
n	1,838	990	663	373	179	49

Reflecting past work that girls are more concerned with social integration (if not status) than boys (Collins, Welsh, & Furman, 2009; Giordano, 2003), boys were more likely than girls to be in the category of teenagers who reported no feelings of not fitting in and girls were more likely than boys to be in the categories of teenagers reporting multiple feelings of not fitting in. Among both girls and boys, the proportion of youth from higher SES families (defined here in terms of parent education and family structure) declined as feelings of not fitting in increased, but there were racial/ethnic differences across the two genders. Among boys, Latino/as and youth attending minority-concentrated high schools were overrepresented at the upper end of the not-fitting-in distribution. For girls, whites were overrepresented at the upper end, and the school composition trends were less pronounced.

Thus, the norm among American teenagers is to have at least some feeling of not fitting in at high school, but some teenagers' feelings extend well beyond this "normal" range. As I discussed in the opening chapter of this book, what I am concerned with are teenagers' perceptions of social marginalization, which this scale of not fitting in captures. Some of the teenagers scoring high on this scale may actually be quite socially integrated in and respected at their schools, while some scoring low may actually be quite marginalized. What matters, I argue, is teenagers' own views of their social situations at high school as much as their objective positions in the social arena of high school because their views – their readings of the fit between them and the environment, whether correct or incorrect – are what they react to when charting their way through high school. As I discuss shortly, these reactions are the very crux of how informal education can filter into formal education.

Another thing to note here is that, as of yet, we do not really know why some teenagers feel that they do not fit in and others feel that they do. Is it something very internal, or is it rooted in the way they are treated by others? If the latter, is it something about the way they look or how they act or their social background? In the next chapter, I turn to a couple of reasons why some teenagers may feel like they do not fit in, but, for the moment, I maintain a general focus on teenagers who have these feelings, regardless of why they do.

Moving from the Social to the Academic

If, according to educational psychologists (Marsh, Trautwein, Ludtke, Koller, & Baumert, 2005; Marsh, 1987), the concern over teenagers who feel that they do not measure up academically is that these feelings may lead to problematic academic outcomes, then that concern also likely applies to teenagers who feel that they do not measure up socially. Put another way, feelings of not fitting in at high school might not only pose risks to mental health and general well-being, but also undermine educational attainment.

As touched on in the discussion of the integrative model of informal and formal education in Chapters 3 and 4, curricular reforms and school reorganization in recent decades have created a situation in which, more and more, academic success and the route to college are defined by teenagers' accrual of highly valued academic credentials in a heavily differentiated, often optional curriculum. These credentials include good grades, of course, but also credits in advanced coursework. Taking such classes, especially when they are no longer required, and earning top grades in the process, signals to colleges, especially elite colleges, that teenagers are up to the challenge of postsecondary education. Staying on this curricular trajectory and meeting the expectations and standards of teachers in the classes in this trajectory require concentration, confidence, and persistence. This is particularly so because persistence in most curricula besides English becomes more voluntary over the course of high school and, moreover, because coursework is so cumulative that "bad" curricular decisions are very difficult to reverse once certain trajectories are under way (Crosnoe &

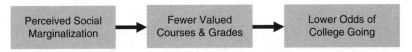

Figure 5.2. The Long-Term Effects of Not Fitting In at High School.

Huston, 2007; Morgan, 2005; Plank & Jordan, 2001; Schneider & Stevenson, 1999).

To the extent that teenagers who doubt themselves socially come to doubt themselves academically, that teenagers who are disillusioned with the social contexts of their high schools become disillusioned with the academic side of schooling, and that teenagers who worry about their social situations are distracted from their academic activities, therefore, we would see a pattern in which teenagers who feel that they do not fit in socially accrue fewer academic credentials during high school, credentials that so powerfully predict college going. This basic idea is captured in Figure 5.2, which is a partial rendering of the not-fitting-in pathway presented in Chapter 1. For now, we are focusing only on the short- and long-term *academic* outcomes of perceived social marginalization. If this pathway bears out in reality, then the view that social problems in high school are a phase that teenagers eventually get over, something that does not ultimately matter very much once high school is done, is called into question. After all, in the modern economy, college going has historically powerful effects on lifelong socioeconomic attainment and the multiple life course trajectories related to it. Moreover, in the aggregate, college-going rates are important components of economic productivity and social stability for society at large.

NOT FITTING IN, ACADEMIC PROGRESS,
AND COLLEGE GOING

To test the abbreviated pathway depicted in Figure 5.2, I first looked at which teenagers in Add Health enrolled in a 4-year college in the years immediately after high school.[4] Echoing the full population patterns from the census, the college-going rate among the Add Health teenagers was 34% and tilted toward girls (female college-going rate = 37%, male college-going rate = 30%).

Next, I examined whether the odds of going to college after high school differed as a function of feelings of not fitting in socially during high school. In modeling these odds in a multilevel logistic regression framework, I was concerned about factors that might be confounded with what appeared to be an effect of not fitting in on college going. Misattributing cause is especially problematic in research attempting to inform policy, but, even though nonexperimental studies can never establish cause, researchers can take steps to improve causal inference. Consequently, these models needed to statistically control for many factors that might lead teenagers to feel like they do not fit in at school and also affect their odds of college going.

Of such confounds, three sets were particularly important. First, recall my earlier assertion that how teenagers perceive their social situations matters above and beyond what their objective social positions are. Thus, I accounted for various aspects of teenagers' social relations, including the number of friends they had, their popularity within the school, and their dating status.[5] Second, recall that an important

---

[4] I created a binary measure of college enrollment based on a series of questions in the Wave II In-Home Interview about educational attainment. In this measure, young people who were currently attending or who had graduated from a 4-year institution of higher education received a 1, and those who did not meet these two criteria (including those who had never attended such institutions, those who had dropped out of such institutions, and those who were enrolled in or had graduated from 2-year institutions) received a 0. I then predicted this binary outcome by a set of independent variables with logistic regression in the glimmix macro in SAS. This macro adapted the mixed procedure (the SAS version of multilevel modeling) to the logistic framework, allowing for the accurate estimation of school effects (by partitioning the outcome variance into between- and within-school components).

[5] Sociometric reports in the Wave I In-Home Interview allowed the identification of the number of friends (a count of friends nominated by the teenager; $M = 3.16$,

conclusion of educational psychology research is that feelings of academic inadequacy have effects regardless of actual academic ability, as well as my argument that social problems can affect the educational trajectories of even capable students. The models of college going that I estimated, therefore, controlled for teenagers' scores on standardized cognitive tests as well as entry-level (e.g., start of high school) academic indicators.[6] Third, a major theoretical thrust of this study is that problems rooted in adjustment to high school peer cultures can matter academically regardless of the actual academic values of those cultures. Reflecting this position, I drew on the census-like nature of Add Health's first school-based survey (in which almost all students in each school reported certain information) to measure and then control for the prevailing academic norms (e.g., average achievement, educational aspirations, and course enrollment) of the student body of each high school.[7]

SD = 2.66). Sociometric reports by all students in each sample school allowed the construction of full network measures, including the popularity of teenagers defined as ego-based received network (e.g., count of nominations of teenager by others as a friend; M = 4.53, SD = 3.65). Romantic involvement was a binary measure, where 1 = teenager reported having a serious boyfriend or girlfriend (57%) and 0 = no such relationship.

[6] Add Health participants took a modified version of the Peabody Picture Vocabulary Test (PVT) in the Wave I In-Home Interview. Scores were converted to percentiles (M = 50.79, SD = 28.19). The high school transcripts in Add Health allowed the measurement of the first grade point average recorded in high school (M = 2.56, SD = 0.88).

[7] Following work I have done with Add Health published in *Child Development* (2008) and *Social Problems* (2007), student reports of grades (averaged across four subjects into a conventional four point GPA; M = 2.77, SD = 0.23), educational expectations (on a scale from 0 = no chance to 8 = it will happen; M = 6.21, SD = 0.53), math/science enrollment (1 = enrolled in either or both in last year, 0 = enrolled in neither; M = 0.71, SD = 0.13), and principal estimates of the percentage of graduates going on to college in years past (divided into quintiles; M = 2.70, SD = 0.95) were averaged among all students in each school to create three school-level variables. These variables were then converted to z-scores (to account for the different metrics) and then averaged into a single scale of academic press among school peers (α = .66; M = 0.02, SD = 0.62).

In addition to these three sets, other confounds could have, if left uncontrolled, produced observed effects of not fitting in on college going that were not trustworthy. Thus, the statistical models I estimated also included controls for stage of development and schooling (e.g., grade level, age), demographic characteristics (e.g., race/ethnicity, immigration status),[8] parents' characteristics (e.g., parents' marital and educational statuses),[9] and other key aspects of school structure and composition (e.g., public vs. private sector, size of school, racial/ethnic composition, socioeconomic composition).[10]

Fortunately, Add Health included data that could tap into these important confounds. Unfortunately, Add Health contained no data on other theoretically important confounds. As a social demographer, I am also acutely aware that other confounds might not even be known or identified by theory regardless of how easy or hard they may be to measure if known. A good example of this problem of "unobservable" confounds concerns genetic traits. Teenagers may have heritable dispositions related to their self-perceptions and academic behavior that, if not taken into account, can present the false appearance of a link between the two. Such an occurrence could reflect a cluster of known traits or, even more problematically, factors that are completely unidentified and unknown. Obviously, dealing with such confounds,

---

[8] Race/ethnicity was measured with dummy variables for non-Latino/a white (52%), non-Latino/a African American (20%), Latino/a (17%), Asian American (8%), and Other race/ethnicity (3%), all based on teenager self-reports.

[9] Family structure was a binary measure based on teenager self-reports, where 1 = teenager lived with both biological parents (56%) and 0 = other family form. Parent education represented the maximum level between parents on a 5-point scale reported by the teenager (1 = less than high school graduation, 2 = high school graduate, 3 = some college, 4 = college graduate, 5 = postgraduate). The mean for the sample was 2.96 ($SD = 1.26$).

[10] Sector (1 = private, 0 = public) and size were based on the reports of school administrators at Wave I. Approximately 9% of the sample was in a private school, and the mean school size was 1,381 ($SD = 829$). Reports of parent education and race/ethnicity on the In-School Survey were aggregated within high schools to measure the proportion of students in each school who were nonwhite ($M = 48.84$, $SD = 33.79$) and had at least one parent with a college degree ($M = 0.34$, $SD = 0.15$).

genetic or otherwise, is difficult. Here, I attempted to do so by calculating post hoc robustness statistics that quantified how big of an effect some unknown confound would have to have on both the predictor (e.g., feelings of not fitting in) and outcome (e.g., college going) for the control of that unknown confound, if it was known and could be measured in Add Health, to eliminate the observed effect of the predictor on the outcome.[11]

In discussing findings from my analyses of Add Health in this and subsequent chapters, I focus on results from statistical models that persisted despite the control of observable confounds, and that appeared to be robust to the potential control of unobservable confounds. Again, these results do not prove cause, but they are relatively high on the spectrum of causal inference for analyses of survey data.

The College-Going Rates of Teenagers Who
Feel Like They Do Not Fit In

Figure 5.3 presents the predicted odds of college going for teenagers at each point on the not-fitting-in distribution. These predicted odds were derived from the fully controlled logistic regression models described in the section above that were estimated for each gender.[12] In this figure,

---

[11] The Impact Threshold for Confounding Variables (ITCV) quantifies how large an unobserved confound would have to be to reduce a focal coefficient to nonsignificance and, therefore, negate causal inference (Frank, Sykes, et al., 2008). The ITCV was calculated for the coefficients of the not-fitting-in variable in each model and then, in later modeling iterations, for the academic status variable and the socioemotional functioning variables. The ITCV equation is $r_{xy} - r^\#_{xy} / 1 - r^\#_{xy}$, where $r^\#_{xy} = t / \text{SQRT}[(n - q - 1) + t^2]$, t is the critical t-value, n is the sample size, and q is the number of model parameters. When covariates are included in the model, the equation becomes $\text{ITCV}_{\text{no covariates}} \times [\text{SQRT} (1 - R^2_{xg})(1 - R^2_{yg})]$, where g is the set of covariates, R^2_{xg} is the R^2 value from a regression predicting the focal independent variable by the covariates, and R^2_{yg} is the R^2 value from a regression predicting the outcome by the covariates.

[12] To arrive at these predicted odds, I multiplied the model coefficient for the not-fitting-in scale by each possible value on the scale, multiplied the female coefficient by 1 and 0, and then added each possible value to the intercept value (the

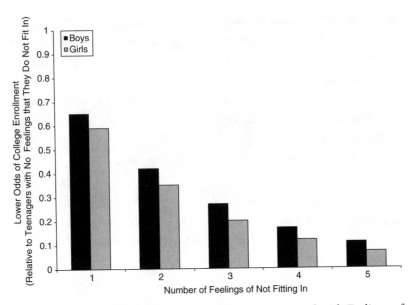

Figure 5.3. Lower Odds of College Enrollment Associated with Feelings of Not Fitting In at School.

each bar represents the odds of going to college for teenagers with that number of feelings of not fitting in relative to same-gender and otherwise highly similar (i.e., matched on controls) teenagers reporting no such feelings. Since all bars, for girls and boys, are below 1.0, they indicate that teenagers with any feelings of not fitting in at high school had lower odds of going to college after high school than their otherwise comparable peers who did not feel in any way that they did not fit in at high school. Indeed, with each additional feeling of not fitting in, teenagers' odds of going to college after high school declined iteratively. This trend was more pronounced among girls than boys. The gap in college-going odds between those with feelings of not fitting in and those without such feelings was bigger for girls at each point of the distribution than it was for boys, even though girls were more likely to attend college after high school overall than boys.

model constant added to the product of each model coefficient besides these two focal ones and their respective means/modes).

Importantly, the effect size of the association between feelings of not fitting in socially at high school and college going after high school was large for both girls and boys (50% of a standard deviation in the college-going measure for girls, 40% for boys). Such effect sizes meet conventional thresholds for what constitutes an empirical pattern with policy relevance, in other words, a pattern that might justify investment (McCartney, Burchinal, & Bub, 2006).

Academic Progress as a Linking Mechanism

According to the hypothesized pathway in Figure 5.2, one explanation for the lower college-going rates of teenagers who feel like they do not fit in at high school is likely. Because of their social situations, such teenagers do not accrue the kinds of valued academic credentials in their cumulative high school careers that improve their competitive advantage in college admissions and that enable to them to persist in college if they are admitted.

To test whether the statistically significant, large, and robust link between feelings of not fitting in during high school and college going after high school in Add Health was mediated by high school academic progress, I followed the lead of sociologists of education, such as Barbara Schneider and Chandra Muller (Schneider, 2007; Riegle-Crumb, Farkas, & Muller, 2006; Stevenson, Schiller, & Schneider, 1994), and drew on official transcripts to count how many of three valued academic credentials teenagers were able to obtain during high school: persisting in the math curriculum past Algebra II, persisting in the science curriculum past Chemistry, and accumulating a final grade point average of 3.0 or higher. These thresholds represent tangibly elite academic credentials that make teenagers very attractive to colleges. Importantly, according to studies conducted by the U.S. Department of Education, they also represent critical thresholds in academic preparation for college.[13] In other words, the more such thresholds teenagers

---

[13] As two examples, see the 2006 and 1999 reports by Clifford Adelman.

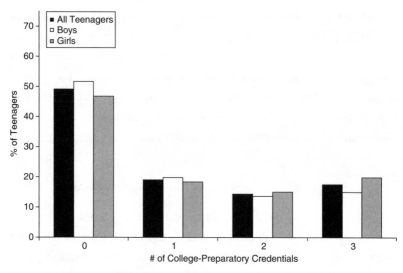

Figure 5.4. Number of College-Preparatory Credentials Accumulated by the End of High School.

reach in high school, the greater their later chances of matriculating in and then graduating from 4-year colleges. Of course, other domains of achievement, academic and otherwise, matter to college enrollment too. Looking at these three indicators, however, provides a parsimonious but powerful window into what helps and hurts teenagers on the path through high school to college.

Figure 5.4 presents the distribution of Add Health teenagers on this scale of academic progress, defined by end-of-school outcomes (e.g., before graduating or dropping out) tapping navigation through a differentiated, cumulative, and highly optional curriculum.[14] A

---

[14] Because the math/science curriculum in American secondary education is largely standardized into a hierarchy of less advanced to more advanced classes, the AHAA transcripts were used to create variables measuring location in math and science course sequences for each year of high school as well as the ultimate level achieved by the end of high school (Riegle-Crumb, Muller, Frank, & Schiller, 2005). Coding schemes were similar to those previously applied to the National Educational Longitudinal Study (Schiller & Hunt, 2003; Schneider, Swanson, & Riegle-Crumb, 1999). Each class on a transcript was assigned a

near majority of the teenagers in Add Health accrued none of these academic credentials by the end of high school, primarily because they made Cs or even lower grades at one or more point of their high school careers and because they stopped taking math and science around their junior years of high school. Again, this distribution was gendered. Girls were overrepresented at the high end of the distribution, reflecting the documented pattern that girls have caught up with or surpassed boys in math/science coursework and generally make better grades across subjects (Shettle et al., 2007; Bae, Chow, Geddes, Sable, & Snyder, 2000).

To establish end-of-school level of academic progress, so defined as a mediator of the already established link between feelings of not fitting in socially at high school and college going after high school, I had to first document that feelings of not fitting in were significantly and inversely associated with academic progress during high school. Simple comparisons revealed that the average teenager with no feelings of not fitting in at high school accrued more than one (1.3) of the focal academic credentials before graduating from or dropping out of school and that the average teenager with four or five of these feelings accrued less than one (0.82), a difference representing just less than half (41%) of a standard deviation in the academic progress scale. This

CSSC (Classification of Secondary School Courses) code designating the course subject, using the standard taxonomy created for all National Center of Education Statistics data sets. For math, these codes were collapsed into 10 hierarchically ordered categories (0 = No Math, 1 = Remedial Math, 2 = General Math, 3 = Pre-Algebra, 4 = Algebra 1, 5 = Geometry, 6 = Algebra II, 7 = Advanced Math, including Algebra III and Statistics, 8 = Pre-Calculus, 9 = Calculus). For science, they were collapsed into six categories (1 = Basic/Remedial Science, 2 = General/Earth Science, 3 = Biology I, 4 = Chemistry I, 5 = Advanced Science, such as Biology II or Chemistry II, 6 = Physics). Transcripts also gave the letter grade earned by students in each course of the high school career, which were averaged across classes and semesters to calculate a comprehensive GPA ranging from 0 (failure) to 4 (A). Each of these three items was dichotomized (7–9 for the math sequence, 5–6 for the science sequence, and 3.0+ for GPA) and then summed (M = 1.00, SD = 1.22).

difference was even bigger among girls, at 55% of a standard deviation. Indeed, girls who reported five feelings of not fitting in at high school had the lowest average level of academic progress (0.41) of any subset of the sample examined.

Because this link between feelings of not fitting in and academic progress could also be spurious, I turned to a Poisson multilevel model in which the academic progress scale was regressed on the not-fitting-in scale as well as all of the measured confounds discussed in the Not Fitting In, Academic Progress, and College Going section for the college-going model.[15] For both girls and boys, academic progress declined significantly and substantially (although somewhat less substantially than in the simple mean comparisons) as feelings of not fitting in rose. Unlike in the simple mean comparisons, however, this association did not differ by gender.

The next step in establishing the mediational power of end-of-school level of academic status was to add it to the original college-going model and assess the degree to which its inclusion attenuated the previously observed effect of feelings of not fitting in on college going. For both girls and boys, academic progress by the end of high school was – not surprisingly – powerfully associated with later college going. Each increase on the academic progress scale was linked to a more than one and a half standard deviation decrease in the odds of college going for teenagers of each gender. Furthermore, the inclusion of the academic progress scale in the model led to a 30% attenuation in the size of the coefficient for the not-fitting-in variable among girls and a corresponding 42% attenuation among boys. Both links in the focal pathway – between not fitting in and academic progress, between academic progress and college going – were deemed robust by post hoc statistical tests.

---

[15] Poisson estimation techniques were needed because of the countlike nature of the academic progress variable. These models were also estimated with the mixed procedure and the glimmix macro in SAS.

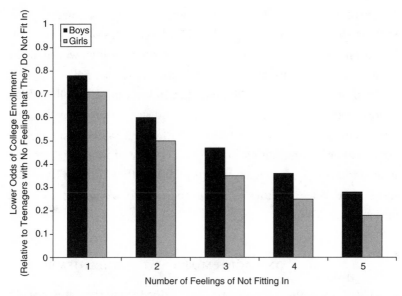

Figure 5.5. Lower Odds of College Enrollment Associated with Feelings of Not Fitting In at School among Teenagers with the Same Levels of Academic Progress by the End of High School.

To the extent that such attenuation reflects a causal process, then, a significant portion of the differences in college-going rates between teenagers who did and did not feel like they fit in socially at high school occurred because the latter group of teenagers made lower grades and persisted less far in the math and science curricular pipeline than the former group of teenagers. Based on these models, Figure 5.5 presents the predicted odds of college going for teenagers at each point on the not-fitting-in scale after adjusting for differences across categories in the academic progress levels of teenagers. Comparing Figures 5.3 and 5.5, the differences in odds between teenagers with each number of feelings of not fitting in and teenagers with no such feelings were smaller in Figure 5.5. As one example, looking at the smallest difference in both figures, boys with one feeling of not fitting in had 48% lower odds ([1.0 – .52] × 100 = 48) of attending college after high school than otherwise similar boys with no such feelings (refer back to

Figure 5.3). After holding constant academic progress, however, boys with one feeling of not fitting in had 22% lower odds of attending college than otherwise similar boys with no such feelings who had the same level of academic progress by the end of high school.

In short, teenagers who felt like they did not fit in socially at high school demonstrated less persistence and achievement in the academic curriculum and, partly as a result, were less likely to enroll in college after leaving high school. The next line of inquiry, therefore, is to understand why teenagers who felt like they did not fit in followed academic trajectories that put their chances of going to college at risk.

FOCUSING ON SOCIOEMOTIONAL MECHANISMS

In all likelihood, the mechanisms connecting teenagers' feelings of not fitting in socially with their academic trajectories through high school and into college are numerous and complex. As a developmentalist, I am interested in a particular piece of the puzzle. Drawing on the work of scholars from Piaget to Sameroff to Cairns (Cairns & Cairns, 1994; Sameroff, 1983; Piaget, 1955), I am interested in teenagers' attempts to create a semblance of equilibrium in their environments, to adapt to or change their immediate situations as a way of bringing stability to their lives. In other words, past theory suggests the value of looking at how teenagers in trouble attempt to cope with their troubling situations, sometimes with positive results, but also sometimes with problematic results. The latter outcome is what I focus on here – how teenagers' well-intentioned attempts to cope with their feelings of not fitting in at school ultimately do more harm than good. This phenomenon is captured by the full not-fitting-in pathway presented in Chapter 1 and then again in an abbreviated form earlier in this chapter (see Figure 5.6).

Like many developmental perspectives on individual and social problems that have been erroneously viewed as examples of blaming

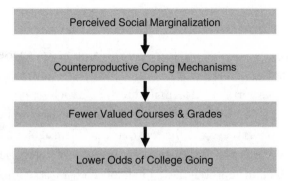

Figure 5.6. The Long-Term Effects of Not Fitting In at High School – Revised.

the victim,[16] this perspective may be criticized for focusing too intently on what teenagers are doing at the expense of what is being done to them, for seeming to place the fault of their lower odds of college going too much within them. I take an alternative viewpoint, however, stressing that this perspective emphasizes another quality of teenagers for which they do not often receive enough credit: their agency.

Like adults, teenagers are agentic beings, meaning that they perceive their lives as under their own control.[17] Consequently, when in trouble, they try to take charge. Sometimes, these attempts are healthy and developmentally positive. For example, a girl who feels like she does not belong in school may get involved in sports as a way of finding her social niche. Even if she ultimately does not find her social niche, she may locate her own field of personal success that counterbalances what she believes she may be missing socially. Yet, what may be more common is that teenagers, so entrenched in the concerns of the present that they have trouble seeing into the future, engage in coping responses that are self-protective in the short term but are problematic, even disastrous, in the long term.

---

[16] Here, I am thinking of such conceptual models as the family process perspective on poverty (McLoyd, 1990; Elder, 1974), which views poverty's developmental risks as at least partially filtered through parenting.

[17] See reviews of self-efficacy by Bandura (2000, 1997).

Coping in Three Counterproductive Ways

Although positive attempts to cope with troubling experiences are certainly not uncommon and are quite central to understanding the link between informal and formal education in high school, I will wait to address them in later chapters, instead focusing now on more risky coping responses that are at the root of the problem at hand. In particular, past research and theory point to three general categories of what I refer to as counterproductive coping mechanisms, the final piece of the full pathway presented in Figure 5.6.

In the first counterproductive coping mechanism, *internalization*, teenagers manage their feelings of not fitting in by altering their own assessments of the self to be in line with their image of how others see them. This mechanism, reflecting the basic insights of the Looking Glass Self and other social psychological theories of the self, suggests that teenagers will accept their perceived lack of social value – their difference or exclusion – as a means of making sense of their social situations. In one light, downgrading one's own sense of worth and devaluing one's life seem like psychological or health *outcomes* of some social process, but we can also look at such actions as *channels* in a process, as actions taken by young people to bring order to their worldviews and an element of expectancy to their lives.[18]

In the second counterproductive coping mechanism, *self-medication*, teenagers try to numb the pain of feeling like they do not fit in at high school by turning to quick fixes. As demonstrated in the work of Hussong, Aseltine, and other psychologists and health researchers, alcohol and drugs are often such quick fixes for feeling better.[19] If perceived social marginalization in high school is the malady, alcohol and drugs may be viewed by some teenagers as the appropriate medicine.

---

[18] For more on internalization, read about the Looking Glass Self (Yeung & Martin, 2003; Cast, Stets, & Burke, 1999; Cooley, [1902] 1983).

[19] For more information about self-medication among teenagers, see articles by Hussong, Hicks, Levy ,Curran (2001) or by Aseltine and Gore (2000).

For example, teenagers who feel rejected may try to play physician or pharmacist to themselves, administering treatments (e.g., beer, pot) that they hope will eliminate the feelings of loneliness, emptiness, and fear that this rejection causes.

Finally, the third counterproductive coping response is *disengagement*, which is derived from Merton's social psychological conceptualization of anomie and social strain.[20] A seemingly logical response to feeling left out or excluded at high school is to avoid or reject high school. Such action can take both explicit and implicit forms. As one example, a teenager who feels like a nobody at school may stop going to school or cut classes. As another example, problematic experiences at school may lead a teenager to not like school, not just the school itself but also everything (e.g., academic achievement) it represents. Devaluing school, not trying in school, and checking out of school in these ways are attempts to reduce the immense power that school – and the people in it – has over a teenager.[21]

For teenagers, these three kinds of coping responses may represent perfectly rational reactions to the experience of not fitting in socially at high school. They assess their social situations in school and make calculated decisions about how to protect themselves. In the short term, they are often correct in these assessments, in the sense that these three coping responses can be effective means for making sense of or dealing with the pain caused by their social experiences in high school. After attempting to cope with perceived social marginalization in these ways, teenagers often feel better or at least have a sense that they understand what is happening to them.

If coping in these three ways at least has potential for self-protection in the short term, the long term is a different story. What is self-protective for the present may be self-defeating for the future.

---

[20] See Merton's 1957 book, *Social Theory and Social Structure*.

[21] The oppositional culture research offers one important, albeit controversial, view on the protective power of disengagement from school (Ogbu, 1991). The work of Dance (2002) is also informative.

College going is one good example of how these short- versus long-term trade-offs may play out in teenagers' lives. Not only is college going now far more important in a socioeconomic sense than it ever has been before, today's American teenagers now overwhelmingly view going to college as the appropriate and desired next step in their lives after leaving high school. Indeed, this viewpoint cuts across socioeconomic and racial/ethnic lines – it is the normative outlook of teenagers.[22]

Yet, my own research with Add Health has demonstrated that behaviors and feelings that map onto internalization, self-medication, and disengagement all disrupt teenagers' paths to college, primarily through declines in academic effort and achievement (Crosnoe, 2006; Crosnoe, Riegle-Crumb, & Muller, 2007; Crosnoe, Muller, & Frank, 2004). First, negative self-concept (a sign of internalization) lowers teenagers' future aspirations and reduces their motivation to achieve these aspirations. Second, drinking and other forms of self-medication impair cognitive functioning, undermine conventional norms of behavior and achievement, and put teenagers at great health risk. Third, disengaging from school – in the form of truancy or downgrading the importance of school – clearly interferes with the accumulation of valued academic credentials in high school. Triangulating this research poses a hypothesis that teenagers who try to cope with their feelings of not fitting in at high school by internalizing, self-medicating, and/or disengaging are likely disrupting their academic trajectories in ways that could truncate their long-term educational trajectories.

Testing the Relevance of Counterproductive Coping Mechanisms

Add Health offers several ways to measure different dimensions of the three counterproductive coping mechanisms viewed as mediators of

---

[22] Barbara Schneider's 2007 report for the Gates Foundation on college-going high school communities gives a nice overview on the new norms about college enrollment in the United States.

the association between feelings of not fitting in socially in high school and end-of-school academic progress, an association that, in turn, I have linked to college going. To capture aspects of internalization, I measured teenagers' feelings of self-rejection, suicidal ideation, and depression.[23] To capture self-medication, I measured rates of drinking alcohol and smoking marijuana.[24] Last, to capture disengagement, I measured truancy.[25] Table 5.2 presents the average levels of each of these socioemotional factors by gender across the two waves of Add Health. In general, girls had higher levels of internalization while boys had higher levels of self-medication and disengagement. To the extent that the latter factors capture externalizing behaviors, these trends echo long-standing patterns of gender difference in socioemotional well-being in the literature (Leadbeater, Blatt, & Quinlan, 1995; Ge, Lorenz, Conger, Elder, & Simons, 1994).

Again, following the steps of mediation, I first examined the degree to which feelings of not fitting in were associated with each of the socioemotional factors. Worth noting is that, in order to take a more dynamic developmental perspective, as well as to guard against reverse causality, my multilevel lagged modeling strategy actually examined how

---

[23] The rejection measure was binary, indicating that the teenagers disagreed with the statement that they liked themselves just the way they were (8% at Wave II). For suicidal ideation, teenagers reported whether they had seriously considered committing suicide in the last year (11%) or not. In a modified version of the Center for Epidemiologic Studies–Depression Scale (Radloff & Locke, 1986), students reported how often they experienced 15 symptoms of depression, including loneliness and anxiety. Responses ranged from 0 (never or rarely) to 3 (most or all of the time). The sum measured depression ($M = 7.52$, $SD = 5.97$; $\alpha = .86$).

[24] Based on prior Add Health research (Crosnoe, 2006; Resnick et al., 1997), teenagers' responses to a series of items about timing and frequency of substance use were collapsed into two 6-point scales (0 = none in the last year, 1 = 1 or 2 days in the last year, 2 = once a month or less, 3 = 2 or 3 days a month, 4 = 1 or 2 days a week, 5 = 3 to 5 days a week, 6 = nearly every day), one for alcohol use ($M = 1.20$, $SD = 1.56$) and one for marijuana use ($M = 1.08$, $SD = 2.14$).

[25] Truancy was the count of teenager-reported unexcused absences from school (0 = 0 days, 1 = 1–2 days, 2 = 3–5 days, 3 = 6–9 days, 4 = 10+ days; $M = 2.31$, $SD = 3.68$).

Table 5.2. *Average Levels of Socioemotional*
Conditions and Behaviors, by Gender

	Average Levels	
	Boys	Girls
Self-rejection (%)		
First year	0.06	0.15
Second year	0.04	0.11
Suicidal ideation (%)		
First year	0.10	0.17
Second year	0.05	0.13
Depression (0–45)		
First year	6.67	8.42
Second year	6.71	8.27
Drinking (1–6)		
First year	1.20	1.05
Second year	1.34	1.07
Marijuana use (1–6)		
First year	1.15	0.97
Second year	1.17	1.00
Truancy (0–5)		
First year	1.78	1.66
Second year	2.51	2.12

these socioemotional behaviors and conditions changed over time. In other words, I predicted each socioemotional factor from Wave II by the not-fitting-in scale from Wave I, as well as the Wave I version of each socioemotional factor. Consequently, an example of the question that I was really asking is, does the depression of a teenager with feelings of not fitting in at high school escalate at a faster rate across 2 years of high school than the depression of a highly similar teenager with no such feelings?[26] This series of models revealed that feelings of

---

[26] I predicted the various socioemotional factors by the independent variables (including all control variables, the not-fitting-in scale from Wave I, and the Wave I version of each socioemotional factor), using logistic regression for binary outcomes and Poisson regression for countlike outcomes (both in the mixed procedure in SAS with the glimmix macro).

not fitting in were significantly associated with over-time increases in every indicator of counterproductive coping except alcohol use. This pattern was the same for girls and boys, with effect sizes ranging from small/moderate (not fitting in → depression) to moderate/large (not fitting in → truancy).

The next step was to determine whether these socioemotional factors that were predicted by teenagers' feelings of not fitting in predicted, in turn, their academic progress. To do so, the previously estimated models in which academic progress was the outcome and the not-fitting-in scale was the focal independent variable were reestimated, with variables capturing Wave I to Wave II changes in the six socioemotional factors added iteratively. For both girls and boys, over-time increases in three socioemotional factors (depression, marijuana use, truancy) during high school were significantly associated with lower levels of academic progress by the end of high school. These associations persisted above and beyond the numerous developmental, demographic, family, social, and academic confounds that could be observed and were also robust to the potential control of confounds that could not be observed.

Thus, of the six socioemotional factors hypothesized to be counterproductive coping mechanisms, only three could conceivably act as mediators of the association between teenagers' feelings of not fitting in and their academic progress. Adding all three of these socioemotional factors to the academic progress model revealed that the coefficient for the not-fitting-in scale was attenuated by 36% for girls and 40% for boys. Thus, the counterproductive mechanisms put forward in the pathway in Figure 5.6 accounted for some, but certainly not all, of the lower levels of end-of-school academic progress of teenagers who felt like they did not fit in at high school. Either other mechanisms are at work or the three hypothesized mechanisms are not being captured fully by Add Health data.

As a final step, the college-going model was supplemented by adding the full set of factors tapping over-time socioemotional functioning.

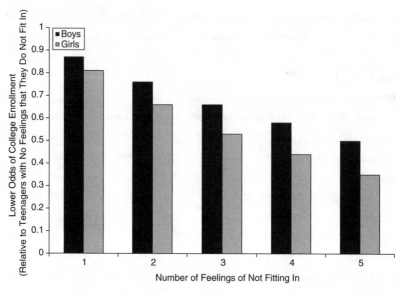

Figure 5.7. Lower Odds of College Enrollment Associated with Feelings of Not Fitting In at School among Teenagers with the Same Academic Status and Socioemotional Adjustment.

For girls and boys, greater changes in self-rejection, marijuana use, and truancy were associated with lower rates of college going. Adding these factors attenuated the already established association between teenagers' feelings of not fitting in at school and their odds of going to college by 38% for girls and 45% for boys. Indeed, this association was no longer statistically significant for boys after their over-time socioemotional functioning was taken into account.

Based on these models, Figure 5.7 presents the predicted odds of college going for teenagers at each point on the not-fitting-in scale after adjusting for differences across categories in the academic progress levels and socioemotional functioning of teenagers. Compared to Figure 5.5, the differences in odds between teenagers with each number of feelings of not fitting in and teenagers with no such feelings were smaller. For example, looking at the biggest difference in both figures, girls with five feelings of not fitting in had 82% lower odds of attending college after high school than otherwise similar girls with no such feelings (look at the very last bar in Figure 5.5). After holding constant socioemotional functioning (in addition to academic progress and all behaviors/circumstances/conditions captured by the control variables), however, this difference in odds of college going fell to 65%.

Basically, this last set of analyses revealed that marijuana use and truancy helped to explain why teenagers who felt like they did not fit in at high school were less likely to go to college, in part because these behaviors disrupted academic progress and in part because they were more directly related to college going regardless of teenagers' academic progress. At the same time, the role of depression in linking feelings of not fitting in with college going was entirely channeled through academic progress. Conversely, teenagers' feelings of self-rejection appeared to disrupt college going completely independently of academic progress.

SUMMARY OF FINDINGS

Following the conceptual model of not fitting in that was derived from the integrative model introduced and elaborated on in Chapters 3 and 4, the analyses of Add Health discussed so far indicated that teenagers who felt like they did not fit in at high school were less likely to go to college. This disparity in college going was not a function of key aspects of teenagers' school location, family background, demographic statuses, more objectively measured social positions in school, cognitive skills, or prior academic skills, and it appeared to be robust to the potential control of other aspects of teenagers' lives and developmental ecology that could not be measured in Add Health. For both girls and boys, the majority of these disparities were accounted for by the interplay of teenagers' socioemotional functioning and academic progress.

For girls, 57% of college-going disparities linked to their feelings of not fitting in were explained by socioemotional functioning and academic progress. Of this 57% portion, slightly more than half (54%) was accounted for by the pathway captured in Figure 5.6. Feelings of not fitting in were associated with increased depression, marijuana use, and truancy over time, which were associated with lower-level academic progress by the end of high school, which was associated with lower odds of going to college. The remainder of this 57% portion (46%) was accounted for by feelings of self-rejection that disrupted college going regardless of academic status and by the leftover significance of marijuana use and truancy for college going that was not channeled through lower-level academic progress.

For boys, 68% of college-going disparities linked to their feelings of not fitting in were explained by socioemotional functioning and academic progress. For the most part, this reflected the pathway in Figure 5.6: feelings of not fitting in → increased depression, marijuana use, and truancy → academic progress → college going. Yet, as for girls, we also saw that some (38%) of the portion of these disparities related to socioemotional functioning were accounted for by direct links among feelings of not fitting in, socioemotional functioning, and college going regardless of academic progress. The observed consequences of not fitting in for college going were *weaker* for boys than girls overall, therefore, the hypothesized pathway between feelings of not fitting in and college going provided *greater* explanatory power for these consequences among boys than girls.

What cannot be stressed enough is that I also looked into variability in this not-fitting-in pathway by race/ethnicity, immigration status, and socioeconomic status.[27] I did detect some differences in various pieces of the pathway, but the strongest pattern emerging from these analyses was that *teenagers from diverse social and economic groups were much more similar than different in their experience of the*

---

[27] Focal racial/ethnic groups included white, African American, Latino/a, and Asian American teenagers. Socioeconomic status was defined by family income and parent education. First, second, and third generations of immigrants were examined.

not-fitting-in pathway. Thus, this pathway is more generalizable across groups than it is group specific.

In short, the pathway depicted in Figure 5.6 provided the single best (i.e., majority) explanation of college-going disparities related to not fitting in socially at high school across diverse groups of teenagers, but there is still more to know about why teenagers who do not fit in at high school are less likely to go to college after high school. What we have here is a good start. The take-home message is that even if the social struggles of not fitting in at high school are something that teenagers get over eventually, their attempts to get over them might set in motion a chain of bad things before they have a chance to get over them. Up to this point, our attempts to understand this problematic developmental process have been agnostic to why teenagers might feel as though they do not fit in socially at high school. In the next chapter, this changes.

6

Teenagers at Particular Risk

If not fitting in socially during high school threatens the future educational trajectories of teenagers in an era in which the lifelong returns to college going are at an all-time high, then, for the purpose of policy intervention, we need to ask, who is at risk for feeling like they do not fit in at school? As with so many developmental issues, the answers to this seemingly straightforward question cross many domains of behavior, adjustment, status, and trait and vary a great deal by setting and context. Because I could not look into all of the reasons that teenagers might feel like they do not fit in socially at high school, I decided to couple theory with timely policy interests to narrow the focus.

In short, working from classic social psychological theory and with an eye toward major public health initiatives in the United States, I focused in general on the idea that some subsets of the population can carry social stigma and in particular on two groups that, historically, have been stigmatized: teenagers who are obese and teenagers who are lesbian/gay. Importantly, focusing on social stigma is true to the basic argument underlying the work presented so far; specifically, that teenagers may be affected by feelings of not fitting in whether those feelings "accurately" reflect their social positions or not. The known, widespread existence of a stigma in some cultural context – be it a peer network, a school, a community, or society at large – can subject someone to social devaluation from others but also cultivate self-perceptions of social devaluation even when it is not actually happening.

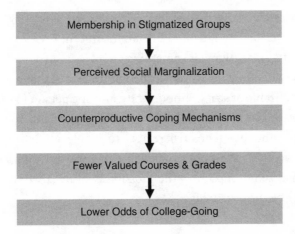

Figure 6.1. The Long-Term Effects of Not Fitting In at High School – Further Revised.

Exposure to social stigma, therefore, is hypothesized to be a factor that can engender teenagers' feelings of not fitting in at high school and the associated socioemotional and academic consequences of these feelings. This elaboration of the not-fitting-in pathway that was the basis of the empirical analyses in the preceding chapter is depicted in Figure 6.1. In this chapter, I further motivate this elaboration and then test it with data from Add Health.

STIGMA

Most closely associated with Erving Goffman,[1] stigma is a collective rather than individual characteristic. It refers to groups of people defined – either internally or externally – by a common trait with a negative label. According to one formal definition, a stigma singles out groups "about which others hold negative attitudes, stereotypes, and beliefs, or which, on average, receive disproportionately poor inter-personal or economic outcomes relative to members of the society

[1] See Goffman's 1963 book *Stigma: Notes on the Management of Spoiled Identity*.

at large because of discrimination" (Crocker & Major, 1989, p. 609). Thus, as described by Link and Phelan in a recent review of research on social stigma, a stigma is something about a group of people – how they look, what they do, who their people are, etc. – that makes them seem undesirable or scary.[2] Importantly, any one person in that group might escape the stigma of that group, but, regardless, all people in the group are at heightened risk relative to people not in the group for being viewed negatively or devalued. In other words, being a member of a stigmatized group raises the probability of negative social treatment but does not ensure it.

Obese Youth, Lesbian/Gay Youth, and Social Stigma

Obviously, many traits are stigmatized in American society in general and in American youth culture in particular. I decided to highlight obesity and homosexuality here for two related reasons. One reason is that they capture so well some of the main tenets of the basic theoretical conceptualization of social stigma. The other is that, today, these two subsets of young people are viewed as developmentally at risk from a public health perspective and, consequently, are targeted by policy intervention.

First, Goffman laid out several categories of social stigma. Because he was writing for a different time, his terminology seems offensive by contemporary standards, but his basic ideas are still quite instructive. According to Goffman, two of the strongest and most destructive stigma are abominations of the body and blemishes of character. His descriptions of these regrettably named categories of stigma explain how they encompass a variety of stigma related to physical appearance and to personal beliefs and behaviors outside the mainstream. Obesity and homosexuality clearly fit these definitions and, indeed, often serve

---

[2] See their 2001 entry, "Conceptualizing Stigma," in *Annual Review of Sociology*.

as focal examples in scholarly discussions about the nature and origin of social stigma (Link & Phelan, 2001).

Second, Goffman also made a crucial distinction between discrediting stigma and discreditable stigma that is still fundamentally important to understanding the developmental significance of stigma. The former refers to a stigmatized trait that is immediately visible to everyone, like obesity. When an obese boy walks into a room, his weight is often the first thing that others register about him. In others' eyes, it puts him in a category of people with a generally known social status. A discreditable stigma, on the other hand, might not be visible to everyone, but it is activated if and when others become aware of it. A girl's classmates might not be aware that she is a lesbian, but she may fear that, if they find this out, there will be consequences. In some ways, then, she suffers from the potential of stigma, even if she is not actually stigmatized. She has not yet been placed in a category of people with a generally known social status, but she easily could be. As a result, according to Bos, Sandfort, de Bruyn, and Hakvoort, being gay can make a teenager feel different even if no one knows she is gay.[3]

Third, focusing on these traits brings different demographic groups into the spotlight. For example, obesity is much more common among the poor and among racial minorities, and it tends to be experienced more negatively by girls than boys. At the same time, however, homosexuality seems to be more or less randomly distributed across the American population (Anderson & Butcher, 2006; Savin-Williams & Cohen, 1996). By studying both groups of teenagers at the same time, therefore, I can be more sure that I am not simply studying a phenomenon that is unique to only one segment of the American youth population, be it historically disadvantaged youth or historically advantaged youth, girls or boys.

---

[3] This conclusion was made in a 2008 article in *Developmental Psychology* about gay teenagers in Holland.

Fourth, ample evidence has been accumulated over the years that these two personal traits are rated low, on average, by Americans, from national opinion surveys about homosexuality to experiments in which young people rate pictures of subjects with different body types (Carr & Friedman, 2005; Russell & Joyner, 2001; Crandall, 1994; Goffman, 1963). In general, Americans do not tend to see obese and/or lesbian/gay individuals in a very positive light. Instead, they often see them as unattractive or undesirable partners, friends, co-workers, and neighbors and, in the extreme, as defects and even immoral. Again, this is a group perspective – how Americans feel about these groups as a whole, not how they feel about a specific obese or lesbian/gay person, especially one they know.

Fifth, the National Institutes of Health (NIH) have identified obese youth and sexual minority youth as special populations of interest in efforts to improve public health. The special attention to obese youth is not new. Obesity has been a priority of the Healthy People initiative for some time. It is a direct result of the obesity epidemic that began in the 1990s and is primarily motivated by concerns about physical health.[4] Yet, the research generated by this priority has expanded beyond the physical health domain to include aspects of social, emotional, and socioeconomic functioning that have been directly linked to the stigmatization of obesity in American culture.[5] The emphasis on sexual minority youth is newer. Indeed, such youth were added as a Healthy People priority for the first time for the 2010 report, which came with a special companion document on GLBT health from the Gay and Lesbian Medical Association. Justifying this addition are the social psychological risks faced by lesbian/gay

---

[4] For statistics on the obesity epidemic, see the Weight Control Information Network from the National Institute of Diabetes and Digestive and Kidney Diseases (http://win.niddk.nih.gov/statistics/).

[5] My own work on obesity, including the research in this book, has been supported by NIH for these reasons.

youth, largely as a result of stigmatization, because of their sexual identity/orientation.[6] Following these points, focusing on the stigmatization of obese and/or lesbian/gay youth as a way of understanding the connection between informal and formal education in general and the educational consequences of not fitting in at school in particular is theoretically motivated, empirically justified, and policy relevant. Obese and/or lesbian/gay youth constitute stigmatized groups in American society. According to theory, a member of a stigmatized group is under threat of social exclusion and, as a result, has to work much harder than others to make a case for his or her own value and/or to socially integrate (Link & Phelan, 2001; Puhl & Brownell, 2001; Goffman, 1963). Thus, being subjected to social stigma, either real or perceived, can psychically separate teenagers from their surroundings, increasing the likelihood that they see themselves, accurately or not, as not fitting in socially at high school. In this way, obese and/or lesbian/gay youth may be at risk for lower academic progress and truncated rates of long-term educational attainment even though obesity and homosexuality are not known impediments to cognitive or intellectual development.[7] This risk is well aligned with the general spirit of NIH priorities for public health policy and intervention.

Two Additional Points of Consideration

One thing that is important to note is that emphasizing the role of stigma in this process alleviates some of the "blaming the victim" connotation of work on the developmental troubles experienced by obese and/or lesbian/gay youth. According to psychological theorists such

[6] See the report from the Gay and Lesbian Medical Association (http://www.nalgap. org/PDF/Resources/HP2010CDLGBTHealth.pdf).
[7] I discuss how social stigma can link social and academic experiences more in a 2007 article in *Sociology of Education*.

as Hegerty,[8] stigma is something done to teenagers. It is an externally imposed obstacle to healthy development that their peers from non-stigmatized groups do not face. As such, studying such youth through the prism of stigma moves their well-documented problems out of the realm of inherent pathology and into the realm of social context, which is far more amenable to policy intervention than individual development.

Another point worth mentioning is that although some stigma are global in the sense that they are widely shared among diverse groups of people, even the most global stigma will vary in intensity across local contexts. In other words, just because something is devalued in the United States in general does not mean that it is devalued everywhere in the United States (Link & Phelan, 2001; Goffman, 1963). According to sociological research, for example, the degree to which obesity is viewed as attractive or unattractive varies considerably across societies and, within a given society, across different segments of the population. As a result, the degree to which obesity affects mental health also varies considerably across and within societies (Pinhey, Rubinstein, & Colfax, 1997; Ross, 1994). The conclusion I take from this research, which maps onto theories about stigma more generally, is that a general stigma observed in American youth culture at large may be turned up or dialed down by the particular peer culture or subcultures in any one American high school. Such school-level variations in stigma then lead to an amplification or modulation of a teenager's need to cope with that stigma depending on where she or he attends high school. The extent to which being obese and/or lesbian/gay disrupts a teenager's sense of social belonging in school and related life trajectories, therefore, is in part dependent on the prevailing values about obesity and homosexuality specific to that high school.

---

[8] See Hegerty's 2009 essay about gay/lesbian/transgender youth in *Developmental Psychology*, which was a rejoinder to articles in a 2008 special section of that journal on sexual minority youth.

THE SOCIOEMOTIONAL AND ACADEMIC EXPERIENCES
OF OBESE AND/OR GAY/LESBIAN YOUTH

Of the Add Health teenagers I studied, slightly over 10% were obese according to the standards put out by the Centers for Disease Control and Prevention. Specifically, their weight to height ratios were in the 95th percentile for their age and gender according to population tables developed prior to the contemporary spike in child obesity.[9] The obesity rate was slightly higher among boys than girls in Add Health.

Following the lead of psychologists like Henny Bos and sociologists like Stephen Russell, I looked at teenagers who reported that they were same-sex attracted. Given the developmental nature of sexual identity and, in particular, coming out, they have argued that same-sex attraction, which is one stage of the process, is the appropriate way to categorize sexual minority youth (Bos et al., 2008; Russell & Sigler-Andrews, 2003). In Add Health, 7% of teenagers reported that they were sexually attracted to other youth of their same gender, with, again, a slightly higher rate among boys than girls.[10]

Although a similar proportion of Add Health teenagers (7% to 10%) fell into each of these stigmatized groups, the same teenagers did not make up that 7% to 10% in both. Indeed, only 1% of the sample was both obese and same-sex attracted. The overwhelming majority of obese youth were not lesbian/gay, and the overwhelming majority of lesbian/gay youth were not obese.

After identifying the teenagers in each of the two groups, the next step was to examine whether they were less likely to enroll in college

---

[9] The official threshold for obesity in the youth population is greater than or equal to the 95th percentile of body mass index – weight (kg) / [height (m)]^2 – for age and gender category. The BMI × Age × Gender tables are published by the CDC (http://www.cdc.gov/nccdphp/dnpa/bmi). Height and weight were self-reported by teenagers in the Wave I In-Home Interview.

[10] Teenagers reported on their same-sex attraction in the Wave I In-Home Interview. Because the question did not ask teenagers to self-identify as gay or lesbian, the proper designation is same-sex attraction, not homosexuality.

after high school than their peers and, if so, whether these disparities were related to the focal pathway connecting teenagers' feelings of not fitting in, socioemotional coping, and academic progress captured in Figure 6.1. These analyses followed the same multilevel modeling plan from Chapter 5, with one important change. I also drew on cross-level student by school interactions (e.g., teenager obesity × schoolwide body size norms) to gauge the extent to which the apparent consequences of being in a stigmatized group varied across high schools in which that stigma was likely to vary in intensity.[11]

College-Going Disparities Related to Obesity

Figure 6.2 presents the predicted odds of obese girls going to college relative to nonobese girls with the same general demographic, family, social, academic, and school profile, calculated from the results of multilevel logistic regressions.[12] In general, regardless of the average body size of girls in the student body, obese girls had 78% lower odds ($[1.0 - .22] \times 100 = 78$) of attending college than nonobese girls,

---

[11] The modeling strategy was the exact same plan used for the analyses presented in Chapter 5: logistic and Poisson mixed models in SAS with the glimmix macro, depending on whether the focal outcome was binary (college going, several of the socioemotional indicators) or countlike (not fitting in, academic progress, some of the socioemotional indicators), with ITCV estimates calculated post hoc. In each model, I added an interaction between an individual stigma variable and a school-level stigma variable: 1) mean BMI of girls and boys in the school for obesity, measured by the mean BMI score for the representative subsample of Add Health respondents in the Wave I In-Home Interview in each school, and 2) the proportion of students in the school who were same-sex attracted, measured by aggregating respondents in the representative subsample of Add Health respondents in the Wave I In-Home Interview in each school.

[12] Again, the coefficient for obesity was added to the sum of the products of the coefficient and mean/mode of each control variable and then converted to an odds ratio. For the school-specific predicted odds, the product of the school coefficient and one of two values (one standard deviation above or below the mean) and the product of the interaction, the focal obesity value, and the focal school value (again, either one standard deviation above or below the mean) were added to the total. These summed totals were then converted to odds ratios.

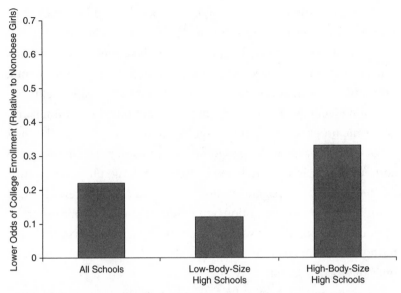

Figure 6.2. Lower Odds of College Enrollment Associated with Obesity among Teenage Girls, by Average Body Size of Girls in School.

matched on a host of characteristics, including race/ethnicity and socioeconomic status.

Importantly, however, this disparity in college going varied according to the average body size of other girls in obese girls' high schools. As the average body size of girls in the high school increased, the gap in college going between obese and nonobese girls declined. Thus, the risks that obese girls would miss out on college after leaving high school were maximized when they attended high school with large numbers of thin girls. Indeed, they had almost 90% lower odds of going to college than nonobese girls when attending low-body-size schools, defined as schools with an average body mass index among female students one standard deviation below the mean in Add Health. Alternatively, these risks were less pronounced, albeit still large (about 67% lower odds), when they attended high schools with heavier girls, regardless of other characteristics (e.g., race/ethnicity, socioeconomic status) of their schools.

To understand these college-going disparities and how they were related to the working conceptual model depicted in Figure 6.1, I first examined the degree to which obesity predicted feelings of not fitting in at high school, socioemotional functioning, and academic progress and then investigated the effects on the obesity coefficient of adding feelings of not fitting in, socioemotional functioning, and academic progress to the college-going model for girls.[13] In the final model, the disparity in college going between otherwise similar obese and nonobese girls was reduced by 22% by taking into account similarities between obese and nonobese girls in their perceived social marginalization, socioemotional functioning, and academic progress. Moreover, the significant variation in this disparity across schools differing in the average body size of female students was no longer seen once these other factors were held constant.

Slightly more than one-fifth of the obesity disparity in teenage girls' college going, therefore, was explained by the processes highlighted by the conceptual model. Furthermore, summarizing across all of the analyses conducted, 88% of this portion of the college-going disparity was explained by the exact paths specified in the conceptual model. First, obese girls scored significantly higher on feelings of not fitting in socially at high school, with an effect size equal to one-third of a standard deviation in the not-fitting-in scale in general and reaching one-half of a standard deviation in high schools with low average body size among female students. This association was robust to the control of both observable and unobservable confounds. Second, replicating what was reported in Chapter 5, the more girls felt like they did not fit in, the more likely they were to be depressed, smoke marijuana, and skip school and, as a result, the lower the level of academic progress they demonstrated in high school and the less likely they were to go to college.

---

[13] Again, these modeling steps followed the same plan used in Chapter 5, with the same control variables.

The role of feelings of not fitting in, socioemotional functioning, and academic progress in college-going disparities related to obesity, however, did not always take this exact sequential form. Models also revealed evidence of direct linkages among obesity, self-rejection, and college going that were independent of feelings of not fitting in and academic progress as well as direct linkages among obesity, academic status, and college going that were independent of feelings of not fitting in and counterproductive coping mechanisms. Other models showed that variations in the links among obesity, not fitting in, and depression among girls across high schools varying in the average body size of girls in the school accounted for all of the previously reported school-to-school variation in obesity-related disparities in college going.

Adding these related pathways to the specific pathway in the conceptual model, a sizable portion of the lower odds of obese girls going to college was explained. Unfortunately, however, the majority of this disparity was left unexplained. Other things were at work, but the not-fitting-in phenomenon at the heart of the conceptual model is an important starting point.

Turning to boys, the picture that emerged from these analyses was far simpler. Recall that the conceptual model linking not fitting in socially at high school to college going after high school depicted back in Chapter 5 did more to explain the lower college-going rates of boys who felt like they did not fit in than it did for similar girls. The elaboration of this model to include obesity as a stigmatized group triggering the not-fitting-in process did not add much when looking at boys. Indeed, obese boys had only marginally lower college-going rates than nonobese boys once their basic demographic, family, social, and prior academic profiles were taken into account. What little difference that did remain was primarily explained by the lower levels of academic progress of obese boys. They were not more likely than nonobese boys to feel like they did not fit in socially at high school and, for the most part, did not demonstrate more problematic socioemotional conditions or behaviors.

For boys, therefore, whatever long-term educational consequences of being obese that existed were academic, not social or psychological, in nature. These patterns are in line with past evidence that the stigma attached to obesity in American society is much stronger for women and girls than for men and boys. This gendered nature of social stigma, however, is less true for the stigmatization of homosexuality, which we turn to next.

College-Going Disparities Related to Being Lesbian/Gay

Girls who reported being same-sex attracted in Add Health were somewhat less likely than otherwise similar girls who reported being opposite-sex attracted to attend college after high school. The former had about 50% lower odds of college going than the latter once the full set of demographic, family, social, academic, and school controls was taken into account. In contrast to what was seen for obesity, this disparity did not vary according to the proportion of girls in the student body who were also same-sex attracted, perhaps because of the lack of variability in same-sex-attracted girls across high schools.

In another contrast to obesity among girls, almost all of the college-going disparity related to same-sex attraction among girls was explained by the exact paths specified in the conceptual model in Figure 6.1.[14] In other words, same-sex-attracted girls were more likely to feel as though they did not fit in socially at high school, which appeared to trigger increasing rates of depression, marijuana use, and truancy, which, in turn, were associated with lower-level academic progress during high school that predicted lower odds of attending college after high school. What was most powerful in this pathway

---

[14] Again, I am summarizing across a series of models in which same-sex attraction was the focal independent variable in models predicting the not-fitting-in scale, each socioemotional factor, and the academic progress scale and in which all of these factors were added iteratively to the model predicting college going.

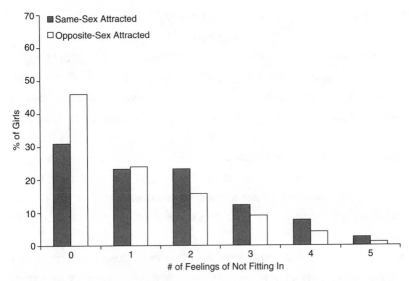

Figure 6.3. Number of Feelings of Not Fitting In at School Experienced by Girls, by Same-Sex or Opposite-Sex Attraction.

was the link between same-sex attraction and feelings of not fitting in among girls. This link is depicted in its simplest form – mean differences with no other factors taken into account – in Figure 6.3. In a multivariate framework,[15] this link had an effect size of almost one-third of a standard deviation on the not-fitting-in scale.

One final note about girls is that a slight variation on the exact pathway specified in the conceptual model accounted for some of the college-going disparity related to same-sex attraction. Specifically, girls who were same-sex attracted were also more likely than opposite-sex-attracted girls to consider suicide and drink alcohol, regardless of their feelings of not fitting in at school, and both of these socioemotional conditions/behaviors were significantly and inversely associated with college going independently of academic progress.

[15] In other words, a multilevel Poisson model in the mixed procedure with the glimmix macro in which the not-fitting-in scale was the outcome and same-sex attraction and the control variables were the independent variables.

Recall that, in general, the stigma of homosexuality is not as tilted toward girls as is the stigma of obesity. Yet, again, considering same-sex attraction added little to the conceptual model linking not fitting in at high school and later college going among boys. In short, although same-sex-attracted boys did have poorer overall socioemotional health (e.g., more depression and suicidal ideation) than otherwise similar opposite-sex-attracted boys, the former were no less likely to attend college after high school than the latter, nor did they have lower levels of academic progress during high school. Interestingly, same-sex-attracted boys were also no more or less likely than their opposite-sex-attracted peers to report feelings of not fitting in socially at high school.

In short, the socioemotional and academic consequences of not fitting in socially at high school were a major part of why same-sex-attracted girls were less likely to go to college but in almost no way captured the high school experiences of same-sex-attracted boys.

SUMMARY AND LOOKING FORWARD

In the past chapter, we saw that both girls and boys suffered long-term educational consequences through the short-term socioemotional and academic risks of not fitting in socially at high school. For the most part, these patterns reflected the exact sequence specified by our conceptual model or some modification of this sequence. In this chapter, we saw that, for girls, this phenomenon could also be leveraged to explain some or all of college-going disparities related to two major social stigma in American culture: being obese and being same-sex attracted. For boys, however, this phenomenon was more or less unrelated to such stigma.

These population patterns reveal an example of how informal and formal education can come together in ways that hurt teenagers and schools and, at least for girls, how this interplay of informal and formal education maps onto major public health initiatives targeting specific subsets of the American youth population. Yet, still more can be known about how all of this plays out. At this point, we still know little about how teenagers come to see themselves as not fitting in socially and why these feelings trigger counterproductive coping mechanisms that put them at risk academically in the short term and educationally and socioeconomically in the long term. Such knowledge is crucial to helping teenagers and schools facing such problems, but the kinds of statistical approaches and survey data offered by Add Health are not as helpful for delving into such highly nuanced and complex social psychological dynamics.

7

How Teenagers Know What They Know
and Why It Matters

The educational risks of not fitting in socially at high school are by no means universal. After all, feelings of not fitting in did not perfectly predict college going (or socioemotional functioning or academic progress either) in Add Health, and being obese and/or gay/lesbian did not perfectly predict feelings of not fitting in. The not-fitting-in pathway that I have put forward and tested, therefore, is a probabilistic one. Feeling like one does not fit in at school raises the probability of various psychological and behavioral mechanisms that lower the probability of going to college, but there is nothing guaranteed or absolute about this pathway. That variability in how this pathway plays out among American teenagers – variability in the potential risks of not fitting in and in the actual experience of not fitting in – is important. Figuring out who feels like they do not fit in (and who does) and who reacts to such feelings in problematic ways (and who does not) tells us which teenagers need help the most and points to different strategies for helping them.

To gain such an understanding, focusing more narrowly on the central piece of the not-fitting-in pathway – in other words, focusing on feelings of not fitting in themselves – is necessary. After all, if teenagers who may be vulnerable to feeling as though they do not fit in never develop those feelings or if teenagers who feel like they do not fit in manage to cope with those feelings in healthy ways, then the full pathway breaks down. In this chapter, I attempt to fill in some of the intervening steps in this pathway, looking at what happens just before and just after teenagers feel like they do not fit in at school. In short, I wanted to know how feelings of not fitting in socially (including those related to social stigma) are activated in school and how this activation leads some teenagers to change their own thoughts and behaviors while not affecting other teenagers in the same situation. Such information provides valuable insights into the educational risks of not fitting in but, importantly, also sheds light on the more general link between informal and formal education in the United States.

This investigation is grounded in sociological and psychological theories about the social nature of the self. Drawing on such theory, I expand on that central piece of the not-fitting-in pathway and add to it a consideration of information processing and identity discrepancy.

INFORMATION AND IDENTITY

Figure 7.1 presents a two-piece schematic of the focal segment of the not-fitting-in pathway and depicts my hypotheses about how information processing and identity discrepancy factor into this pathway. Basically, theory suggests that teenagers' active attempts to digest the information they are gathering about themselves and their social environment (e.g., the high school) will point to a particular kind of mismatch between the two for some; specifically, a mismatch in which the teenager comes out as inferior to or unwanted in the environment (the A piece of the schematic). This perception of person-context mismatch may, in turn, lead a teenager to see his or her personal identity as somehow under suspicion, fraudulent, or misconstrued and, consequently, encourage personal action to reduce the vulnerability he or she may feel (the B piece). In the following sections of this chapter, I unpack each piece of this hypothesized sequence.

Information Processing

As a first step, consider the part of Figure 7.1 denoted by A, which captures a hypothesized mechanism by which teenagers come to see

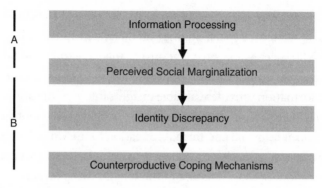

Figure 7.1. A Closer Inspection of Not Fitting In.

themselves as not fitting in socially at high school. According to social and cognitive psychologists,[1] individuals develop knowledge within their social contexts, observing the world around them to gather data that they can then sort through, weigh, assess, code, and output as socially derived "facts" and judgments that help to determine their courses of action. In general, such information processing favors efficient processing of large amounts of information over thorough processing of small amounts of data.

This very human tendency reflects our basic social condition – we understand the world by living in the world. It is also a central component of most theoretical perspectives on child and adolescent development, including Piaget's.[2] Not surprisingly, then, information processing is useful for understanding how teenagers come to feel as though they do not fit in socially at high school. Basically, they derive different kinds of messages about themselves and their fit with the school from others at or around school. They collect data and then mine these data, but, importantly, they do so with varying degrees of skill and accuracy. Furthermore, these data that teenagers process about

---

[1] See the chapter by Taylor in the 1998 *Handbook of Social Psychology* or the chapter by Howard in *Sociological Perspectives on Social Psychology* (1995).

[2] See Piaget's 1955 *The Child's Construction of Reality.*

their fit with the high school are multisourced. Here, I focus on the information they collect that is socially generated or self-generated.

First, teenagers receive data from external sources when, for example, others at school speak to them or act in a certain way toward them. I refer to this source of information as *social feedback*. A discussion of academic self-evaluation is useful for illustrating how social feedback works. If teenagers are asked to provide some evidence-based assessment of how smart they are or are not, they will invariably bring up their grade point averages, test scores, and other academic criteria as evidence for whatever position they take. In doing so, they are following a concrete protocol in which they process official feedback coming from the context – the high school – most relevant to the question. This same protocol is followed when the self-assessment is social, rather than academic, in nature. The high school, in its role as the site of peer culture, is still the most relevant context, and the feedback coming out of this context can be both official (e.g., winning a student election, being voted some social honor) and unofficial (e.g., number of friends or dates, treatment by others). Just as when they make an academic self-assessment, teenagers then construct an evidence base of external evaluations within a school as a foundation for making their own assessment of their social value and position in that school.

For assessments of how teenagers fit in socially at their high schools, the most important source of social feedback will likely be the other students in the school. As described so well by Brown and Klute, Giordano, Hartup, and others, most high schools house a peer world that is organized into levels of contact, interaction, and identification that make up concentric circles of peer dynamics (Brown & Klute, 2003; Giordano, 2003; Hartup, 1993). The most intimate level consists of dyadic friendships, which are embedded within slightly larger, tightly knit friendship cliques characterized by frequent interaction and some degree of emotional bonding. These cliques, in turn, are embedded in wider, more diffuse bands of peers – peer crowds or status groups like "brains" and "populars," what I refer to as PLUs (people like us) – that encompass teenagers who share the same academic and/ or social space in high school. Such a peer group is usually a collection of several cliques who share some commonality or a collection of young people who take the same kinds of classes and serve as a pool of potential friends and romantic partners for each other. Even if teenagers do not know all of the people in their band of peers, they tend to use this level of the peer world as the primary reference point in school. These larger bands of peers are, in turn, embedded in the student body as a whole, serving as subsets or subcultures of the school.[3]

Typically, developmental research emphasizes the influences of teenagers' closest friends on their behavior and general well-being, and educational policy and related research (e.g., on segregation/ integration) focuses on peers at the school level (Kahlenberg, 2001; Hartup & Stevens, 1997). Yet, my reading of the relevant literature is that the middle level of the high school peer context should matter most to teenagers' feelings of not fitting in.

Specifically, recent theoretical developments suggest that the intermediate band of peers in high school – larger and less intimate than cliques and more personal, less diverse, and involving more sustained interaction than the student body as a whole – may be a danger zone for teenagers (McFarland & Pals, 2005; Milner, 2004; Eckert, 1989). Indeed, Peggy Giordano has referred to this band of peers as a developmental stretch in that it simultaneously represents an opportunity for achievement and status for some teenagers but also an arena of social vulnerability and exclusion for many, if not most, others (Giordano, 2003). Because social ties on this level tend to be somewhat tenuous, they do less to protect teenagers from each other. In contrast, strong emotional bonds and shared histories keep *friends* together despite differences and disagreements – they help *friends* look past what they do not like about each other or what others do not like about them.

---

[3] See my 2008 article on peers in *Child Development* with Riegle-Crumb, Field, Frank, and Muller.

Absent these personal emotional bonds, then, a teenager is always vulnerable to being penalized or isolated in his or her peer crowds and status groups. Much less is protecting a teenager from social penalty and exclusion if he or she goes astray of social norms. Instead, he or she can simply be dropped with very little loss for the entire collective. At the same time, however, there is an upward bound on this phenomenon, as the sense of internally felt and/or externally imposed identity of peer crowds and groups makes the forces of conformity on this level greater than what is seen in the student body at large.

Second, teenagers also generate their own data by, for example, studying themselves within the setting of the school. I refer to this source of information as social comparison. Something of a subset of social feedback, social comparison was originally delineated by Leon Festinger.[4] This concept contends that one of the most common ways that individuals figure out where they stand in a social setting is to evaluate themselves in comparison to some standard in the form of another person or group of people. Typically, they do this by looking at whomever is nearby or whomever is viewed as a similar other. Going back to the academic self-evaluation example used earlier in this section, teenagers can best use their grade point averages as evidence for their self-evaluations if they know how the people around them score on the grade point average scale. Their absolute ranking on the scale means less than their relative ranking (Marsh & Hau, 2003; Eccles & Wigfield, 2002). In a sense, individuals who rely on social comparison are generating their own external feedback about themselves in order to understand their "rank."

Similar to my attempts to understand social feedback, I approach the role of social comparison in teenagers' feelings of not fitting in at high school primarily through the lens of peer dynamics. In short, I view school peers as the most relevant standards for teenagers making

---

[4] Festinger's 1954 article in *Human Relations* provides an overview of the formulation of social comparison theory.

social comparisons to understand their own social situations in school. And, again, I view the intermediate band of peer crowds and groups – rather than friends or schoolmates – as the level of the high school peer world from which social comparisons will be drawn. As elucidated so well by McFarland and Pals, Barber and colleagues (Barber, Eccles, & Stone, 2001), Akerlof and Kranton, Kinney, and others (McFarland & Pals, 2005; Akerlof & Kranton, 2002; Kinney, 1999), a major role of such midlevel peer collectives in adolescent development is precisely to serve as a reference group – both for teenagers making assessments of the self and for others trying to make social judgments about the teenagers. This role is rooted in the nature of peer crowds, which categorize large collections of teenagers (i.e., the student body of a high school) into a more manageable, parsimonious set of categories of teenagers who are like each other; hence, my use of the term PLUs (people like us) to designate such peer crowds. As such, these peer crowds are the natural venue for social comparison, with teenagers comparing themselves to similar others within their self-identified or externally imposed peer crowds or to similar others in contiguous or competing peer crowds.

The standards that are used for social comparison vis-à-vis others in the same peer crowd range from seemingly objective to entirely subjective. As both sociologists (e.g., Frank and colleagues, Milner) and psychologists (e.g., Halpern and colleagues) studying teenagers' social statuses have argued over the last decade, teenagers are often hyper rational and extremely literal when making social considerations, in contrast to adult views that they are irrational and emotion driven (Frank, Muller, et al., 2008; Milner, 2004; Halpern, Udry, Campbell, & Suchindran, 1998). In other words, they tend to focus on black and white and avoid shades of gray. As such, I would expect that teenagers would put more weight on what they view as objective criteria when making social comparisons on the peer crowd level as a means of assessing how well they fit in socially at high school. By objective, I refer to official school-based social distinctions, such as elections, club memberships, or sports activities that signal popularity. Also viewed as higher in objectivity would be quantifiable aspects of peer dynamics, such as numbers of friends, parties attended, and dates, as well as peer crowd membership itself. More subjective appraisals, such as comparisons of physical attractiveness or sociability, may still be important while also not being the first line of social comparison.

Following this discussion of two modes of information processing, my working hypothesis is that teenagers will determine the degree to which they fit in socially at high school primarily by sorting through social feedback that they receive in the intermediate band of peer crowds and groups (PLUs) in school and by making social comparisons about perceived objective markers of fitting in within and across such peer crowds. I make this working hypothesis well aware of two important caveats.

First, in both socially and self-generated mechanisms, teenagers process the information they have – by interpreting actual and perceived external feedback to decode the messages they think they are receiving from others or by interpreting the layout of the social system as a way of determining their place in it. In some sense, both mechanisms are social *and* self-generated.

Second, I recognize the paradox of focusing on peer groups, intimate or diffuse, to explain how teenagers come to see themselves as not fitting in socially at high school. After all, the most basic form of social marginalization is being isolated – having no friends, no peer group to call one's own. This reality is one reason that focusing on peer crowds, as opposed to friendships or cliques, is potentially insightful. Even when teenagers do not have friends and/or do not identify with any peer crowd, they are likely identified by others as being a part of a peer crowd, usually a negatively labeled one that serves as a catchall categorization of isolates, rejects, and undesirables. This external identification, of which the teenagers in question are often well aware, allows the hypothesized mechanisms of social feedback and social comparison to still take effect (Bearman & Moody, 2004; Kinney, 1999).

Identity Discrepancies

Having established an approach for understanding how teenagers come to feel like they do not fit in socially at high school (the A piece of Figure 7.1), we now turn to the question of why such feelings of not fitting in might engender coping mechanisms that ultimately prove to be counterproductive to short-term academic progress and long-term educational attainment (the B piece). Recall from Chapter 3 my argument, based on the work of other social and behavioral scientists, that personal and social development is the primary theoretical link between high school peer culture and the academic consequences of living in such a culture. The same holds true in this specific case study. That information that teenagers receive about their value and worth in high school through social feedback and social comparison can translate into counterproductive behavior when it endangers how they see themselves or how they want to see themselves. In this way, identity – the development of which is one of the key tasks of adolescence, according to Erikson (1968) – is the linchpin.

This hypothesized mechanism is grounded in decades of social psychological and developmental research demonstrating that the core of personal and social development, identity, is inherently social in nature as well as multidetermined.[5] Contrary to naïve but widely held beliefs that identities represent stable, intrinsic properties, humans, including and especially teenagers, develop their identities in a fluid process through interactions with other people over time. These "others" can include friends and loved ones, strangers, or some collective other like the media. The classic social psychological theory, the Looking Glass Self, and its many updates and offshoots offer one way of thinking about the social nature of identity (Yeung & Martin, 2003; Cast, Stets, & Burke, 1999; Cooley, [1902] 1983). This

---

[5] For thorough descriptions of identity, the self, and identity development, see reviews by Baumeister (1998) and Gecas and Burke (1995).

perspective contends that humans come to a semiconscious, semi-unconscious understanding of their own *social* worth by seeing how they are treated by others, including how others react to them and either engage with or disengage from them (e.g., the social feedback and comparison processes described in the prior section). Because we have evolved as such a social species, that collective judgment, whether real or perceived, comes to shape our own sense of self-worth. Consequently, how we navigate the outside world filters into our innermost selves. In turn, our innermost selves represent bundles of multiple pieces of information that most of us slowly work into an integrated whole. We are, according to social psychologists, many different and occasionally contradictory things that fit together in intricate ways (Stryker, 1987; Markus & Nurius, 1986).

The highly social nature of the development of multifaceted identities, however, also injects a great deal of risk and vulnerability into adolescent development. These ongoing identity projects that consume so much of teenagers' mental energy can pose problems when there is conflict between what teenagers see in themselves or want to see and what information processing is revealing to them about themselves. Feeling as though they do not fit in at school is related to such an identity problem if teenagers feel as though they should fit in or that they are being unfairly excluded. Specifically, feelings of not fitting in socially at school map onto two different but related kinds of identity discrepancies. First, an actual/ideal identity discrepancy occurs when "the person you are is not the person you want to be." Teenagers who feel like they do not fit in at school may come to think that their social struggles result from their failure to live up to their own potential value. Second, an actual/ought identity discrepancy occurs when "the person you are is not the person others think you ought to be" (Harrison, 2001; Ewell, Smith, Karmel, & Hart, 1996; Higgins, 1989). Teenagers who feel like they do not fit in at school may come to think that their social struggles result from a failure of others to see their own value.

A particularly acute form of identity discrepancy, what Goffman referred to as "spoiled identity" (Goffman, 1963), is relevant to understanding how teenagers react to their feelings of not fitting in that have been generated by social stigma (e.g., of obesity or being lesbian/gay) within schools. A spoiled identity occurs when that intricately complex thing that is the self gets boiled down to one stigmatized trait that holds the most weight with others, when one piece affects the whole package. In this case, the actual self and/or the ought self do not line up with the ideal self because the former are viewed primarily through the prism of a stigmatized trait while the latter is viewed in full. For example, negative associations with obesity and/or homosexuality in the wider culture may be so strong that they override all else about a person and become a label that erases or contaminates other information about that person, that dissuades others from getting to know the full person. That the person in question does not have any negative association with that trait or correctly sees it as only one piece of who he or she is often does not matter. Again, the consequences are real. Furthermore, prolonged experience with a spoiled identity may spoil the identity of someone even through his or her own eyes.

Such identity problems are indeed problems, in the sense that they are both painful and stressful. As already argued at several points in this book, teenagers are agentic beings, and this is especially so when dealing with their social selves. According to Peter Burke and other identity theorists (Burke, 2004; Cast & Burke, 2002), humans facing identity problems have a fundamental drive to solve these problems, and one of the most consistent ways that they enact this drive is by creating consistency between their views of the self and the social views of the self that they perceive from others. They try to match social information to their views of themselves, alter their behavior to elicit desired information, alter their views of themselves to be less discrepant with the information they are receiving, and, if all else fails, engage in behavior that reduces the negative affect associated with the identity discrepancy between self- and social views.

The self-verifying responses to identity discrepancies that are so central to identity theory connect back to the various kinds of counterproductive coping responses that teenagers seem to have to feelings of not fitting in socially at high school. For example, one theoretically highlighted and well-documented self-verifying response is a passive, nonenhancing one: adjusting views of the self downward so that they are aligned with the perceived social judgment of the self even if it is a negative one. The internalization mechanism of the not-fitting-in pathway is an example of such a response. If the inconsistency between the self-view and the social view of the self is causing distress, reducing that inconsistency is the key to self-protection. Internalizing negative feedback into one's own identity certainly does not improve one's sense of self-worth, but it can introduce a degree of order and expectancy into one's life. Everything makes sense and is predictable. In some cases, this self-verification strategy is so strong that teenagers might even seek out social interactions and settings that then further confirm this negative judgment about themselves (Sedikides, 1993; Taylor, 1989).

As another example, some self-verifying responses to identity discrepancies are more active and can also be emotionally enhancing, such as when teenagers try to manipulate their social experiences to match their own views of the self rather than the other way around. The disengagement mechanism of the not-fitting-in pathway illustrates such an active self-verifying approach. By disengaging from their schools, teenagers can pick social contexts and social interactions in which they can be sure that they will get positive feedback about themselves or at least reduce the negative feedback that will come their way. They can also selectively process, interpret, or rationalize any negative feedback that they do get. In effect, disengaging teenagers are trying to control the social views of the self that they receive by choosing who is able or unable to produce those social views for them (Carter, 2006; Dance, 2002; Swann, Stein-Seroussi, & Giesler, 1992). Self-medication is also a form of active self-verification to the extent that such behavior allows teenagers to present a different face to the peer world, especially if they attend schools in which risky behavior is high status or admired. More generally, however, self-medication represents the "if all else fails" scenario mentioned earlier in this section – teenagers who, having given up trying to fix identity discrepancies, focus on anesthetizing themselves so that they cannot feel the pain of such discrepancies (Allen, Porter, McFarland, Marsh, & McElhaney, 2005; Crosnoe, Muller, & Frank, 2004; Hussong, Hicks, Levy, & Curran, 2001).

In all three of these cases, the understandable attempts that teenagers make to cope with identity discrepancies related to their feelings of not fitting in may be self-protective in the short term but self-destructive in the long term. In this way, identity discrepancies are a key to understanding why feelings of not fitting in among teenagers are a threat to the educational mission of high schools. As such, my working hypothesis is that feelings of not fitting in socially at high school will make teenagers more likely to suffer from actual/ideal and actual/ought identity discrepancies generating internalizing, self-medication, and disengagement responses. Of the three kinds of counterproductive self-verifying actions, ones that are active and/or self-enhancing (e.g., disengagement, self-medication) will be the first line of defense, while a more passive, nonenhancing approach (e.g., internalization) will be less likely.

Turning to Lamar

These two sets of working hypotheses – one set about information processing and its role in feelings of not fitting in, one set about identity discrepancies and their relation to such feelings – need to be tested empirically. Unfortunately, as valuable as Add Health is for studying the social experience of young people in modern American high schools, it does not provide much help in unpacking and deconstructing these two additional linkages in the not-fitting-in pathway. As a nationally representative study, Add Health is about breadth, not depth, and its impersonal surveys do not offer sufficient traction when looking into an experience that is so highly personal. Thus, my tests of these two sets of hypotheses drew on qualitative, ethnographic data from Lamar High School, including discussions centered around the Lamar teenagers' Who I Am projects and their social networking sites.

HOW MESSAGES ABOUT FIT ARE TRANSMITTED AND PROCESSED

All teenagers at Lamar reported that, at least occasionally, they felt as though they did not fit in socially at Lamar. These feelings ranged from fleeting and mild among about five teenagers to stable and intense for about five others, with most falling in between. As predicted, the teenagers at Lamar came to see themselves as fitting in or not primarily by sorting through the information that they received or derived from their interactions with peers. Yet, their experiences did not completely align with the hypotheses that I put forward about how such information processing would work. Although the PLU level of peer dynamics was the primary venue for social feedback and social comparison, other levels of the peer world – from friends all the way up to youth culture, as represented by the media – mattered in important ways. Moreover, both mechanisms had the biggest impact on teenagers through very subtle, subjective means. Indeed, the subtlety of messages delivered to or perceived by teenagers about their social value in school was precisely why these messages had such an impact.

Social Feedback from School Peers

All but one of the teenagers at Lamar reported having at least one or two close friends, regardless of how much they felt like they did not fit in or not. Seeing how these friends could participate in the social feedback process that might lead teenagers to see themselves as not fitting in socially at high school, however, is decidedly tricky for two reasons. First, the strong, often intense emotional bonds that keep cliques together over time can block the flow of negative or hurtful informa-tion to any teenager in the clique, especially such information com-ing into the clique from the outside. Indeed, this feature of friendship group bonds is one of the real *advantages* of being in a clique during high school. Second, on top of this feature of the friendship group (or maybe because of it), teenagers have such a strong tendency to idealize their friends that they are often unwilling to recognize or admit even a small degree of rejection or disapproval in their friendship group. As voiced by two teenagers at Lamar as they described their friends,

> We're all different, like I said, but we complement each other and we're all just fine with each other. It's like, don't change who you are. (Juanita, Latina 9th grader)

> They know who I am. I don't have to worry … they know who I am. So, I don't have to try to like show anything or prove anything. (Ali, Middle Eastern 10th grader)

These same comments, slightly reworded, were made by just about every teenager at Lamar. The obvious sincerity of teenagers when talk-ing about their friends this way speaks to something very important about the sometimes rocky path from childhood to adulthood, namely that the romanticized view of friendships is grounded in the power of tightly knit friendship groups to facilitate teenagers' necessary and developmentally appropriate establishment of social and emotional independence from parents. At the same time, this function of friend-ship groups in the social feedback process also means that the flow of information to the teenager is incomplete, which can be both positive and negative. On the plus side, the accepting norms of close friends can be self-protective. They block out the bad stuff, they shield. On the minus side, this apparently self-protective role of friendships may represent an incomplete or even misleading view of reality among teenagers. Moreover, even if the discrepancy between social feedback inside and outside the friendship group is accurately perceived, it may grow so large that it becomes problematic for teenagers.

When pressed, most teenagers reluctantly admitted that their friends *did* critique them. They could see how their close friends policed them when they get off track socially or were at risk of breaking known social rules in the larger Lamar peer culture or its many subsets. The way that friends did this policing, however, often had an altruistic patina. As explained by James, a Latino 10th grader, male friends got their point across through an affectionate form of teasing. "They would probably tell me by like joking about it, like making it seem like good fun." In this way, he was able to receive a potentially hurtful message but then shake it off. As another example, friends also pointed out teenagers' risk of social marginalization by offering to help them stay on track socially and/or correcting whatever the "problem" may have been. According to a white 10th grader named Madeline, her girlfriends tended to say "You can do better" to her. She found this approach "more helpful" than criticizing, which is what her parents and other adults did, and recognized that it still gets the point across that she needs to make some changes.

Importantly, the teenagers at Lamar often described these two different, somewhat gender-specific ways that friends police each other in terms of body size and sexuality. Of the Lamar teenagers, about a quarter were overweight. Because of district rules, we could not ask questions about sexuality, and no teenagers revealed to us, unprompted, that they were same-sex attracted. Yet, teenagers still drew on these two examples of peers who might not fit in at Lamar as a way of illustrating their views on social exclusion and acceptance at the school. They did so from the perspective of teenagers being marginalized as well as from the perspective of teenagers doing the marginalizing. Both perspectives are crucial to understanding how information processing works within the not-fitting-in pathway.

For example, many boys talked about social feedback issues in terms of a boy who engages in behaviors that might make him appear gay to others at Lamar. Going out for drama was one scenario highlighted by several boys at Lamar. They described how his male friends might respond – by joking with him, ribbing him, as a way of letting him know that he is opening himself up for trouble in general, even if *they* are cool with him and what he is doing.

As another example, girls tended to focus on body issues when discussing social feedback. They discussed how, if a girl starts to gain weight, her friends might help her diet or exercise because, at least nominally, they care about her and want the best for her.

In both of these examples, the teenagers at Lamar understood that friends could give messages to someone that he or she was running afoul of the rules. They also believed, however, that such messages would be far less devastating to teenagers than if the messages had come from someone less close to them. Friends, they explained, cloaked warnings in good feeling.

Compared to friends, larger, more diffuse peer crowds and status groups (or PLUs) were viewed by the Lamar teenagers as playing a much bigger part in the social feedback process of not fitting in. The Lamar teenagers focused primarily on two aspects of this process – why peer crowds mattered so much and how they provided information to teenagers.

The key role that PLUs played in teenagers' lives, according to those at Lamar, was as a reference point – telling a teenager as well as other peers what his or her social location and, therefore, general profile was in the school. Having a PLU as a reference point was particularly important, they argued, at a school like Lamar, where the large size and diversity of the student body interfered with the ability of any one teenager to make a name for himself or herself. As a young white student named Christian explained, "[Lamar] is so big that it's like different groups of people are cool," as opposed to individual people. In this climate, teenagers were judged and evaluated on superficial information, with these initial impressions then influencing whether time and effort would be devoted to knowing more about the teenager in question at the expense of knowing more about some other teenager in the mix. As a result, a teenager's PLU – whether self-identified, assigned by others, or some combination of the two – went a long way toward determining the opportunities for socializing, interaction, and achievement that teenagers had in the high school. As this arena for first impression, the PLU wielded a great deal of power, both positive and negative.

Indeed, in contrast to friendship groups, these PLUs were not romanticized or idealized by teenagers at Lamar. The main feeling I got from them was that "my friends are all right but everyone else's friends are not." As predicted by developmental theory on peer dynamics, then, the intermediate band of peers in the school was where teenagers got into trouble.

At Lamar, every teenager could list different social subsets of the school student body and generally place everyone in one group or the other, although they typically viewed themselves (and themselves alone) as crossing multiple subsets. What they said about Lamar was strikingly similar to peer crowd research in other high schools in different states at different times, although the names of the different groups often varied. The jocks and the mean girls (or the plastics) came up a lot, as did the goths, and the Latinos were viewed as one single monolithic peer group to all non-Latinos in the school. What mattered was not just the group identities and names but the clear boundaries that divided one group from the others. As a white 9th grader named Cooper explained about the mix of PLUs in Lamar,

> It's like the groups are pretty strange ... it's just a whole web of people who weren't allowed to hang out with certain people and people who aren't supposed to even come near other people.

Not surprisingly, then, the teenagers at Lamar were quite clear that this PLU level of the peer culture was where all of the pressure to conform and the exclusion happened. It was never they and their friends who were participating but, instead, always this more ambiguous, often faceless mass of teenagers out there. As Olivia, an African American girl, explained about what she witnessed going on in the school,

> Yeah, if they are ... like some of the goths or something, or if they are special. I know some people – not *my* friends, but *some* people

would look at them different. Think that they are mutants or whatever. I look at them the same way as being a human. I mean, they still have blood. They have veins.

According to Olivia, she and her friends saw past the superficial, but all of the other teenagers at school could not. The PLU level was a superficial level and, as a result, an arena in which teenagers were vulnerable to being misjudged or pressured to live up to some judgment, accurate or not. This vulnerability applied to teenagers playing by the rules of their own PLU, trying to gain access to some desired PLU, or falling victim to a clash between different PLUs.

What struck me most when hearing about how these PLUs operated their influence at Lamar was how nontransparent that influence often was. Yes, the Lamar teenagers would describe how they had seen someone who was different (often an overweight girl or an effeminate boy) ridiculed in the hall, but these instances were the exception rather than the norm. Instead, social feedback on the PLU level possessed a degree of *subtlety* that teenagers are not often credited with having. Some of this subtlety was similar to the thinly veiled social aggression perfected by girls that was described in the book *Queen Bees and Wannabes*, which was later made into the movie *Mean Girls* (Wiseman, 2002). In short, what I mean by subtle is feedback that is deliberately opaque as a way of providing the person giving the feedback plausible deniability. Because this feedback could be plausibly denied, it tended to be more stinging. As Ava, a white 9th grader, explained,

> They are trying. They try to be subtle. But it comes across more than they ever originally intend it to be.

Often, this kind of subtle social feedback is transmitted through ostensibly private talk directed outward, which girls appeared to be especially skilled at doing. For example, a group of teenagers making jokes that the target of their jokes could overhear was a widely recognized maneuver. One female 9th grader explained this feedback thusly,

People saying stuff behind your back and making fun of you, to where you come upon a conversation and you hear them actually saying it, that has a lot greater impact [than anything else].

A variation on this externalized private talk was the inside joke, in which teenagers were made to feel as though they were being discussed but were not exactly sure what was being said. What they could be sure of, the Lamar teenagers explained, was that such discussion was unlikely complimentary. Cooper described the inside joke from his own personal experience:

Like, some people might make jokes that other people might not understand, because it's more part of their group and what they do.

Another mechanism of social feedback on the PLU level of peers at Lamar was double speak, or saying one thing that is objectively nice but may or may not have another less positive meaning. Again, the Lamar teenagers viewed this strategy as being primarily one taken by girls. As a Latino boy, Miguel, commented about how much more *stealthily* hurtful girls could be with words than boys,

Because you can know in your head, like you have a feeling that they are talking about you like that, but you might not know. With a guy, he's telling you straight up. Like, you know he told you that. But with a girl, it's like, did she just say that? I mean, wait a minute.

A third common ploy recognized by the teenagers at Lamar involved a nice compliment that itself actually implied the opposite. "Oh, that is a nice shirt" or "I think you're losing weight" or "Are you dating anyone?" Both girls and boys used this ploy at Lamar much more often than pointing to someone and openly making fun of him or her.

By far, the most commonly cited example of nontransparent feedback on the PLU level at Lamar was "the look." More than anything else, teenagers at Lamar would say that they knew that they were crossing some social line when they received looks from other people. These looks were not necessarily dirty or mean. They could be quizzical or register surprise or even fear. As Katrina put it, "Sometimes, like random people I don't know just look at me weird." A look, whether real or perceived, neutral or value laden, conveyed a message to teenagers. The flipside of "the look" was not being looked at ever. According to one 9th grade girl, a key way a girl at Lamar knew that she has no social value was when boys never looked at her in the hallway. "Probably one of the biggest things would be guys not looking at her," she said when asked how a girl at Lamar would know that she is not measuring up socially.

Whatever the form, these looks (or lack thereof) registered with teenagers *if* they happened often enough. In the eyes of the teenagers at Lamar, the most pernicious thing about "the look" was that it was completely open to interpretation and, at the same time, could be totally a function of the teenager's imagination. One never knew for sure. As a result, how "the look" was interpreted was often more a function of the teenager himself or herself than of the actual social feedback being given, if, in fact, it was being given intentionally.

Overall, the teenagers at Lamar sometimes saw a clear degree of intent in these various forms of nontransparent negative social feedback, but sometimes they saw no such intent. Often, they explained, the social feedback emanating from PLU interactions at Lamar was not intended to hurt or police teenagers. Indeed, it could even be transmitted when the teenager receiving the feedback was completely unknown to the teenagers sending it. Two examples really made me understand the Lamar teenagers' point.

The first example, described by a female 10th grader, involved an overweight girl overhearing a conversation that was not targeted at her personally (the speakers might not even have known that she was there) but that was relevant to her. That conversation might have been a discussion of how ugly fat people are among a group of boys. Those boys might not have been talking about the overweight girl who overheard them – they might have edited themselves if they had known she was listening or, perhaps, might not have even perceived her to be overweight. Even in such circumstances, the girl would have received a clear message about her social worth from overhearing this conversation.

The second example, described by a female 9th grader, involved a teenager being the recipient of talk about a third person that was relevant to that teenager even if the speakers were not aware that it was relevant to that teenager. Consider a boy who was sexually confused even though no one else at Lamar had any reason to know this. If that boys repeatedly hears homophobic talk in the hallways and classrooms at school, he will recognize that this talk speaks to his social worth even if those people doing all of the talking do not know that it does.

Social Feedback from Outside the School

Of course, even as friendship groups are enveloped in PLUs and PLUs are enveloped in the student body, all of these groupings are enveloped into the larger youth culture of the United States and its various subcultures. Social feedback from that larger youth culture, therefore, is often transmitted to teenagers through their more intimate social groups, but the media play a big role too. They both reflect and shape messages in youth culture about what the standards of appearance, behavior, and thought are.[6] The media, then, are another direct source of social feedback that may make teenagers feel as though they do not fit in at school. Partly, this role of the media is channeled through the PLU level, but not entirely so.

Historically, the effects of the media on young people's views of the self have been described in terms of teenagers as somewhat passive recipients of media messages. In this perspective, teenagers learn what

[6] The 1992 edited volume on media and adolescents by Greenberg and colleagues provides an overview of the role of media in youth culture in the United States, although it predates the widespread use of the internet.

is expected of them by consuming media. Although this perspective certainly has some evidence behind it, the Lamar teenagers revealed different ways of thinking about the connection between the media and the specific developmental issue of feelings of not fitting in. Importantly, their thoughts and experiences also reflect the critical nature of the "new" media in understanding teenagers' socially oriented perceptions of themselves. I want to discuss two examples of this process.

First, today the media talk back. Teenagers can interact with the media personally rather than passively consume media content. When making a Facebook page, for example, a teenager is making his or her own media, putting it out for public display, and almost immediately generating feedback from others. This quick turnaround can be quite thrilling and self-validating. As Cathy explained about why she loved MySpace,

> It's like, yeah. Refresh page. New comments! Oh, my God, I'm so happy! Like, when you put a new picture up, it's like you get comments right away on it, and it's just exciting.

In short, many Lamar teenagers had a venue in which they could control what feedback they received about themselves. Indeed, the comments sections on most of their social networking sites typically overflowed with positive commentary about the owner of the page. Going back to an example from Chapter 4, Katina, an immigrant 10th grader, used her social networking site page to present an image of herself that was diametrically opposed to how she was viewed at Lamar. Shy, polite, and bookish at school, she depicted herself online – whether accurately or not, I am not sure – as what is often described as a riot grrrl. According to the comments posted on her page, however, this self-presentation appeared to have brought her and her friends a certain amount of respect, respect that she clearly craved.

At the same time, the Web also provided a media venue in which more negative feedback could be given anonymously. Of late, the news has been filled with stories about teenagers being harassed online, often with horrible consequences like suicide. The teenagers at Lamar told me stories about this, although it was usually something that happened to someone else, never to them. In this way, the Web had become an interactive channel of feedback from the high school culture, one that teenagers had more control over but also one that could never be turned off.

Second, the Lamar teenagers spent a great deal of time surfing the Web for news and information. For the most part, this activity was one they enjoyed and viewed as a positive, with the Web surpassing all other media platforms in keeping them informed about the world and also offering them a great deal of choice in how they kept informed. Yet, some teenagers detected a form of negative social feedback about themselves in the news stories and blogs that they came across on the Web covering current events and/or research findings, stories that were unlikely written with any sort of intent or underlying message.

The best illustration of this phenomenon given to me at Lamar was from a girl with body issues who was mortified by reading news stories about the "obesity crisis" in the United States. As for other examples, one could imagine a boy who is confused about his sexual orientation reading a recent *Newsweek* cover story on a California boy murdered in his high school for being gay, an economically disadvantaged boy seeing a series of stories in the newspaper documenting the scientific evidence about the low likelihood that poor teenagers will ever make it out of poverty, or an overweight girl seeing that widely circulated article in the *New York Times* about girls at an Indiana university being kicked out of their sorority for not being thin. In all of these scenarios, a teenager might come away with the message "I am in trouble" even if that was the very last thing that the reporter or the scientist or the blogger would *ever* want.

Social Comparison

At Lamar, teenagers either relied on social comparison less than social feedback when assessing themselves or, more likely, were less cognizant of the social comparisons that they made. Still, they were able to describe several different kinds of social comparison, each with its own advantages and pitfalls.

As expected, the most common target of social comparison consisted of other teenagers at Lamar. Typically, teenagers compared themselves to peers in the same grade and of the same gender who were (or were at last perceived to be) 1) at the top of the social hierarchy, 2) right where the teenager wanted to be or thought he or she should be in the hierarchy, or 3) at the bottom of the hierarchy. Triangulating among these three school-based comparisons seemed to give teenagers a sense of how they were doing and whether they were in trouble.

Again as expected, the first-response standards of social comparison with school peers were obvious, more objective markers of social status like school honors, recognitions, and status roles (e.g., elected class president, star athlete). By far, the most important of these "obvious" factors was perceived success with the opposite sex. Who dated and who had romantic/sexual experience both represented the yardstick on which a teenager at Lamar was measured socially.

Yet, although teenagers at Lamar initially focused on these objective markers of status, they quickly turned to more subjective or idiosyncratic standards. Examples mentioned included,

> How many people you see walking with them in the hall and stuff. I mean, that's not even a big deal, but I've seriously been.... This girl, she's always like, "Oh, my god! That guy never walks with anyone. He's such a loser!" (Madeline, white 10th grader)

> There is a lot of special coffee places, I guess, that a lot of people would go to, just so they can say they went there. They may hate coffee, but it is just the well known cool place to go. (Romina, Latina 10th grader)

Who walked with the most people through the hallway, who went to which after-school hangout, who got the most hellos from older students, who parked in a certain lot, who ate lunch inside the building or outside. In a teenager's eyes, these were seemingly concrete pieces of data that could be used to assess who ranked high or low at Lamar, data that could be used to evaluate one's own social position at the school. What the teenagers at Lamar told me about how social comparison worked within the school setting can be best illustrated using a vignette of an overweight girl, which was stitched together from many different but highly similar responses to my inquiry about how a hypothetical girl might know that her weight was a problem at Lamar. Even if no one ever made fun of her or let her know in any overt way that her body was a social liability, this hypothetical girl might come to understand her social marginality at Lamar through a simple *empirical* process in which she looked around and determined that she had less experience with boys than the girls who made cheerleader in her grade. Perhaps even more importantly, she might have determined that she also got less attention from boys, fewer invitations to parties, and fewer welcome looks at lunch than girls who were not so popular but who were thin. More evidence could come from comparing herself to other overweight girls in her grade, which might reveal that all overweight girls in her field of vision led similar social lives. Adding things up, she would surmise that her body was marginalizing her despite her many other qualities. At this point, another kind of social comparison might be triggered, as she compares herself to the clear outcasts in her grade and concludes that she, at least, is not totally marginalized. Along with the more negative social comparisons this girl has made, this more self-protective social comparison would help her pinpoint her exact place in the social hierarchy of Lamar.

Although the social comparisons that Lamar teenagers made were predominantly relative to other school peers, they were also made relative to others outside the school, even if understanding one's social positions at Lamar was the point of the comparison. For example, older siblings provided a very reflexive target of social comparison for the teenagers at Lamar. They felt that this social comparison was forced on them by their parents and teachers, and so it seemed like a natural one to make themselves even if they nominally rejected it. Sometimes this social comparison was self-enhancing (e.g., one girl at Lamar got a great deal of satisfaction out of being viewed as the good one from her family in the school), sometimes less so (e.g., one boy felt that he would never live up to his brother's legacy at the school). As another example, the ideal physical/body types put forward in the media constituted a major source of social comparison, for boys and girls. In other words, teenagers at Lamar compared themselves to peers at school according to how well each of them measured up against media ideals, especially in terms of thinness for girls and musculature for boys.

Still, when it came to figuring out one's value on the social market at Lamar, the social comparison process was almost overwhelmingly directed at other teenagers at Lamar. Most of the time, these within-school social comparisons were focused on teenagers who were not close friends but were not complete strangers either. Again, that inter-mediate level of the peer world was important. Having said this, I also want to acknowledge that the teenagers at Lamar had a very difficult time seeing how they made social comparisons within the school setting. The insights I gleaned from them primarily derived from less personalized discussions, such as by asking them to discuss the plights of other students they knew at Lamar or by giving them hypotheti-cal scenarios. This tendency to overlook or deny social comparison is quite natural. Just as teenagers are driven to do it, they seem to be driven to not see that they are doing it.

The Interplay of Social Feedback and Social Comparison

One night, when I was listening to the tapes that my graduate students had made of their interviews with the Lamar teenagers, I came across a conversation that one of them had with a young boy named Cooper. He was actually talking about his parents, but it struck me as capturing the social experience of high school and how teenagers come to know what they know.

COOPER: I guess ... I have an idea of something, but I can't really put it into words. Hmm.

MY STUDENT: Would it be in relation to family or friends?

COOPER: I think my parents want me to be something a little different, but I'm not sure what.

MY STUDENT: So you somehow get....

COOPER: I don't know. Something. I don't know.

MY STUDENT: But you're not sure what exactly it is that they would want.

COOPER: Right. I just think they think I'm too ... I'm not even sure what they think I'm too much of, but it seems like it. I have a feeling. I've got a gut feeling.

MY STUDENT: Like you kind of sense something?

COOPER: Yeah.

MY STUDENT: Huh. That's interesting. Like you sort of sense something is there.

COOPER: Mm-hmm.

MY STUDENT: But it's not like they've ever said to you....

COOPER: Right.

Cooper is not sure what he knows or how he knows it, but he feels like something is off, that something is just not right. That is what I discovered at Lamar. Teenagers just *know* that they do or do not fit in. Some of the teenagers appeared to be wrong – their perceptions of themselves as not fitting in or as on the margins of social life did not bear much resemblance to what I observed. Going back to the Thomas theorem, however, whether the knowledge produced through various forms of information processing is based on reality or misperception does not always matter. What matters is whether the consequences of this knowledge are real.

WHY MESSAGES ABOUT FIT MATTER

The teenagers rarely used the terms "identity" or "the self" when discussing their experiences at Lamar, but their discussions absolutely centered around these very concepts. They tended to talk about "who I am," "the real me," and "what makes me me." Indeed, whether commenting on their own lives, the experiences of friends, or the experiences of other teenagers they witnessed at school, they demonstrated a great deal of agreement that it was these very aspects of the self that were most likely threatened by social struggles at Lamar. When asked why not fitting in would be difficult for teenagers' academic careers, the teenagers all eventually touched on identity issues. In doing so, they confirmed my *general* hypothesis about the role of identity discrepancies in the academic consequences of not fitting in socially at school, although they also demonstrated several ways in which my more *specific* hypotheses about this phenomenon were off base.

The Social, Multifaceted Nature of Teenage Identities

Recall that, from a theoretical perspective, the first step in understanding how identity serves as a channel between teenagers' problems on the informal side of high school and the socioemotional conditions and behaviors that pose risks to the formal side of high school is to grasp just how complex and socially embedded teenagers' personal identity development is. Having the teenagers at Lamar make Who I Am projects provided much needed insight into the process of identity development *from a teenager's point of view*. I gave them cameras, poster boards, and art supplies and asked them to make a collage in order to let us know who they were. Importantly, these Who I Am projects led several teenagers to invite us into their personal Web pages on social networking sites; they realized that their Web pages were simply digitized Who I Am projects.

In line with social psychological and developmental theory, the most consistent theme across all of the teenagers' projects was that they could not discuss who they were – "the real me" – without discussing the relationships, groups, and institutions in which they lived their lives. Without any sign that they recognized the inherent

Figure 7.2. Lizzie's Who I Am Project.

contradictions of what they were saying, the teenagers stressed that they were their own independent, autonomous persons, always true to themselves, but also explained in great detail how knowing the people they knew and living in the places where they lived had made them who they were.

Figure 7.2 presents the Who I Am project made by Lizzie, a white 10th grader from a middle-class, somewhat bohemian family. Lizzie was a varsity athlete and great student involved in several school clubs, and she took her project quite seriously and enjoyed talking and writing about it. I present Lizzie's project here because it captures the general theme of identity development that arose from almost all Who I Am projects – specifically, that personal identity was developed within a system of interwoven social contexts, with the peer culture of high school at the center.

With almost no exception, the teenagers at Lamar viewed their *school* friends as the single most important reason that they were who they were. For example, Lizzie included several friends on her project (although they had to be blacked out), and she wrote in an accompanying essay that everything she put on this project (e.g., the pictures of concerts, local hangout spots, and elements of pop culture) was there because it symbolized something about her friends at Lamar. Indeed, she told us that she would have found it impossible to describe who she was without talking about her friends. As another young woman with a Who I Am project very similar to Lizzie's project explained about her friends at Lamar,

> They, like, make up me. They, like, help me, like, shape – they shape who I am and everything. So it's basically, like, they're, like, they make me who I am.

The dominance of school friends as a window into personal identity was especially striking considering the comparative absence of parents in the teenagers' Who I Am projects. Only a minority of the Lamar teenagers included images or symbols of their parents in their projects, and, interestingly, most of those who did were racial/ethnic minorities or from more working-class backgrounds. Among the most privileged teenagers, parents were basically invisible. I should stress that *all* of the teenagers at Lamar talked about their parents a great deal, but they were very unlikely to think about their parents when we asked them to tell us who they were. For them, personal identity was not about family, it was about friends.

Indeed, one young Latina, Juanita, centered her Who I Am project (pictured in Chapter 1) as well as her personal Web page around a pink Post-it note on which she had handwritten an old Mexican saying that she had adopted as her own personal mantra:

> *Digame que sus amigos sean y le dire que usted sean* (Show me who your friends are and I will tell you who you are).

Although Juanita was an ambitious, headstrong, and confident young woman who held the "To Thine Own Self Be True" messages of youth culture in high esteem (again, refer back to her Who I Am project in Chapter 1), she had a great deal of difficulty separating who she was from who her friends were when asked to talk explicitly about herself. All of her friends, in turn, were also students at Lamar.

Although the Lamar teenagers did not connect the role of friends in their identity development to home or even neighborhood, most articulated how they saw their friendship groups – and themselves – as embedded in a set of ever-larger social systems. Most importantly, they almost exclusively viewed their friendship groups as a part of Lamar itself. To them, Lamar *was* their friends. Indeed, this connection between friends and Lamar was the primary reason that the majority of the teenagers (Lizzie being one exception) had a picture of the actual Lamar building prominently featured on their Who I Am projects and/ or personal Web pages. When questioned, those who included such pictures explained that being a student at Lamar was a major source of identity for them. Importantly, several of the teenagers who did not include such pictures on their projects echoed this same sentiment at some point in our conversations with them. They felt that telling someone that they went to Lamar revealed fundamental information about who they were. This information had almost nothing to do with the institutional structures of Lamar. Instead, the teenagers seemed to think that such information was important because it located them in a group of teenagers of a specific, identifiable kind.

Although the friends and peers embedded within Lamar were the focal point of identity discussions, many teenagers went beyond this narrow focus to consider larger social systems. In doing so, however, they were far less likely to discuss the direct effects of these systems on who they were than to discuss the indirect effects of these systems through their school friends and peers. For them, who they were was embedded in their friendship groups and peer groups, which were embedded in Lamar, which was embedded in broader cultures.

The two most commonly discussed of these broader cultures were the city of Austin and certain segments of youth culture defined by music and media.

First, two-thirds of girls and one-half of all teenagers at Lamar included pictures of Austin landmarks on their Who I Am projects, as did the majority of teenagers with personal Web pages. Lizzie's project, for example, featured a picture in the lower left of Barton Springs, a natural swimming hole that is a major community meeting point in the city. She did so, she explained, because she viewed her friendship group – and, to a lesser extent, Lamar, which she saw as the "real" Austin compared to other schools – as capturing the spirit of the city.

Second, the teenagers at Lamar often saw their friendship groups as two-way conduits between themselves and the larger youth culture. In this way, the music that they listened to, the games they played, and the movies they loved were all elements of youth culture that shaped who they were and who their friends were but also, importantly, provided them and their friends with an outlet to demonstrate to the world who they were and to link up with other teenagers out there who were like them.

Lizzie's Who I Am project, for example, featured pictures of the White Stripes and of the Austin City Limits Music Festival, which meant something to her not because liking such things made her unique but because it identified what she shared with her friends. Other teenagers (about two-thirds of those who made Who I Am projects) featured pictures of favorite CDs, drawings of favorite musicians, movie posters, book covers (primarily *Harry Potter*), and shots of video games. The same representations were also found on personal Web pages, with one girl, Sara, dedicating her entire Web page to a list – written encyclopedia style – of hundreds of the musicians and songs that mattered most to her and her friends.

Thus, the Lamar teenagers came at the issue of personal identity in different ways but with many commonalities. The most striking of these commonalities was their view that their experiences with other teenagers within the micro-, meso-, and macrolevel contexts of their lives were what made them who they were. This widely held, consistently articulated view, which aligns well with social psychological and developmental theory, became the foundation on which their attempts to understand why not fitting in at school mattered so much were built.

School-Based Problems in Identity Development

In the eyes of Lamar teenagers, the high school was a primary setting in which they figured out who they were and what they were "worth." Initially, they all presented this process in a positive light; school was where they met their friends, who helped them be who they were supposed to be. Few featured pictures or images on their Who I Am projects that would depict them more negatively or that alluded to struggles that they might have been having, acknowledged any potentially stigmatizing characteristic (e.g., obesity), delved into more problematic peer processes at school, or discussed identity problems within the context of school – at least at first. When we followed up their positive discussions of friends and the self with a few simple questions, however, their linear, bump-free depictions of their identity development got far more nuanced. "Being in your group of friends at Lamar has obviously been quite important to making you the person you are, but, Lamar is a large school filled with many different groups – have your experiences been more positive, more negative, or the same when you move outside of your group?" was one such question. Another was, "Some teenagers figure out who they are and like who they are, others have trouble figuring out who they are, and still others figure out who they are but are unsure they like who they are – where do you (and your friends) fit and why?"

The conversations opened up by these probes were not nearly as consistent across the teenagers at Lamar as conversations of other subjects, but one recurring theme was that one of the worst problems a teenager could have, at least emotionally, would be to not be accepted at school for who he or she really was. As Lizzie explained long after going through her Who I Am project,

> It's important for people to like you. It's more important for you to like yourself, but it's hard to like yourself if other people don't like you. It's hard for people to like you when you don't like yourself. It's kind of like a never-ending link there.

Although Lizzie and the teenagers discussing such problems were not familiar with social psychological theory, the images that they used are remarkably similar to the main principles of the Looking Glass Self. They talked a great deal about the differences between how teenagers saw themselves and how others at school saw them. Indeed, some even talked about how hard it would be for one of the marginalized teenagers at Lamar to look into a mirror in the bathroom and fear that something was wrong with him or her because of what happened every day at school. In other words, the teenagers at Lamar saw the peers at school, collectively, as a sort of looking glass in which they could view themselves. If this looking glass was limited to friends, then the reflected appraisals were often, although not always, positive and self-affirming. If the looking glass was expanded to encompass the larger bands of peers at school, then the reflected appraisals were much harder to predict or control.

This looking glass metaphor that came out of discussions with Lamar teenagers captures the linked social feedback and social comparison processes described earlier in this chapter. When these processes led teenagers to feel as though they did not fit in socially at Lamar, the looking glass at school showed them something that was different than what they saw in the bathroom mirror. For most teenagers at Lamar, these discrepancies were not severe and did not last long. For others (both teenagers we interviewed and the friends that they talked about), these discrepancies were more enduring. Of the various kinds of identity problems suggested by theory as potentially important, the more general actual/ought discrepancy and the more specific spoiled identity syndrome were the two that the teenagers at Lamar felt or saw most clearly.

Again, talking about identity discrepancies was difficult at Lamar. Using the standard questions for getting at identity discrepancies – "Do you ever feel like the person you are is not the person you want to be?" and "Do you ever feel like the person you are is not who others want you to be?" – yielded very little information (Harrison, 2001; Ewell et al., 1996; Higgins, 1989). These questions were followed up with additional prompts, and we reworded the questions and related probes in various ways. Although some teenagers admitted to feeling something akin to an actual/ideal identity discrepancy in the past, feelings that they eventually got over, only one admitted to having such feelings in the present. That one teenager was Ray, a white 9th grader, who described how entering high school had made him doubt himself:

> And it seems like everyone is doing things and they are getting ahead of me and I feel like I am losing myself sometimes. I feel like I am not really … I don't feel like I am as much as I was.

At first, no teenager would admit to have any degree of actual/ought discrepancy either. The Lamar teenagers' prolonged exposure to the key "be real" themes of American youth culture and youth-oriented media that I have mentioned previously was likely a factor in their reluctance to talk about identity problems. These themes capture the widespread tendency for teenagers to react to adult perceptions of teenagers as mindless followers with an exaggerated projection of independence, self-reliance, and disdain for conformity (Milner, 2004; Coleman, 1961). Indeed, almost every teenager at Lamar voiced, at some point, a variation on this theme:

> I always be myself. I don't try and be anyone else … it never works out. So, it is, like, it doesn't really matter, because then you won't be happy if you try and be someone else. (Wes, white 9th grader)

> Just confident in who I am. Able to stand up and say, "Yeah, this is me. Take it or leave it." (Juanita, Latina 9th grader)

I … what I believe in is just be who you are … I just don't feel that I should I be somebody else that other's want me to be. I just like to be who I am and if nobody likes it, then oh well. (Sylvia, Latina 10th grader)

Basically don't care what other people say, be who you are and just do what you do. (Althea, African American 9th grader)

Underneath this self-presentation, however, some other feelings were lurking that came out when more oblique inquiries into actual/ought identity discrepancies yielded a bit more self-reflection. A back-end way into this topic was asking if other people at school, maybe a friend, ever felt such a discrepancy. "Oh, I'd say most kids do," answered Christian without hesitation. Even more effective was asking, "If your parents were to make a collage about who you are, would it look the same?" The majority of teenagers would ponder this question and then slowly start talking. No, they would answer, and then work through their feelings about how much this hurt or, alternatively, how much it drove them. Eventually, the conversation would turn to their friends and, even more commonly, the other students at school who were not their friends (e.g., the PLU). The outburst from Ray recounted in Chapter 3, about his struggles with being called Kelso, actually emerged from a discussion about this kind of identity discrepancy.

In the end, every teenager interviewed eventually described his or her own struggles with an actual/ought discrepancy or talked about helping a close friend through such struggles. Importantly, almost all of these teenagers linked such a discrepancy back to some variation of not fitting in at school. Feeling off in school, like one does not measure up, appeared to be – at least according to them – a trigger for looking inward and revaluating the self. Although some teenagers would respond to feelings of not fitting in by laying the "blame" on others ("What do they know?" "Who cares what they think?"), a more common response seemed to be to eventually doubt the self ("What is wrong with me?, "Why don't they like me?").

In Goffman's conception, a spoiled identity is not an identity discrepancy, although it can lead to one. According to Goffman, a spoiled identity occurs when a stigmatized or socially devalued aspect of the self overwhelms all other personal characteristics; to the world, that one part of the self stands for the self as a whole. One of the most powerful themes arising from discussions with Lamar teenagers was that teenagers could be pigeonholed or stereotyped very early on in their high school careers in ways that would set into motion the link between feelings of not fitting in and identity problems. Again, they never used the spoiled identity terminology – or, indeed, any identity language at all – but certainly echoed its basic meaning.

To the Lamar teenagers, something like a spoiled identity happened because Lamar was such a large, heterogeneous school that finding one's place was quite difficult. In this environment, external or known traits became easy-to-use, first-response standards on which judgments about whether to get to know or befriend someone were based. Explained Christian,

> I try not to be prejudiced, but certain times you just can't … I'd say a lot of kids will look at someone and make an idea of them just like that … I think physical appearance … is more in the short-term, like, people decide if they're going to talk to them or not.

In other words, the sheer vastness of the market of relationships at Lamar required that a great deal of immediate categorization and sorting occur. According to two of Christian's classmates, this sorting process occurred within minutes and had long-term effects on who interacted with whom. Consequently, the "real" self mattered far less than superficial aspects of the self or reputation. Ali, a young Middle Easterner at Lamar trying to make his way through high school in a post-9/11 world, provided a personal example of how this process could occur at Lamar. He explained that he knew that, no matter what he did or who he really was inside, people saw him as terrorist first. His experience poignantly illustrated how a spoiled identity was something that happened to a person, something imposed from the outside in.

Being overweight was the most common scenario that Lamar teenagers used to illustrate how someone could be immediately and lastingly disadvantaged on the PLU level by superficial characteristics that foreclosed on the prospect of future social interaction and status. Among the other examples offered were being gay, but only for boys and by boys.

Coping with Identity Problems

As already explained, the link between feelings of not fitting in and identity discrepancies (and its link, in turn, to stigma) was almost universally viewed among the Lamar teenagers as one of the worst fates possible for a high school student. "Painful," "awful," "torture," and "unbearable" were just a few of the words they used to describe how teenagers would feel if they began to doubt themselves because of their social positions at school.

Not surprisingly, then, the teenagers at Lamar had many ideas of what someone in such a situation could do, including many ideas derived from their own experiences or the experiences of close friends or siblings. Importantly, when discussing other people, they drew a distinction between what they would like that person to do and what they thought that person would do. As expected, the scenarios they described were much more active and aimed at self-enhancement than passive and solely concerned with aligning self-views with social position. Indeed, the teenagers at Lamar would admit to more passive responses to school-based identity discrepancies, such as internalizing social views into the self, only in the past – "when I was young" or "back in middle school." As one girl said, "I hated myself then." For the most part, they were far more likely to recognize this passive, self-verifying response in others, especially friends who were just outside of their group of best friends. "This one girl I know ..." was a typical way that they would start discussions about internalizing coping responses, which were almost always couched in terms of self-esteem. A socially isolated girl coming to see in the mirror what others saw was cited as an example by more than one teenager.

Even though more passive self-verifying responses to school-based identity problems were acknowledged by teenagers at Lamar, they overwhelmingly concentrated on more active self-verifying responses, especially those that helped them feel better about themselves in the process. One common response discussed by the Lamar teenagers, one that aligns with well-documented theoretical mechanisms of self-protection, was taking a selective approach to social contexts. For example, a teenager whose school experiences make him doubt himself may avoid school. Even if he keeps going to school regularly, he may reconfigure his feelings about school so that not fitting in at that school is a self-affirming badge of honor rather than a source of shame or confusion. Indeed, several teenagers at Lamar discussed this strategy as something that they had done, would do, or had seen someone do:

> Instead of letting the people disown them, they disown the people instead. So that makes them feel better about it. (Cooper, white 9th grader)

> Well, I guess I try to withdraw myself. I try … I honestly … I will try to become a hermit. I will try to … and it is just, I don't know, it is kind of a cycle. It gets worse. (Ray, white 9th grader)

> Yeah, like, once school gets out, we're the first people out of the freaking school, you know. (Miguel, Latino 10th grader)

Although the teenagers at Lamar also discussed alcohol and drug use as responses to the personal pain of social problems at school, how they viewed this response did not tap into the hypothesized self-medicating strategy. Instead, they viewed drinking and drug use as possible attempts to find a peer crowd in which one fit, to forge a new kind of social identity. In other words, substance use behaviors might have represented, to some teenagers, a way of self-protectively selecting or prioritizing a new reference group in or around school. Substance use was social, not medicinal.

In line with the not-fitting-in pathway, these responses involved short-term protections with long-term risks. Both active and passive responses to identity problems, including those linked to social stigma, are, at best, quick fixes. They might improve life now, but they create roadblocks in the path to higher education in an era in which higher education has increasingly taken on a make-or-break quality. Thus, issues of identity were significant to understanding multiple pieces of the not-fitting-in pathway. Not only did they help to explain how feelings of not fitting in might translate into educationally counterproductive coping mechanisms, they also explained how being in a stigmatized group could engender feelings of not fitting in at school.

Ava

The links among social turbulence in high school, identity development, and coping responses with long-term risks were illustrated by a young white, middle-class 9th grader named Ava, whom I first described back in Chapter 4. For whatever reason, this intelligent young woman had come to see that she was viewed as a nerd (or dork or geek) by others at school. Even though she thought of herself as a nerd too, she knew that this social label was not a positive one in the eyes of others. She had come to believe that others found her weird, a belief that she experienced in different ways depending on her general mood.

This marginality at Lamar – despite the fact that she had several close friends – clearly affected Ava's own sense of self in ways that often caused her to act. She admitted to undergoing a major identity crisis in middle school when she first felt pushed to the side by old friends who were developing new ideas about what was cool. She said that she gave it everything she had to keep up, changing the way she dressed, the music she listened to, and even the way she talked now that her androgynous clothes, black-humor-laden conversation, and taste for metal rock were verboten. For example, when her "friends want me to dress differently, I will just wear a normal pair of jeans and like a black shirt to school. And they will be a little more friendly to me." Among the teenagers I interviewed, she was the one most conscious of doing things specifically to get positive feedback from other people at school.

Yet, taking these specific actions did not make her happy, and so she took another tack. Basically, as she transitioned into high school, she removed herself from the more preppy, upper-middle-class circles of her middle school friends and tried very hard to find her own niche at Lamar. She had a palpable need to have a group to call her own, and she felt that she had found it in two ways: 1) in a group of friends she developed within the school marching band and 2) on the Web with other teenagers, in and out of her school, who shared similar interests (including science fiction and Japanese anime). In these supportive settings, she was protected from a spoiled identity. She found some measure of consistency and enhancement.

Despite finding her niche at Lamar, Ava's effortful, if not conscious, identity work was clear to any adult observer. She was doing a lot of what social psychologists call self-presentation, both in person and on the Web. In other words, she was trying to create a social persona, her idealized identity, and push it out into the world. As a reaction to the conformity of her middle school years and her rejection of those who had rejected her, this idealized identity was of a punk rebel, an independent free spirit who did what she wanted when she wanted. She dedicated her personal page to musical acts she viewed as tough and anarchic and filled her lengthy Web postings with tough, blunt, oppositional language. In the process, she developed a personal philosophy about the value of difference.

AVA: I like being really, really different … I like people to look at me and I like to see their reactions, with them saying, "She is weird." And whatnot. So.…

ME: So, difference is a goal for you?

AVA: Yes.

ME: So, how do you do that?

AVA: A lot of the time, it is just by kind of the way I dress. I will act really weird around certain people. Just to kind of make them wonder what is going on.

ME: OK. So, you value difference.

AVA: Yes.

ME: And being different.

AVA: Very much.

As part of this new philosophy, she tried to reconstruct the relationship between her and the larger PLUs at Lamar. She did this by developing a new theory that anyone at Lamar who did not like her was not rejecting her but, instead, was afraid of her. Fear, not dislike or disrespect, was the problem she faced. Yet, one saw cracks in this idealized identity, this effortful simultaneous attempt at self-enhancement and self-verification.

When talking about her many musical loves, she told me that what she liked best about the metal rap group Insane Clown Posse was that they wear masks. If they wear masks, she explained, they can "go out into normal life and not be like bombarded." She said that she wanted to be able to do that. When talking about her fervent love of anime, she expressed her desire to go to Japan and find people like her, the goths, because she "would like to have a lot more people like me," a "community" that appreciated her. In both cases, after realizing what she had said, she backtracked immediately, reiterating and emphasizing that she was "perfectly content with myself." Still, the cracks in the façade showed, and they were telling, as when she wrote on her blog that her greatest fear was "being alone."

So, Ava was doing identity work to protect herself from the vulnerability she felt at school, and although some of it was positive, it was not enough. Her identity was under attack, and over time her coping responses turned more problematic, even if she could not see the connection so clearly. She did not turn to drugs or crime. Instead, she just stopped caring about school, at least as much as a middle-class girl with well-educated parents could. For her, school was about "them," and she did not want to buy into it. She did not study. She did not ask for help from teachers. By the end of the year, this clearly bright girl had failed her science class, which meant that she could not follow the curricular pathway through the next couple of years that most of her fellow students coming from the same privileged middle school would.

The last time I saw Ava, she told me that she wanted to get out of Austin one day and go to Colorado or some place like that, and – true to her social class – she viewed college as her ticket. I asked her if she thought that failing science now might thwart her plans then, and she seemed genuinely taken aback by that prospect.

TURNING THE PAGE

The discussions in this chapter about social feedback/comparison and identity development, together, answered the "why?" question – why do some teenagers try to cope with feelings of not fitting in at school in ways that hurt them in the long run? The other important question raised by the general not-fitting-in pathway tested with Add Health data and Lamar data is "why not?" In other words, why do some teenagers in the same situation cope in different ways and, partly as a consequence, have more promising prospects for the future. This "why not?" question is addressed in the next chapter.

8

Sources of Resilience

As laid out in the preceding chapters, some teenagers respond to the identity crises triggered by feelings of not fitting in socially at school in ways that are *protective* in the short term but *harmful* to long-term mental health and socioeconomic attainment, and other teenagers respond in ways that promote their future prospects. The differences between these two scenarios tap into the concept of resilience. Resilience refers to the phenomenon of overcoming the odds – the success stories in a segment of society characterized by bad odds of success.

To be more specific, resilience is derived from epidemiology and represents a specific combination of risk, protection, and outcome. A risk factor characterizes a population with an elevated probability of a problematic outcome. A resilient individual, then, is a member of that at-risk population who avoids that negative outcome or, alternatively, achieves a positive outcome. A protective factor is something about the person, her or his life or social world, that reduces or breaks that link between the risk and the negative outcome. In other words, a protective factor is what helps someone be resilient in the face of risk. In epidemiology, the negative outcome might be cancer. In this scenario, an at-risk population would be smokers, and the protective factor might be some genetic trait that helps a smoker's body somehow resist the carcinogens contained in cigarettes (Jessor, Van Den Bos, Vanderryn, Costa, & Turbin, 1995; Garmezy, 1985). In human development, a classic example of resilience is when schooling helps a poor youth grow up to be an economically successful, healthy adult.

For some time, social and behavioral scientists, such as Werner, Masten, and others, have been trying to elucidate the mysteries of resilience among young people. A general conclusion is that there is really no such thing as a resiliency trait. Outside of the realm of physical disorders and illnesses, people are not born with a capacity for resilience. Instead, the social context in which people live presents resources – protective factors – on which some people, especially those with certain skills and talents and personality characteristics, can draw to become resilient. In this way, resilience is not so much an attribute of the person as it is an intersection between the environment and the ability of the person to tap into something in that environment.[1]

Not fitting in socially at high school does indeed seem to be a risk in that, in the general population, it lowers the odds of matriculating in college and, likely, the many things associated with higher education, such as future earnings, marital stability, and health. Thus, a resilient teenager would be one who comes out fine despite feeling as though he or she does not fit in at school. Why this might happen and what the protective factor(s) may be then become important issues from both a theoretical and intervention perspective. The focus on the link between feelings of not fitting in and the counterproductive coping mechanisms within the general not-fitting-in pathway identifies a developmental issue in need of more investigation. Specifically, the issue at hand is why some teenagers coped with their feelings of not fitting in (and associated identity discrepancies) in ways that exacerbated the problems of those feelings while others, the resilient ones, did not take counterproductive coping actions or were somehow able to turn such a negative situation into a positive.

[1] Masten and Coatsworth provide a great review of resilience in their 1998 essay in *American Psychologist*. Werner's book on children in Kaui is a good resource for getting into this literature.

POTENTIAL PROTECTIVE FACTORS

Protective factors that counteract risks come in many forms. In developmental research, three kinds of protective factors are particularly prominent. Personal factors refer to personality attributes and psychological characteristics that allow teenagers to persevere through adversity, interpersonal factors refer to relationships that give young people strength and support to overcome obstacles in their lives, and group/organizational factors refer to aspects of social systems that pull teenagers out of problematic circumstances or help blunt their impact (Scaramella, Conger, & Simons, 1999; Masten & Coatsworth, 1998; Jessor et al., 1995).

These different kinds of protective factors vary considerably in their amenability to policy intervention. Personal and interpersonal factors, for example, are difficult to manipulate externally on a larger scale, and attempts to do so bring up ethical questions. Organizational factors, on the other hand, are often targeted by policy intervention, although they might be less strongly associated with positive outcomes than more proximal processes (Huston, 2008; Coleman, 1990). Still, these three kinds of protection provided a theoretically grounded starting point for discussions of resilience with the teenagers at Lamar. We told them to think about themselves or, alternatively, a friend or someone at school who they knew was having trouble at school because they did not fit in and then asked them to ruminate on what would help them or those other teenagers do better. A complementary strategy was to tell the Lamar teenagers to think about two teenagers who felt like they did not fit in at school, one who was still happy and doing well academically and one who was not, and reflect on what might account for the difference in outcomes between the two. In doing so, we prompted them to think about personal, interpersonal, and organizational factors – e.g., "what is it about you/them, the people you/they know, or the groups you/they are a part of that helps so much?"

The teenagers at Lamar had a lot that they wanted to say on this topic of resilience, and their responses demonstrated a remarkable degree of consistency. Overwhelmingly, they highlighted interpersonal factors. Furthermore, even when they discussed organizational factors, they tended to highlight interpersonal relations within organizational settings as a reason for the positive impact of those factors.

Interpersonal Protection

Not surprisingly, given the quantitative and qualitative results presented so far and the subject matter of the Who I Am projects, the teenagers at Lamar highlighted peer relations first and foremost as the most important resource for resilience. With few dissents, these teenagers believed that peers – the very source of the problem at hand – were also the most likely source of help. Like all paradoxes, this one makes more sense after it is deconstructed.

Remember that the teenagers at Lamar drew a clear distinction between their close friends and the larger peer crowds (people like us; PLU) that subsumed their cliques. The same distinction is important for thinking about resilience. If the PLU level of the high school peer culture was the problem, then the friend level was the solution. Again and again, having friends – especially more than one – was what the teenagers at Lamar figured would make the most difference in the life of a teenager at their school under some sort of social threat. Importantly, they personalized this line of questioning by saying that this is what *they* personally had that *someone else* in such trouble would need to have.

For girls, having a friend who was there for emotional support and for talking difficult things through was the consensus choice for most important protective factor. As Cathy, who had not had a lot of trouble at school herself, responded, "talking and sharing with girlfriends" was what gave her strength in life, and so she figured that this is what would save someone else in trouble. In her view, friends allowed teen-agers to process through their conflicted feelings and, in doing so, plan a course of action. Boys often agreed that this sort of personal, sup-portive exchange with friends would be a major source of protection, but they mostly talked about such an exchange vis-à-vis their female friends. For example, Cooper described the nightly phone calls he had with a long-time, platonic female friend, ending with, "[She] helped me solve a lot of my problems. In turn, I helped her solve some of her problems."

In the majority view among boys at Lamar, a male friend was not someone for sharing and talking but instead someone who was in your corner, who would stand up for you when you needed it. As Miguel explained,

> My best friend is like my brother ... you know, like, we call him a brother from another mother, you know ... [because] he always has my back.

Consequently, Miguel diagnosed the problem with anyone having trouble at school socially as not having a friend who has his or her back – without that someone, life at school could be scary, and fear makes people do strange things. Many boys at Lamar focused on this aspect of friendship when talking about resilience. This basic gender difference reflects a lot of research over the decades detailing the differ-ent things that boys and girls – and men and women for that matter – prioritize in their same-sex friendships (Giordano, 2003; Prinstein & La Greca, 2002; Hartup & Stevens, 1997).

Another aspect of the peer world that connects the more imper-sonal arena of the PLUs to the more intimate relations of friendship groups is romance and dating. In recent years the national media have been fixated on this idea of "hooking up" and the concomitant decline of traditional dating relationships in adolescence and young adulthood. The debate about whether this is a real phenomenon or an exaggerated urban myth aside, many teenagers at Lamar did follow the more traditional model of adolescent romance. They had boyfriends and girlfriends, and, moreover, they often cited these relationships as a source of support that might serve as a protective factor for a teenager in trouble at school. Interestingly, this potential protective factor was cited more often by boys than girls, perhaps because, as recent mixed-methods research by sociologists has shown, romantic relationships with girls are often teenage boys' main (if not only) venue for emotional connection and expression.[2]

The irony of this consistent focus on peers as protective factors in discussions of resilience is twofold. First, as already mentioned, teenagers consider peers to be a source of risk and of resilience in the face of that risk, and they rarely acknowledge the connection, or any tension, between these two roles of peers. Second, a socially marginalized teenager is, almost by definition, less likely to have close relationships with friends and less likely to have a romantic partner. In this light, teenagers are focusing on a potential protective factor that the most at-risk youth are least likely to have. What I want to stress, however, is that such supportive peer relationships are not impossible for these youth to access and maintain, and that might be the key. Perhaps these kinds of relationships could make a difference if and when they are present.

Although the Lamar teenagers were primarily interested in discussing resilience in terms of peers, they did acknowledge the potential for families to offer protective factors that counteract social risks in high school. Indeed, parents and other aspects of family life were mentioned by most teenagers at Lamar in relation to resilience, although they were not discussed in as great of detail as friends and romantic partners were. Mostly, two aspects of parent-teenager relationships were highlighted as resources for resilient youth in high school.

---

[2] See Giordano, Longmore, and Manning's 2006 article in *American Sociological Review* for more on gender differences in adolescent romantic relationships.

First, being able to express fears and struggles to parents and hear their advice was considered to be very important. Said Madeline, a white girl,

> Good communication, you can save yourself a lot of trouble like that because ... it's kind of hard to go through alone, especially when you are a teen and all that. So if you have really close relationships, I think it helps a lot.

For Justin, a Latino freshmen, this value of communication was why he believed that eating dinner with his parents every night had made a difference in his life.

> It helps, because they have time to talk about anything. They feel like they have something that's there for them. Whereas, people who don't have that, they don't have any reason to care, because no one cares for them.

Second, just having someone who provides positive feedback and support to counteract the negatives could not be underestimated, according to the Lamar teenagers. For Olivia, an African American teenager who felt caught between different social groups at Lamar, it was all about having "parents ... tell her that she's smart and she has talent." For most teenagers, simply knowing that love is coming from somewhere, from anyone, offered some solace when they were having social difficulties at school.

For the most part, however, the teenagers at Lamar mentioned their families, and their parents, only in passing during their discussions of risk and resilience. They did not elaborate too much on why their parents would be important to them in times of trouble. I believe that this lack of detailed discussion about parents as protective factors probably reflects something more positive than what it appears, at first glance, to say about the distance and detachment in relationships between teenagers and their parents. For the teenagers at Lamar, that their parents would be supportive of them and help them when they were down was a given. "That's just what parents do," some of them said. Consequently, that they would need to highlight or explain this seemingly obvious role of parents in a teenager's life was not easy to comprehend. If my interpretation of these discussions about parents is right, then the relative imbalance of parents versus other sources of support and assistance, in teenagers' discussions of resilience can be viewed in a more positive light.

Other Potential Protective Factors

Beyond friends and families, four potential resources for resilience were mentioned consistently by at least a substantial minority of teenagers. The first was clearly an interpersonal factor, and the last was clearly a personal factor. The middle two were more like hybrids between two or more types of protective factors. Importantly, how these resources were discussed was also quite consistent from teenager to teenager.

First, some teenagers mentioned having a nonparent *adult mentor* in their lives to whom they went for advice and who, in times of trouble, could offer some protection and strength to them. Mostly, the teenagers who talked about mentors were racial/ethnic minorities. For example, the two African American girls at Lamar who participated in the study were the only teenagers who included a picture of nonparental adults in their Who I Am projects – a pastor for Olivia and a set of several male teachers for Althea. In fact, they talked almost as much as about these adults as they did about their friends. Several Latino/a teenagers also talked about adult mentors even if they did not feature them in their projects. White students rarely did. For the most part, the adult mentors who were mentioned were teachers or school personnel. The one prominent minority administrator at Lamar was cited a lot. Others who came up were family friends. Justin, a Latino, talked about his mom's best friend, a long-time teacher whom he felt understood his circumstances. Romina, a Latina, found a mentor in her father's boss, who inspired her to think big. Perhaps not surprisingly in this era of rapid divorce and remarriage, a couple of teenagers found a mentor in their mothers' boyfriends. Like the value of parents, the value of a mentor could be found in talk and communication but also in more unspoken emotional support. As Althea, an African American explained, her mentor told her what to do (and she did it, she said) *and* made her "feel happy and proud of herself."

Second, passion was big for the teenagers at Lamar. They believed that teenagers who could feel passionate about something would be OK in even the worst social circumstances. In this way, they believed that resilience grew out of *special activities and interests*. To the degree that the actual behavior being engaged in provided the protection to young people at social risk, then this protective factor would be a personal one. To the extent that the relationships cultivated by such activities and interests were what mattered, then this protective factor would be an interpersonal one. Yet, because most of these activities were linked to formal programs in and out of school that are directly targeted by policy, then this protective factor would be a group/organization one. Discussions with the Lamar teenagers revealed that all three elements were likely at work.

For some, this resilience-supporting passion came from music, especially making music of their own, or other creative pursuits like art or writing. As mentioned in Chapter 7, most teenagers highlighted music on the Who I Am projects. Although, for the most part, these references to music were about genres of music teenagers listened to and musicians they admired, several of the teenagers discussed the importance of actual musical experience in their identities. For example, Figure 8.1 presents the Who I Am project for James, a 10th grade lacrosse-playing working-class Latino. In addition to his favorite bands, James's project featured his guitar, his amplifier, and pictures of himself playing music (which are blacked out to protect his identity).

Not surprisingly, then, James brought up playing music as a source of resilience in the face of social marginalization at school, as did other teenage guitarists, drummers, and singers. For them, music helped to

Figure 8.1. James's Who I Am Project.

build connections to similar others, provided an outlet for working through stress, and cultivated a strong sense of self that helped guard against identity discrepancies regardless of social circumstances.

For example, Cooper, who was highlighted in Chapter 7 as a teenager dealing with social feedback and comparison issues, described how his experience as a musician ultimately made him a stronger, more resilient person:

> I feel like I've found, like, who I truly am. And I kind of found that through guitar and art.

Cooper went on to say that at the point in his young life when his "thoughts were really dark and desolate and kind of depressing," what got him through was "sitting down and … playing on my guitar" as well as "expressing things through music and poetry and stuff."

For many of the other teenagers, sports were put forward as activities that promote resilience among teenagers who felt as though they did not fit in at school. One of the most important mechanisms was stress relief. As Ali explained,

> When I am playing basketball, it is like it just ... kind of like gets you away. Like to a different world. Like, I am not really sure how to explain it. But when I am playing basketball, it is like I just get away from everything.

Another important mechanism was the protection derived from feelings of achievement. The social recognition that came with sports at Lamar offset other kinds of social feedback, and the personal sense of accomplishment, regardless of the social feedback, was ego enhancing. For female athletes at Lamar, engaging in sports meant that they were already going against some strong social norms (e.g., traditional femininity), which helped them be more immune to potentially damaging social messages more generally. As Sylvia, a Latina who joined the wrestling team, explained,

> And with wrestling, that just challenged me and that was a big challenge, because not too many girls wrestle ... so, it just, like, all these things just made me who I am. And helped me.

Many other interests were mentioned, including school clubs and community groups. The teenagers who talked about these potential protective factors uniformly agreed on what purpose they served. They gave teenagers "an emotional outlet," something to "occupy time" and "get away from life," a chance "to blow off steam," and a venue to "feel good" through challenging oneself. Yet, the focus on sports and other activities in discussions of resilience could not be divorced from interpersonal considerations, especially peer dynamics. All teenagers who discussed sports, hobbies, and clubs as protective factors eventually described how such activities, especially those that were school based, provided opportunities to meet others with the same interests. In this way, activities might be a back-end way of cultivating the protective factors most often cited by the teenagers at Lamar as a source of resilience: friends and, more importantly, a diverse mix of friends who offer different kinds of support. According to Justin,

JUSTIN: Where they can do something. Any sports or anything where you are with people, where you're going to have a group of people who you are with, who all like the same things and stuff.

ME: OK. So you find your? ...

JUSTIN: Yeah.

ME: So do you think that going through school [and] swimming or student council – doing this stuff or doing this has given you something in your life?

JUSTIN: I like these things too, because they are different, like, really different people. Like swimming, there are some people there who are artistic and stuff and people who all they do is swimming meets. Student council, that's just anyone who wants to get involved. They all have something in common, but they are all different. Like football, everyone is all – everyone thinks everyone is all just a jock.

ME: So because you've been in these different activities, you've met different people and....

JUSTIN: Yeah.

ME: And you realize that there are different people out there?

JUSTIN: Right.

Whether the opportunities are social, psychological, or emotional, music, sports, and other activities were viewed by the teenagers at Lamar as an antidote to the social stresses that they encountered at school.

Third, *religion* was mentioned by about a quarter of teenagers at Lamar when asked about what protective factors might exist to help a teenager in difficult social circumstance in high school become resilient. Much like mentoring, religion was most likely to be brought up by racial/ethnic minority teenagers, although a couple of white teenagers put pictures of their (mostly evangelical Christian) churches on their Who I Am projects. Much like sports and activity participation, discussions about religion also overlapped considerably with discussions about the potential interpersonal protections afforded by friends and mentors. Being religiously involved provided access to like-minded peers, mostly through church youth groups or religiously oriented teen social groups like Young Life. These activities facilitated friendship formation while also introducing a host of adults, including pastors, who might be able to guide and mentor. For these teenagers, the mechanisms by which religion might promote resilience were almost entirely social. Indeed, only one girl, Althea, mentioned religion itself – e.g., the words and teachings of her religion or a belief in a god – as a resource for resilience. When faced with social problems at school, she simply thought,

> People hate Jesus Christ. You don't worry about what people … if they don't like you, they don't like you. Just shrug it off and go on with it. Don't worry about it.

Fourth, only one theme in the resilience conversations at Lamar seemed to be primarily personal in nature. It took different forms but generally centered around a concept that I call *future orientation*, which was directly addressed by nearly half of the teenagers at Lamar. Basically, some teenagers said that someone having social troubles in school would be all right if he or she could somehow remember that high school was temporary and that a whole future was awaiting him or her after high school that was more important than anything that was happening right now. To them, a teenager who could say "hey, I have three more years here and then I am done with these people" would make it through high school just fine, no matter what the everyday experience of high school was. As Ali, the Middle Eastern boy, explained about teenagers who got messed up because of what was happening on the social side of high school,

> They are not focusing on what is important. That is about it. Because if you keep worrying about what other people think of you, or if you are not fitting in, just other people … like … I don't know, I think that at this time of age you should just focus on yourself.

Yeah, you should care about other people and stuff, but I am saying don't focus on trying to impress anybody or anything like that. Because later on, like you know, everything you are going through right now will pay off.... Right now you have to focus more on your future, like education and things. What is going to make you successful later on. And like, I mean, friends is like a small part of my life. Like really I want to be successful in the future. Friends are important, but I don't find it like the main thing.

Of course, Ali and all of the other teenagers who touched on this future orientation idea in some way also admitted that thinking in the long term and seeing high school as a blip on the radar of life were *very* difficult things for a teenager to do. Cathy explained that most teenagers she knew "haven't really matured enough ... they don't even care about how their life would be." Those rare few who could see their lives in this long-range perspective, however, had something that the others did not. Some discussed this phenomenon even in terms of a 10-year high school reunion, with showing others how well you turn out *after* high school as the best revenge for being excluded or picked on *during* high school.

The teenagers at Lamar were quite interested in this idea of resilience. It spoke to them in a very meaningful way, and, as a result, they talked a great deal about what would and what would not serve as a protective factor for a socially marginalized teenager. Yet, although their thoughts on this subject were well aligned with developmental theory, much of what they said was hypothetical or speculative. In some cases, they were talking about themselves and their own personal experiences. In other cases, they were clearly just projecting what they liked about their own lives onto others. Given the speculative nature of this discussion of resilience at Lamar, I wanted to test whether their thoughts on protective factors generalized to diverse groups of teenagers outside the halls of Lamar and outside the Austin city limits. To do so, I went back to the thousands of high school students from across the United States who participated in Add Health.

NATIONAL PATTERNS OF RESILIENCE

To explore resilience in Add Health, I looked at 12 potential protective factors that mapped onto the suggestions of the Lamar teenagers: 1) measures of peer relations included involvement with friends and dating activity;[3] 2) measures of family relations included closeness with parents, parental aspirations, parental involvement, and family organization;[4] 3) measures of activities and interests included hobbies, time engaged in athletic activities, participation in school sports, and participation in extracurricular activities;[5]

[3] The friendship involvement construct was the sum of four items (1 = yes, 0 = no): whether, in the past week, the teenager had gone to the friend's house, hung out somewhere with the friend, and talked on the telephone with the friend and whether the teenager had spent time with the friend during the past weekend. This measure was averaged across all friends nominated by the respondent (M = 2.17, SD = 1.05; α = .62). The romantic activity item was described in Chapter 5.

[4] Parent-teenager closeness/support was measured by teenagers' assessments of the degree to which they felt close to their fathers, felt that their fathers were warm, felt that they communicated well with their fathers, and were satisfied with their relationships with fathers. Responses ranged from 1 to 5 and were averaged (α = .89). This same construct was created for mothers (α = .89). The final construct for parent-teenager closeness was the mean of the maternal and paternal constructs if information was not missing for both parents; otherwise the score for the nonmissing parent served as the value (M = 4.21, SD = 0.67). A single item measured educational aspirations of parents, based on parent ratings on a scale from 1 to 4, of how much they wanted the teenager to go to college (M = 2.29, SD = 1.07). For parental involvement, teenagers reported whether or not they had talked about schoolwork or grades with their parents, worked with their parents on a school project, or talked about school things with their parents. These three items were summed (M = 1.25, SD = 0.90; α = .68). For family organization, teenagers responded to three items about each parent: how often that parent was at home when they left for school, returned from school, and went to bed (1 = never, 2 = almost never, 3 = some of the time, 4 = most of the time, and 5 = always). A scale was created for both mother and father by averaging these three items. Teenagers also reported how often at least one parent was at home with them when they ate dinner. Responses were recoded into a new measure, ranging from 1 (no days in the last week) to 5 (6 or 7 days in the last week). The final scale of family organization consisted of the mean of the maternal, parental, and family eating items (M = 3.60, SD = 0.72; α = .78).

[5] Teenagers reported whether they had engaged in 33 extracurricular activities, which were grouped into four categories (academic, performing arts, leadership,

and 4) measures of religion included religious participation and religiosity.[6] Unfortunately, I was not able to adequately measure extrafamilial adult mentoring or future orientation in Add Health. These four sets of factors were then added to the Add Health statistical models presented back in Chapters 5 and 6. Specifically, they were interacted with the not-fitting-in scale to determine whether and to what degree they reduced the association between that scale and any of the already established mediators of observed not-fitting-in effects on college enrollment. As an additional analytical step, I also examined whether such factors interacted with obesity and gay/lesbian status to reduce the association between either status and any of their already established outcomes.[7] These interactions, therefore, could point to possible instances of resilience-promoting protective mechanisms in the lives of Add Health teenagers who felt as though they did not fit in socially at their high schools.

and other) and then summed ($M = 0.75$, $SD = 1.00$). Several of these activities referred to school sports teams, which were grouped into a separate binary marker of whether a teenager was an athlete (44%) or not. A separate set of questions asked about time in various activities outside of school (0 = never to 3 = 5 or more), including hobbies, such as collecting things or music ($M = 1.48$, $SD = 1.06$), and sports, such as swimming or soccer ($M = 1.38$, $SD = 1.15$). These items tapped nonschool activities and time use.

[6] For religion, each teenager estimated how often he or she attended religious services and youth activities in the past year. Responses, which ranged from 1 (once a week or more) to 4 (never), were reverse coded ($M = 1.73$, $SD = 1.21$). Teenagers also rated how important religion was to them on a 4-point scale (from not at all important to very important), which measured religiosity ($M = 2.01$, $SD = 1.07$).

[7] Using the same modeling approach and structure described in Chapter 3, I estimated the association between the not-fitting-in scale and each socioemotional coping factor identified as significant mediators in those earlier models. All of the individual, family, and school control variables were taken into account in multilevel models (with sampling weights), and the estimator (linear or logistic) was determined by the type of outcome variable being studied. After the focal association was established in each model, I then entered an interaction term (not fitting in × potential resource factor). Significant interactions, which indicated that the resource factor conditioned or moderated the association between risk factors (not fitting in, stigmatized group membership) and the outcome, were graphed to determine the form of the moderation.

As described in a recent review by psychologists Ceci and Papierno of "gap closing,"[8] child-focused interventions that attempt to employ some protective factor to reduce the effects of some risk factor on child outcomes often reveal different forms of protection. For example, two interventions might improve the absolute prospects of at-risk children but have opposite effects on the relative prospects (vs. others) of these children.

Consider the protective pattern I refer to as *true protection*. In this pattern, some protective factor helps both at-risk youth and non-at-risk youth do better socially and emotionally, but the benefit is greater for those at risk than it is for those who are not at risk. The end result is that the socioemotional well-being of both at-risk and non-at-risk teenagers improves while the gap in socioemotional well-being between the two groups narrows. In other words, everyone benefits, and the at-risk teenagers make up some ground in the process. Their absolute and relative prospects go up. True protection, then, produces the gap closing discussed by Ceci and Papierno.

Another protective pattern is what I call *halfway protection*. In this pattern, some protective factor helps both at-risk teenagers and non-at-risk teenagers do better socially and emotionally, but the benefit is greater for those not at risk than it is for those who are at risk. The end result is that the socioemotional well-being of both at-risk and non-at-risk teenagers improves while the gap in socioemotional well-being between the two groups increases. In other words, everyone benefits, but the at-risk teenagers lose some ground in the process. For at-risk teenagers, this pattern is a mixture of the positive (their absolute prospects go up) and the negative (their relative prospects go down). Halfway protection, then, produces gap widening, to use the terminology of Ceci and Papierno.

Of course, a third pattern can also result from intervention strategies and attempts to identify protective factors. Here, I call it risk

---

[8] This review can be found in a 2005 issue of *American Psychologist*.

multiplication. In this pattern, some protective factor helps non-at-risk teenagers do better socially and emotionally, but it seems to reduce the chances that at-risk teenagers will do better socially and emotionally. The end result is that the overall socioemotional well-being of at-risk teenagers declines as they also lose even more ground to their peers who are not at risk. Their absolute and relative prospects suffer. This pattern would produce gap widening, but, unlike in halfway protection, gap widening would not also be accompanied by overall improvements in the well-being of at-risk youth.

Given the peer-based nature of the not-fitting-in phenomenon and the clear centrality of peers in adolescent identity development, as demonstrated by both quantitative and qualitative analyses so far, the peer relations protective factors highlighted by the Lamar teenagers would be expected to be the most likely to fit the true protection pattern. At the same time, the family-based protective factors would be the most likely to fit the halfway protection pattern – close ties with parents might benefit teenagers who do not fit in at school in some ways but do less to chip away at their peer-based disadvantages at school. Moreover, to the extent that young people having social troubles at school use close family ties to withdraw or disengage from school, family relations also have more potential for risk amplification than the other sets of potential protective factors brought up by the Lamar teenagers.

In these additional analyses of the not-fitting-in models in Add Health, therefore, I attempted to identify whether the potential protective factors highlighted at Lamar were associated with the socioemotional and academic outcomes of young people in Add Health and with the link between feelings of not fitting in and these outcomes. When these associations were found, I then categorized the potential protective factors according to whether they appeared to show true protection, halfway protection, or risk amplification.

Unfortunately, I could not locate a single factor that protected teenagers against all of the socioemotional and academic problems associated with feelings of not fitting in at school. *Resilience was the exception, not the norm.* Still, I was able to detect some meaningful variation in the connections between feelings of not fitting in on one hand and problematic coping behaviors and academic struggles on the other as a function of these potential protective factors. In most, but certainly not all, of these cases, further inspection of this variation revealed evidence of true protection.

Risk and Resilience among Teenage Girls

Among the girls in Add Health, I looked at 132 cases of potential protection. These cases represented the 12 potential protective factors interacted with 5 already established mediators of observed not-fitting-in effects on college enrollment (self-rejection, depression, marijuana use, truancy, low academic progress), 3 already established mediators of observed obesity effects on college enrollment (not fitting in, self-rejection, low academic progress), and 3 already established mediators of observed same-sex attraction effects on college enrollment (not fitting in, alcohol use, suicidal ideation). Of these 132 cases, 23 revealed some significant role of the potential protective factor. The majority were in line with true protection, with the remainder split between halfway protection and risk amplification.

Beginning with peer relations, being involved in a romantic relationship was associated with lower levels of depression and truancy among girls who felt that they did not fit in, less so for other girls. It was also associated with less alcohol use and suicidal ideation among same-sex-attracted girls, less so for their peers. Thus, when romantic activity was associated with pieces of the not-fitting-in pathway, it was usually in the direction of true protection. Interestingly, involvement with friends looked very different depending on the piece of the pathway examined. Although girls who felt that they did not fit in socially at school closed some of the truancy gap with other girls when they were more involved with close friends (true protection), they also lost ground to other girls in terms of academic status. This latter pattern occurred because girls who did not fit in at school had lower academic progress when involved with friends while girls who fit in at school had better academic progress when involved with friends (risk amplification).

Turning to family relations, girls were more likely to feel as though they fit in socially at school when they were close with their parents, but these observed benefits of closeness with parents were more pronounced for obese and/or same-sex-attracted girls (true protection). Yet, close ties with parents had more complicated associations when looking at teenagers who differed in terms of feelings of not fitting in at school. For example, teenagers who did not have such feelings appeared to benefit more from having close ties with parents in terms of depression, compared to girls who had more of these feelings (halfway protection). Yet, although the former group of girls tended to benefit from close ties to parents in terms of truancy rates, the latter group tended to be higher in truancy when they had close ties to parents (risk amplification). Family organization was associated with lower levels of just about every problem for girls in general, but these protective associations grew weaker as girls' feelings of not fitting in at school increased (halfway protection). In general, teenagers who did not fit in and/or who were same-sex attracted made up ground with peers on academic outcomes (e.g., truancy, academic progress) when their parents had higher educational aspirations for them (true protection). At the same time, same-sex-attracted girls looked worse on the not-fitting-in scale, in absolute and relative terms, when their parents had higher aspirations (risk amplification).

As for activities and interests, girls who were involved in extracurricular and athletic activities at school had higher levels of academic progress, especially those girls who felt like they did not fit in socially (true protection). Moreover, girls who felt as though they did not fit in socially at school had lower levels of depression when they had hobbies, although less so than girls who did not have such feelings (halfway protection). Looking directly at same-sex-attracted girls, they made up ground with other girls on the not-fitting-in scale when they participated in extracurricular activities but actually looked worse relative to other girls in terms of alcohol use when they participated in sports (risk amplification).

Finally, religious factors were generally not associated with any piece of the not-fitting-in pathway, with one exception. When same-sex-attracted girls were religiously involved, they drank more alcohol in both absolute and relative terms (risk amplification).

Figure 8.2 depicts these observed instances of true and halfway protection in the not-fitting-in pathway (instances of true protection italicized). This figure does not present the less numerous instances of risk amplification.

In summary, peer and activity factors provided the most consistent evidence of protection for girls who did not fit in socially at school. Activity participation and sports participation, for example, were associated with fewer academic problems among girls (in absolute and relative terms) and were never associated with a more problematic socioemotional or academic outcome. Furthermore, girls who demonstrated more signs of peer integration, despite feelings of not fitting in or having a potentially stigmatized characteristic, also tended to look better socioemotionally. Protection in the family context presented a more complicated story. In general, teenage girls facing social risks at school (not fitting in, being in a stigmatized group) had better socioemotional and academic outcomes when they were closer with parents who provided more organized homes and had higher aspirations. Yet, this protection was often halfway, so that they lost ground with their peers even though they were doing better overall. Moreover, girls from stigmatized groups were more likely to feel as though they did not fit in when their parents had higher aspirations for their futures, and girls who felt as though they did not fit in were more likely to disengage from school when they had strong family ties. Overall, girls' feelings of not fitting in were more likely to be counteracted (or buffered against)

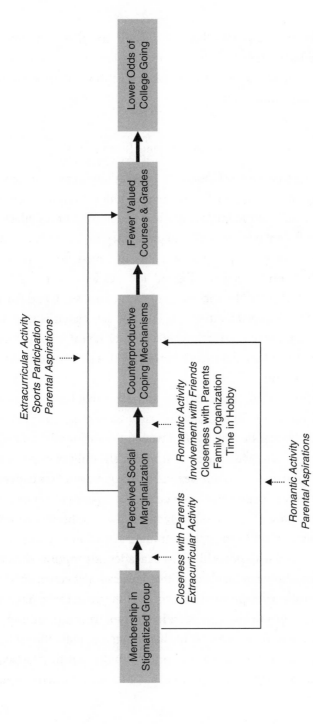

Figure 8.2. True and Halfway Protection in the Not-Fitting-In Pathway among Girls.

by social protective factors than the specific social stigma hypothesized to lead to such feelings, while more positive academic functioning was more likely to result from such protection than more positive
socioemotional functioning.

Risk and Resilience among Teenage Boys

For the Add Health boys, I looked at 96 cases of potential protection.
Specifically, the 12 potential protective factors were interacted with
5 already established mediators of observed not-fitting-in effects on
college enrollment (self-rejection, depression, marijuana use, truancy,
low academic progress), 1 already established mediator of observed
obesity effects on college enrollment (low academic progress), and
2 observed outcomes of same-sex attraction (depression and suicidal
ideation, since same-sex attraction was not associated with college
enrollment among boys). Of these 96 cases, 17 revealed some significant role of the potential protective factor, with a slim majority in line
with true protection.

Of the peer factors, the clearest pattern was that the link between
feelings of not fitting in and alcohol use grew stronger as peer integration (e.g., romantic activity, involvement with friends) increased,
a pattern consistent with risk amplification. The only example of true
peer protection was that same-sex-attracted boys were less depressed
when they were romantically involved with someone. The family context offered more evidence of protection. Teenage boys who felt as
though they did not fit in socially at high school and/or were obese
made up ground with peers in terms of academic progress when they
had parents who were involved in their educational careers and had
higher educational aspirations for them (full protection). Yet, these
same boys lost ground to their peers in terms of truancy (halfway protection). They also lost ground to their peers on and suffered absolute declines in depression, as did boys who did not fit in at school
but were emotionally closer to their parents. As for activity sources

of resilience, extracurricular participation and athletic participation were associated with lower rates of truancy for boys who felt as though they did not fit in at school (halfway protection) and/or were same-sex attracted (true protection). Such participation was also associated with greater academic progress among boys who felt as though they did fit in socially at school (true protection).

Figure 8.3 presents these various instances of true protection (italicized) and halfway protection. Although boys had less opportunity for protection (in that fewer pieces of the not-fitting-in pathway held true for them), they had a higher "yield" of observed protective effects than girls. They also differed from girls in many other ways.

For the most part, boys demonstrated less evidence of risk amplification than girls, and, when they did, these patterns were more easily interpretable. For example, the higher rates of substance use among boys who did not fit in when they had friends or romantic partners likely reflect social activity, of the kind described by the Lamar teenagers in their discussions of identity work, more than self-medication. Overall, however, peer relations appeared less important – protective or otherwise – in the not-fitting-in pathway among boys, and family relations had less negative or ambivalent roles in moderating the various pieces of the pathway. Better academic functioning was a more likely result of buffering/protective processes in this pathway, and more problematic socioemotional functioning was a more likely result of risk amplification processes.

FINAL THOUGHTS

Much of developmental research concerns risk. Resilience research is about the reduction or even reversal of risk. The risks of not fitting in socially at high school were established in earlier chapters, and in this chapter I turned to resilience. Because of how the pieces of the not-fitting-in pathway connect to each other, intervening in any one piece can block the full pathway from playing out. The results presented in

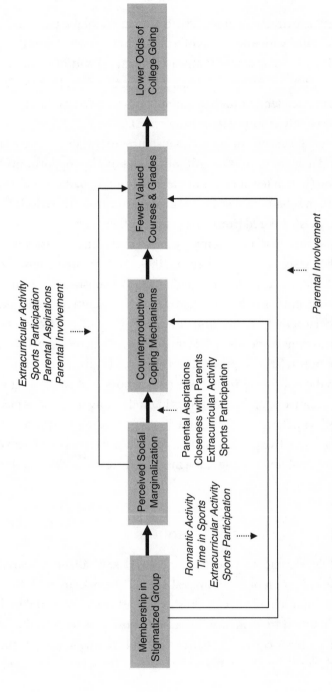

Figure 8.3. True and Halfway Protection in the Not-Fitting-In Pathway among Boys.

this chapter suggest that few things are able to do this and, furthermore, that they are quite difficult to locate. Yet, some things do seem to matter or at least have potential. Teenagers in problematic social situations at school increase the odds of resilience when they are able to draw on social support and/or when they can find some venue that allows them to feel more positive about their lives. That the rewards of such social support or opportunities to achieve are not exclusive to these teenagers in trouble and, therefore, may benefit other peers without such social problems even more is a stark lesson in the often unclear boundaries of intervention. It is also a lesson that, in trying to help, we sometimes have to choose between alternate (e.g., absolute, relative) views of what success is.

PART III

HELPING TEENAGERS NAVIGATE
HIGH SCHOOL

9

Solutions within Schools

At least as far back as the writings of de Tocqueville,[1] the strong emphasis on individualism in American culture coupled with a clear reliance on social integration among Americans has been viewed as a great paradox of the United States. In many ways, the issues discussed so far in this book, including and especially the educational implications of not fitting in socially at high school, are rooted in this paradox, and so are solutions to these issues. Reflecting dominant socialization messages in American culture, U.S. adults are more likely than their counterparts in other countries to stress the value of independence, autonomy, and nonconformity,[2] and, inevitably, they send a clear message downstream – in intimate conversations, teachings, media content – that teenagers should stay true to themselves, that being different is *good*. Consequently, these messages have been internalized by many teenagers and, in exaggerated form, lie at the heart of American youth culture. That is why, when questioned about what influences them, the teenagers at Lamar answered with declarations of nonconformity that were so remarkably consistent that they actually, ironically, signaled a strong sense of conformity.

Beyond ideology and values, however, things get decidedly more complicated. In the "real" world, nonconformity, difference, and

---

[1] See de Tocqueville's 1863 book *Democracy in America*.
[2] See the 2006 *Psychological Science* article by Markus, Uchida, Omoregie, Townsend, and Kitayama about personal agency in different cultures.

standing out from the crowd – as opposed to being unique, which has a more positive connotation in American culture – can be a real risk to teenagers in the social worlds of their high schools, including the virtual, wireless social arenas that are now proving to be an extension of high school peer cultures for many young people. Moreover, that risk to the social and psychological well-being of teenagers seems to be a nonnegligible impediment to school success in an era in which school success is more important to the future than it has ever been.

CONCLUSION WITH CAVEATS

The experiences of the teenagers in Add Health and at Lamar High illustrate this risk. In this way, the educational implications of not fitting in and associated stigma symbolize a larger issue: many great obstacles to improving achievement on the individual level and performance rates on the school level are social in nature – *social*, not curriculum, staffing, or funding. Indeed, the informal education that goes on in high school can and does undercut the formal education that we all agree is what schools were created to provide. This conclusion is motivated by the empirical results on not fitting in I have presented in the preceding chapters, evidence from research directly built on a long line of work on teenagers, peers, and schools by leading psychologists, sociologists, and other social and behavioral scientists. Reflecting some insightful lessons of that rich literature, I also recognize that this conclusion comes with two key caveats.

First, one caveat is that the peer culture of a high school is just as likely to be a valuable resource for teenagers and high schools as it is to be a risk. After all, teenage peer dynamics are not unidimensionally problematic. Instead, much of the past research I drew on to build this study, including work by Steinberg, Eccles, Brown, Hartup, and others, reveals how peer dynamics during this developmental stage are multidimensional and how the positive dimensions often, even typically, outweigh the negative dimensions (Brown & Klute, 2003; Eccles & Barber, 1999; Hartup & Stevens, 1997; Steinberg, Brown, & Dornbusch, 1996). For every teenager whose academic prospects are diminished by struggles with peers about her or his perceived social deficits, other teenagers are going to find help, support, and role models for academic pursuits by being immersed in high school peer cultures that emphasize doing well or treat it as a given (Frank, Muller, et al., 2008). Still others are going to be protected from falling behind when they have personal characteristics that would be social deficits in many other high schools because these same characteristics are socially valued or at least neutral in *their* high schools.

I raise this issue here to contrast common views/biases in the social and behavioral sciences and in American culture more broadly suggesting that peers primarily represent *obstacles* to positive youth development. In fact, my own work – and the work of many other developmental scientists[3] – has consistently shown that peers are more likely *resources* for healthy development and educational success. Moreover, the negative symptomatology that does emerge in the peer worlds of teenagers – excessive conformity, exclusionary practices, risk taking, defiance – often represents short-term "glitches" in the ultimately positive role that peers play in getting teenagers into adulthood and adult roles. Still, the large upside of high school peer culture does not negate the bad things that happen to some teenagers in these peer cultures. The educational risks of not fitting in, I would argue, represent just one of those bad things.

Second, another caveat is that the connection between informal and formal education in American high schools, and the not-fitting-in pathway more specifically, introduces a policy dilemma. Drawing

---

[3] See my 2008 article with Riegle-Crumb, Field, Frank, and Muller in *Child Development* on gender, peers, and math. For reviews, see Giordano (2003) and Hartup and Stevens (1997). For specific applications to education, see Riegle-Crumb (2006), Radziwon (2003), Ma (2001), Nichols and White (2001), Ryan (2001), and Steinberg, Dornbusch, and Brown (1992).

on recent writings by Aletha Huston,[4] I use the term *policy dilemma* to capture the tendency for social and behavioral scientists to study protective factors that contribute to positive child and adolescent development but are also difficult to manipulate from the outside. The dilemma is about the trade-offs between predictive power and "doability."

One example of the policy dilemma concerns parent-adolescent emotional closeness, which has been frequently documented as an all but necessary ingredient in young people's general well-being and academic progress (Crosnoe & Elder, 2004; Call & Mortimer, 2001; Steinberg, 2001; Furstenberg, Cook, Eccles, Elder, & Sameroff, 1999; Grotevant, 1998; Demo & Acock, 1996; Larson, Richards, Moneta, Holmbeck, & Duckett, 1996). While compelling, this large body of research, including my own, begs the question of what we can do with this information. Although a recent review by Berlin, Zeanah, and Lieberman reveals convincing evidence that interventions designed to promote attachment can and do work,[5] the challenge of ratcheting up these relatively small intervention programs to the larger scale is daunting and, when focusing on schools, could raise political, ethical, pedagogical, and financial concerns. The conclusion of many in the policy and education world, then, is that information about the developmental significance of parent-child closeness is important but ultimately difficult to use in a practical sense. Therein lies the dilemma of psychologists, sociologists, and other scientists who want to shed light on developmental processes but also want to inform policies targeting developmental processes. Like parent-child closeness, peer relations also introduce the policy dilemma because few things matter more to how young people turn out but provide less obvious policy recommendations.

[4] Without using the term *policy dilemma*, Huston's 2007 presidential address to the Society for Research on Child Development (printed in the first 2008 issue of *Child Development*) explains the basic idea, as does her 2005 *SRCD Social Policy Report*.

[5] The review by Berlin, Zeanah, and Lieberman is a chapter in the 2008 *Handbook of Attachment*.

For example, some will conclude based on the research presented in this book that we need to reconfigure the peer networks, friendship dynamics, and dating patterns underlying high school cultures, or, more specifically, that we need to create magnet schools for obese or same-sex-attracted girls. These conclusions, however grounded in the empirical results they may be, are also fatally flawed. After all, rejiggering the set of social ties and exchanges within high schools would be extraordinarily difficult, and magnet schools for teenagers from stigmatized groups would provide protections for them at the cost of sacrificing diversity and intergroup contact that we know have important educational and societal benefits that go beyond any one person. In the end, we have to go beyond the obvious but untenable conclusions and think more critically in order to solve the policy dilemma.

With these two caveats in mind, I list and delineate some insights derived from my research for this book into possible avenues of action that schools and educational policy makers can take to gain traction in problems posed by the connection between informal and formal education in general and the educational risks of not fitting in more specifically. Attempting to stay close to the data, my focus is on the level of individual teenagers in vulnerable positions in schools but also on the level of schools and whether they can be viewed as "good" in a holistic, not exclusively academic, sense.

DECOMPOSING THE TEENAGE POPULATION BY RISK

An important step in solving some societal problem is simply knowing where to start. When climbing a huge mountain, deciding where to take the first step is a major challenge that, once made, narrows down to an increasingly, iteratively clearer path. Taking action to address problems associated with the link between informal and formal education in high school is like climbing a mountain. Many, including me, believe that the crucial self-propelling first steps are to acknowledge and name the problem at hand and then focus on where that problem is most severe. This starting approach allows us to craft tailored, specialized interventions and policies as an alternative to implementing the kinds of universal, one-size-fits-all interventions and policies that Ceci and Papierno identified as frequently counterproductive.

Gender as Risk

Reflecting arguments made by Gilligan and others that have filtered into public consciousness and popular psychology (e.g., *Reviving Ophelia*),[6] a dominant stream of thought in developmental research is that the differential socialization patterns of girls and boys results in girls being more affected by social problems than boys. For this reason, I went into this project expecting to see that the risks of not fitting in socially at school would be heightened for girls. Yet, at the same time, a comparison of the well-known American Association of University Women report, *How Schools Shortchange Girls*, to Buchmann, DiPrete, and McDaniel's recent entry in *Annual Review of Sociology* about gender inequality in American education reveals how and why theoretical and empirical attention is shifting from documenting the many disadvantages of girls in the educational system toward explaining why girls do so much better academically, overall, than boys in the system.[7] Moreover, recent attempts to rethink gender differences in social functioning tend to emphasize that girls and boys are both affected by social problems but in different ways (Xie, 2005; Way & Chu, 2003). For these reasons, I should not have been surprised that neither girls nor boys appeared to be obviously more at risk in terms of the connection between the social and educational realms of high school. The actual story was decidedly more mixed and, therefore, calls for a more specific conception of targeted risks.

[6] *In a Different Voice* (1982) is one example of Gilligan's work. *Reviving Ophelia* was published by Mary Pipher in 1994.
[7] The AAUW report came out in 1992. The review piece was authored by Buchmann, DiPrete, and McDaniel and came out in 2008.

Overall, not fitting in socially at high school posed somewhat greater risks for girls' trajectories from high school to college than it did for boys. This pattern is in line with the aforementioned theoretical themes that girls, because they value social integration more, are more harmed when they do not experience social integration. Paradoxically, it also aligns with the aforementioned flip in gender inequality in educational attainment. As a single group, girls are such good students in the United States that their pathways into college are harder to disrupt. On the other hand, boys face more difficulty in high school and are much more likely to be derailed on the path to college. Thus, for girls, the social and emotional difficulties of high school may be the only thing powerful enough to hurt them. For boys, however, these difficulties are merely a "drop in the bucket" among all of the things that threaten to hurt them in the long term. Thus, girls tend to be more successful educationally in general, which means that the problems associated with not fitting in may be a greater threat to their educational careers.

Yet, looking more closely at this pattern reveals that the full pathway between not fitting in and college going that I hypothesized based on past research and theory did not differ substantially by gender. Even though the link between the first (not fitting in) and last (college going) piece of this pathway was stronger for girls than boys, the other links in this pathway (not fitting in → counterproductive coping mechanisms → academic progress → college going) did not differ substantially by gender; if anything, they were stronger among boys. Thus, overall, girls and boys appeared to be more similar than different in this specific connection between informal and formal education. Several differences did emerge, however, and they were telling.

First, according to the quantitative data, two key sources of social stigma – obesity and same-sex attraction – appeared to set the not-fitting-in pathway into motion primarily for girls more than boys. Second, according to the qualitative data, girls appeared to use and receive more subtle, camouflaged, or plausibly deniable peer messages about social worth and fitting in at their schools than boys, although both appeared to be equally affected by social information in terms of their identity development. Third, according to both quantitative and qualitative data, girls had more outlets to express and process their frustration over not fitting in than boys, but, overall, the pieces of the not-fitting-in pathway appeared to be more reactive in protective ways to potential sources of resilience among boys than girls.

Putting all of this together, reconciling the gender difference in the link between not fitting in at school and college going with the greater gender similarity in the chain of mediation in this link suggests that either the pieces of the pathway have not been measured adequately or that the pathway, as conceptualized, is missing important pieces. In any case, identifying the most at-risk segment of the student population by gender is not exactly straightforward and largely depends on the aspect of "performance" that schools are targeting for improvement. If boosting graduation and college-going rates of students in the school is the target, then focusing on girls who are socially marginalized as a critical group would be important. If, however, improving the general health and well-being of students and reducing behavioral and academic problems is the goal, then targeting socially marginalized youth regardless of gender would be appropriate. Furthermore, girls offer an advantage, in terms of narrowing the scope of policy intervention, in that at least two groups of girls characterized by identifiable (at least in theory) social stigma appear to be at risk of social marginalization in ways that set the socioemotional and academic problems of the not-fitting-in pathway into motion. No corresponding subsets of boys have yet been identified.

Critical Periods of Timing

Timing is also key to assessing risk. Although I did not go into the details in previous chapters, the not-fitting-in pathway appears to be strongest during the first 2 years of high school and then fades over time, a pattern that echoes the other research that I have done on the link between the formal and informal education in high school. Indeed, this pattern is why I chose to focus on 9th and 10th graders during my time at Lamar.

Again, this timing effect maps onto important themes in past research, including research on the transition out of middle school by Eccles, Graham, and others as well as research on social development in early and middle adolescence more generally, from Elkind's seminal work to more recent studies by Rudolph and other psychologists.[8] The transition from middle school to high school is a period of great vulnerability for young people. They go into bigger, more impersonal schools that typically mix diverse streams of students from multiple middle schools. A good deal of sorting out has to occur in such a situation. At the same time, young teenagers' developmentally appropriate individuation from parents – which increases their orientation to peers – is also in full swing. As these two phenomena come together, teenagers are much more susceptible to peer influences and much more likely to base self-judgments on the judgments of others. Eventually, most find their place, adapt to their new environments, broaden their social networks, and renegotiate their relationships with parents, and, as they do so, their vulnerability diminishes. Thus, the early years of high school – when, according to sociologists of education like Gamoran, Schneider, and others, foundational coursework, future aspirations, and investments from others set the stage for the highly cumulative long-term educational trajectories that lead to college (Schneider, 2007; Gamoran & Hannigan, 2000) – is when risk is greatest.

---

[8] For work on the transition between middle school and high school, see articles, books, and reviews by Benner and Graham (2007), Barber and Olsen (2004), Eder, Evans, and Parker (1995), and Eccles, Lord, Roeser, Barber, and Hernandez-Jozefowicz (1997). For more on the social orientation of teenagers, start with the classic work by Elkind (1967) as well as newer works by La Greca and Lopez (1998) and Rudolph and Conley (2005).

Race, Class, and Other Issues

A possible reaction to what I have discussed so far is that the problems associated with the link between informal and formal education in high school, and the not-fitting-in pathway in particular, represent a middle-class white phenomenon. According to such criticisms, less advantaged segments of the teenage population face far bigger threats in the educational system than being socially marginalized or having to do identity work. I certainly agree that such criticism is a valid point of discussion. Indeed, the history of American education – as captured in books such as *Savage Inequalities* by Kozol and the many historical works of Labaree – clearly illustrates how many forces are working against teenagers who are from racial/ethnic minority groups, lower socioeconomic strata, or both. Yet, that does not mean that the risks to formal education posed by informal educational dynamics do not also apply to these teenagers.

For example, my analysis of Add Health and Lamar reveals a great deal of consistency in the not-fitting-in pathway across racial/ethnic groups, socioeconomic strata, and immigrant generations. Some pieces of the model were more pronounced in certain groups than in others, but the big picture was largely the same for all of the groups being studied. Granted, these analyses either are painted with broad brush strokes (e.g., national patterns in Add Health) or are specific to one locale (e.g., Lamar High). I have no doubt that among the poorest, most disenfranchised youth attending the most disorganized high schools, the problems of not fitting in are drowned out by the many other risks they face in and out of school. Conversely, I have little doubt that, among the most privileged youth attending the most elite high schools, such as those described by Sara Lawrence Lightfoot in final sections of *The Good High School*, the risks associated with the not fitting in are likely not large enough to water down the enormous advantages that they have over other teenagers in the high-stakes game of education. For the vast majority of the high school population between the far-end tails on the social status gradient of the United States, how-ever, the not-fitting-in pathway has merit. I would venture that the same could be said for other kinds of high school social struggles.

In one compelling way, the issue of racial/ethnic and socioeco-nomic variability intersects with the issues of gender and timing. Young, white, middle-class girls appeared to be the most negatively affected by being a member of a stigmatized group. They were the most likely to feel that they did not fit in because of their appearance or something else about them, to perceive their identities as spoiled, and to take counterproductive actions to stop this spoiling and the pain it caused. This pattern echoes other research I have done with Monica Johnson using Add Health and is a more pronounced version of the gender paradox discussed earlier in this chapter. When examining formal education, white, middle-class girls are – in the aggregate – the most exemplary group of students, but, when turning to informal education, they are also a great cause of concern. As a result, we have to separate out what we know about middle-class white girls' many successes in school from what emerges about the specific dangers they face that chip away at these successes.

If we, as adults, accept that social risks to academic performance, including the not-fitting-in pathway and its relation to social stigma, represent a problem worthy of intervention, then white middle-class girls entering into high school deserve attention. Given that this same group, overall, sets the bar for academic performance and col-lege going among contemporary American youth, targeting inter-vention to them will essentially help the best do better. In this sense, identifying them as at risk means that their full educational potential is not being realized and that, with some help, it could be. How this will play politically is unknown. The "pro" argument is that start-ing interventions with young middle-class white girls will offer help to a group in which mental health needs exceed educational needs. This starting strategy can then eventually be expanded in scope to provide aid to teenagers less socially and emotionally vulnerable to stigmatization and its cascading effects but also less likely to go to college regardless of this vulnerability.

Reconceptualizing Targeted Groups

Risk is a multifaceted concept, and groups become at risk far beyond the boundaries of race, gender, social class, and age. According to the not-fitting-in pathway, social problems in high school make some teenagers less likely to go to college than they would otherwise be. These reductions in college-going rates are not trivial and, in the current global economic structure, contribute to a major societal problem.

Thus, we have a group of teenagers in need of help that could improve their future prospects and, in the process, create a social good. Yet, this group of teenagers is not a prominent at-risk population in educational policy. For example, No Child Left Behind explicitly views low-income youth, English language learners, and students with learning disabilities as targeted populations of interest in the educational system, to name just a few. Consequently, high schools have to disaggregate their testing data for the government and for the public, pulling out the specific data on these, and other, specially targeted groups of young people. When established benchmarks for raising the performance rates in these groups are not met, schools have to come up with detailed action plans and, over time, face increasingly stiff penalties.

This model of targeting certain groups for special attention could be reconceptualized and, in particular, expanded. Socially marginalized youth could be viewed as a targeted group. After all, disparities in college-going rates related to not fitting in socially at school are not all that different from those related to poverty, at least for girls. If the point of explicitly highlighting targeted populations in policy is to hold schools accountable for the academic progress of students in special populations that pull down overall performance rates in the general student population, then paying more attention to socially marginalized teenagers serves this aim. My argument is that we need to let go of our overly demographic conception of students in need (e.g., race, social class, immigration status) and take an *empirical* approach to defining and identifying subsets in which historical underperformance on key academic indicators warrants extra attention. Of course, I realize that this argument raises some very significant concerns.

First, as newly emergent district socioeconomic desegregation plans are demonstrating (Kahlenberg, 2001; Plank, 2000), economic disadvantage can be easily identified by government-set thresholds verified through tax records. Moreover, learning disabilities and language proficiencies can be tested. Yet, identifying socially marginalized teenagers as a group for service is much more ambiguous and difficult. Although some schools may be able to identify such teenagers, they would likely leave great room for error in doing so. The key would be to identify socially marginalized groups for attention and intervention rather than individual students. I have already identified, empirically, two such groups of teenage girls (those who are obese and/or same-sex attracted), and an important future endeavor is to identify more such groups among girls and any such groups among boys in a school-specific way.

Second, if future research is able to identify socially marginalized groups needing special attention, the privacy and ethical issues involved with using such research to enact policy intervention are quite problematic. For example, obese and/or same-sex-attracted girls appear to need help in reaching their educational potential, but gathering information on obesity and/or sexuality in a school will be a challenge. As of yet, I do not have answers to this challenge, but I think that we should at least start the discussion.

Third, even if socially marginalized youth are recognized as needing special attention and can be identified in a way that meets ethical standards, the possibility that targeting such groups with programs and interventions could actually increase their social marginalization is real. In other words, the very act of labeling a group as troubled could reinforce the social dynamics that put that group at risk in the first place. In addition to reinforcing negative social judgments about a group (e.g., "those kids are different"), such labeling could also reinforce negative self-assessments among teenagers in that group (e.g., "we don't measure up"). Historically, this phenomenon has been seen with racial/ethnic minority students in desegregated schools.[9] It also lies at the heart of recent arguments by Hegerty about the risks associated with looking at gay youth as a problem group as well as similar arguments by several scholars, including me, about the negative side effects of widespread public discussions about the obesity epidemic (Hegerty, 2009; Crosnoe, 2007; Gibbs, 2005). I take such concerns seriously. I also know that the more recent history of race/ethnicity-focused intervention efforts offers some insights into this thorny issue. Again, I do not claim to know the answers. My goal, for now at least, is to recognize the problem and put out a call for help to solve this problem.

SCHOOL SERVICES

On a practical level, the reason why identifying certain groups of teenagers as at risk in the educational system is important is because it organizes how services are developed and delivered. For example, when the aforementioned disaggregated school-specific testing trends made public by No Child Left Behind reveal persistent achievement gaps related to many different demographic statuses, schools are required to develop action plans (e.g., organizing parent-school partnerships) to reduce these achievement gaps over time. The same logic applies to risks associated with the informal education of high schools, such as the not-fitting-in pathway. Once at-risk groups are identified, we need to figure out what can be done to address these

---

[9] See the 2008 book *Both Sides Now: The Story of Desegregation's Graduates*, by Wells, Holme, Revilla, and Atanda.

risks. Along these lines, extant services that need to be refocused and niche services that can be ratcheted up to a broader level both present themselves as possibilities.

Directing and Redirecting Extant Services

Over the last century, views about what schools should offer have expanded considerably beyond instructional or pedagogical dimensions. Two examples concern the availability of health services and the scope of the extracurriculum. Now firmly established in American high schools, both represent extant, working policy structures that can be leveraged to address the link between informal and formal education across the high school universe.

Slowly, districts began funding certain health programs (e.g., health education, school nurses, vaccination) in their schools as they recognized the simple truth that students had trouble learning when they felt bad. For the most part, these services have focused on physical health rather than mental health, and their impact has been hard to determine (Thies, 1999; Burns et al., 1995; Millstein, 1988). Still, a basic structure, however imperfect, is already in place that can be utilized.

When teenagers are suffering emotionally, they need a place to go for advice and help. Given that access, convenience, and expense are key considerations in whether they get the help that they need, schools seem to be a good starting point, especially when considering issues of equity and equality. More ambitious than having some mental health equivalent of the school nurse, what I am talking about is a more coordinated effort between the health care system and the educational system, with students referred to mental health services through the school or those services situated in the school. The school-linked services movement that took root in California in the 1980s and 1990s is a good exemplar of how this coordinated health/education effort might work (Kirst, 1994; Gardner, 1993). Such an approach will help to ensure that troubled teenagers do not fall through the cracks between institutional systems designed to serve them separately and that high schools will do more than serve as stopgap stand-ins for other systems when teenagers are in need. Importantly, not only will this approach help teenagers dealing with the not-fitting-in pathway or something similar, it should also help any teenagers attending high school who are dealing with mental health or other socioemotional issues, no matter their root cause.

Another evolutionary change shaping the modern American high school is the addition of (and proliferation of) clubs, teams, and other organized activities to the scope of the educational enterprise. As described in a recent edited volume by Mahoney, Larson, and Eccles,[10] this creation and expansion of the high school extracurriculum serves several purposes. First, it diversifies the venues of achievement for teenagers, offering more opportunities for them to find their niche, identify their special talents, and gain a sense of accomplishment (Dornbusch, Herman, & Morley, 1996; Miller, Sabo, Farrell, Barnes, & Melnick, 1994). Second, it provides new arenas for social exchange among teenagers and among diverse groups of teenagers, in terms of race/ethnicity, social class, or people like us (PLUs) (Eccles & Barber, 1999). Third, it also binds teenagers more closely to the school, occupies their time, and helps to build a shared school identity among teenagers (Crosnoe, 2002). In these ways, the extracurriculum is a plus for both the high school and the teenagers who make up its student body – the very conclusion reached by a panel of experts convened by the Team Up for Youth program to assess the links between a key aspect of the school extracurriculum, sports teams, and major adolescent outcomes.[11]

Consequently, the extracurriculum is also likely to provide some benefits in terms of managing the academic problems associated with

---

[10] This edited volume is titled *Organized Activities as Contexts of Development: Extracurricular Activities, After-School and Community Programs*. It includes a range of articles and studies about the potential benefits of the extracurriculum.

[11] The name of the Team Up for Youth report is *Learning to Play and Playing to Learn*. It came out in 2009 and was authored by Rosewater.

various kinds of social turbulence, including the not-fitting-in path-way. Recall from the previous chapter that, in both Add Health and Lamar, sports, special talents, and organized activities appeared to be school-based or school-related resources that boosted resilience for teenagers dealing with social marginalization in school. As such, they represent opportunities for schools to help teenagers in trouble come out OK. Thus, maintaining a diverse extracurriculum and making concerted efforts to engage all teenagers, especially those in groups known to have higher risk for social marginalization, are two ways to use existing policy structures to address a specific informal threat to formal education in school.

Unfortunately, the recent reductions in funding for schools across many states and the increasing emphasis on formal academic bench-marks on the national level generated by No Child Left Behind have, together, endangered the extracurriculum in many high schools, as described in an edited volume by Meier and Wood titled *Many Children Left Behind*.[12] According to the resilience results presented in this book as well as the general conclusions drawn from the broader literature on extracurricular activities at school and adolescent development and education, this trend would seem to be a mistake not just in terms of individual teenagers. Given the potential of the extracurriculum to boost academic prospects in groups that might otherwise bring down the overall academic performance rates of high schools, it may also be a mistake in terms of the ability of schools to avoid many of the sanc-tions put forward by No Child Left Behind.

Expanding the Breadth of Services

Services that are currently in widespread use in high schools across the United States provide only some help in partnering the informal and formal education in American high schools. We also have to find

---

[12] This edited volume came out in 2004. Its full title is *Many Children Left Behind: How the No Child Left Behind Act Is Damaging Our Children and Our Schools*.

programs that work on the small scale and see if they can be ratcheted up into large-scale policy. In other words, if some approach produces results on the local level, a logical next step is to determine whether it can go national. From welfare reform to class size reductions to marriage promotion efforts, this local to state/national transition is a well-trod policy pathway in the United States.[13]

The challenge is to make schools *safer* for more teenagers. In alluding to safe schools, I am trying to broaden our definition of what school safety is – beyond safety from violence, which was such a major educational policy issue after Columbine – to also encompass safety from threats to socioemotional well-being more generally.[14] Again, promoting school safety in this sense will likely not be predicated on *direct* intervention into school peer dynamics or dictation to teenagers about what their cultural values should be, which are likely to be Sisyphean tasks. Still, adults can take less overt steps to promote school safety, broadly defined, by indirectly shaping how teenagers apply labels to social groups. In the process, they may make some headway in breaking down prejudices among teenagers.

For example, school-based efforts to reduce racial prejudice have a long history in the United States. These efforts generally fall into three categories: 1) a multicultural curriculum, ranging from lesson plans covering the experiences and accomplishments of different groups to more simple and subtle actions like increasing diversity in the photographs accompanying the text in classroom workbooks;[15] 2) cooperative learning, in which collaborative projects are used to connect students in heterogeneous classrooms and allow the different

---

[13] For more on welfare reform, see the 2002 edited volume by Sawhill, Weaver, Haskins, and Kane. For more on class size reduction, see the 1995 review by Mosteller. For more on marriage promotion, see the 2007 essay by Furstenberg.

[14] See the 2004 article by Lawrence and Birkland in *Social Science Quarterly* about the connection between media coverage and legislative activity after Columbine.

[15] A 2007 *SRCD Social Policy Report* by Pfiefer, Brown, and Juvonen provides an excellent summary of school-based and related efforts to reduce racial prejudice.

contributions from different groups to be repeatedly observed by all;[16] and 3) social-cognitive skill development, encompassing activities like role-playing, discussion, plays, and classification exercises that increase the ability of students from different groups to take each other's perspectives and think more critically about group differences.[17] Empirical evidence indicates that each of these approaches, but especially the third, can change the attitudes of young people and increase interracial relationships. Essentially, they change attitudes about racial "difference" that then restructure peer interactions and, more slowly, reconstitute peer cultures. Importantly, because they are directed at the level of the classroom or school rather than at the level of individual students or specific groups, they do not appear to single out at-risk students and student groups for unwanted, potentially risk-amplifying scrutiny, which, as noted earlier in this chapter, is one concern about using risk designations to organize service design and delivery.

Although these efforts to break down racial divisions are still quite ad hoc and largely concentrated in elementary schools, they are relevant to how the not-fitting-in pathway might be addressed, from a policy perspective, in high schools. If such efforts are broadened to encompass multiple sources of social prejudice and tailored to teenagers rather than children, they may influence the peer culture dynamics that lead to the stigmatization of certain groups that, in turn, interferes with the healthy development and academic progress of teenagers in those groups during the high school years. One can imagine, therefore, cooperative learning techniques in economically heterogeneous high school classrooms, or role-playing activities concerning the stigma of obesity. Figuring out the classes or venues in which such activities might be located is something that can be addressed only within a given high school depending on its curriculum and schedule, but if

---

[16] The 1997 edited volume by Cohen and Lotan is a good introduction to cooperative learning.
[17] See the aforementioned Pfiefer et al. report.

piloting such programs yields supporting evidence, state and district policies could encourage individual schools to take such steps.

Similarly, the proliferation of thousands of gay-straight alliances (GSAs) in high schools across the country offers another example for potential actions to make high schools safe. These alliances, which bring together different groups of teenagers to raise awareness about and break down stereotypes regarding sexual orientation, do seem to have an impact at the school level.[18] Specifically, studies have shown that gay teenagers feel safer and have a stronger sense of belonging (and safety) in high schools with GSAs. They also demonstrate that straight teenagers hold more tolerant views of homosexuality in these high schools. Of course, one cannot deny the possibility that high schools with more tolerant, open-minded student bodies facilitate the creation of GSAs more than the creation of GSAs increases tolerance and open-mindedness among students. In other words, GSAs may be a sign rather than a cause of a tolerant school climate. This possibility needs to be assessed more carefully and systematically. Still, the evidence that does exist is hopeful.

In this way, GSAs provide a template on which we can build. For example, forming tolerance alliances – in which various forms of social stigma and prejudice that might lead any group of teenagers to feel as though they do not fit in at school are addressed – may promote more acceptance in general within the student body and reduce the rate of not-fitting-in perceptions among teenagers at the school. In terms of changing peer culture in high schools, the upside of this alliance approach is that it comes from teenagers themselves and is not implemented top-down by school personnel. By targeting social acceptance more generally rather than breaking down stereotypes related to specific groups, this alliance approach also addresses the potential risks of singling out one group of teenagers for help.

---

[18] A 2008 article in the *Journal of Gay and Lesbian Issues in Education* by Russell et al. discusses GSAs and provides evidence on effectiveness. A useful Web site on this issue is www.gaystraightalliance.org.

Having made this argument, I also recognize that attempts to promote the acceptance of diversity in American schools are often quite contentious. The whole idea of multicultural education, for example, has been repeatedly criticized as overzealous political correctness. As another example, GSAs (or really anything having to do with sex or sexual orientation in schools) have generated considerable hostility in many cities.[19] Even antibullying programs, which are not usually tied to specific groups, are criticized for stretching the official mission of schools too far.[20] Expanding these approaches to encompass other aspects of social marginalization and stigmatization – such as obesity, learning disabilities, physical unattractiveness, and many other social risks – will likely also generate opposition.

While acknowledging this possibility, I think that opposition to such programs must be met with the kind of data that I have presented here. For whatever reason, arguments about the economic costs of a problem often do more to sell the strategy than arguments about the social and emotional costs. The debates about federally funded early child care illustrate this point. Conservatives with "profamily" stances have long opposed such funding, but, in recent years, this same constituency has helped to dramatically increase funding for and access to preschool in Oklahoma, Georgia, and other red states because of evidence that quality preschools are an effective and efficient investment for boosting economic productivity in the long run.[21] Similarly, the link between fitting in and/or social stigma and "hard" outcomes, like college going, may do more than the link between social stigma and a "soft" outcome, like self-esteem, to overcome these very real obstacles to making schools safe. The economic calculation of dollars lost can be very convincing to policy makers.

[19] See Fields's 2008 book *Risky Lessons: Sex Education and Social Inequality*.
[20] In 2007, Vreeman and Carroll published a meta-analysis of antibullying programs in *Archives of Pediatric and Adolescent Medicine*.
[21] See Fuller's 2007 book *Standardized Childhood: The Political and Cultural Struggle over Early Education*.

Even if high school peer cultures go completely unchanged, we can still take steps to help teenagers protect themselves in the short and long term. Given the results of my investigation of resilience, providing concrete opportunities for self-actualization in high schools has promise. In other words, we need to identify ways that high schools can help teenagers find their niche, their own domains of achievement, that might counteract hurtful feedback received elsewhere in school. The point here is not to change the quantity or quality of social feedback but instead to change how that feedback affects the identity development of teenagers. Admittedly, this is a tricky proposition for high schools. As discussed at the end of the prior section of this chapter, expanding and supporting the extracurriculum is one possibility, but students would also have to be required to participate in at least one activity – perhaps making that activity an actual period on the schedule – to increase the probability that any one activity will stick.

Recently, a communications scholar, Mary Celeste Kearney, wrote about an activity that connects this niche-selection idea to another major component of the not-fitting-in pathway.[22] Specifically, girls can join groups in which they learn how to *make media*, in the form of films, Web sites, and zines. By producing rather than consuming media under the guidance of trained adults, girls find an outlet to express their feelings and frustrations but also a venue in which they can safely explore their own identities and critically analyze popular culture. True, such media-based activities are largely divorced from the traditional instructional objectives of the educational system, such as teaching math skills. Perhaps this disconnect is artificial. After all, such activities simply represent a very modern take on the fine arts instruction that has long gone on in schools.

Last, strong, supportive connections to adults likely also support resilience – through true or halfway protective means – among teenagers who feel as though they do not fit in at school. High schools

---

[22] Kearney's 2006 book is titled *Girls Make Media*.

cannot do much to strengthen bonds between teenagers and their parents, but they wield far more power to facilitate mentoring relationships between school personnel and students. Their biggest role is simply to create opportunity for these relationships to arise. Many high schools, including Lamar, are experimenting with policies in which students are assigned to one teacher for the entire high school career, with meetings and check-ins required. As a variation on this same approach, "homerooms," in which students start the school day with a short period in the same classroom every day, are assigned at the start of 9th grade and carry over from year to year. Both approaches increase the likelihood that teenagers will have an adult at school to go to in the case of problems and that an adult at school will be able to advise teenagers and help them identify their niches. These approaches represent fairly simple policies that will not eliminate social turbulence in high school but may reduce the number of teenagers who are affected by it in ways that are counterproductive to the education mission of the educational system.

SCHOOL ORGANIZATION

Homerooms and teacher mentors are not really services that schools can provide but instead small variations in the organization of schools. Such variations can be broader and bolder, changing schools to better serve students. I think that two more or less contemporary organizational reforms, implemented for different reasons, provide templates for thinking about the way high schools work can feed into or protect against potentially harmful disconnects between informal and formal education in high schools, including and especially the not-fitting-in pathway.

The Size of Schools

In earlier discussions of the contemporary relevance of the link between informal and formal education in high school, I highlighted the rapid increase in school size. The pros and cons of small and large schools have been seriously debated for decades, and the weight of the evidence suggests two somewhat opposing trends. As argued by Conant in the middle of the 20th century, larger schools are better able to realize economies of scale, which means that they can make their resources go farther by moving beyond critical baseline cost thresholds that any school must face. They can also offer many different kinds of classes and activities without worrying about filling slots.[23] In today's funding climate, these economic and curricular returns to increasing school size are not trivial. Yet, as demonstrated in studies by Lee and colleagues and by my own work with Add Health, small and medium-sized schools encourage more cohesion, sense of belonging, and participation among students. Any one student is likely to interact regularly or semiregularly with a greater proportion of the student body and the teaching staff in such schools compared to larger schools, and students face less competition getting onto teams and into clubs that are offered.[24]

As highlighted in a recent book by Lee and Ready and by recent funding initiatives by the Gates Foundation,[25] one compromise between these two sets of advantages has been the concept of schools within schools, an organizational strategy in which large schools are broken down into separate, smaller academies that operate as independent entities within the same institutional body. In other words, any one school building might contain several different, mostly autonomous schools with different names, student bodies, and curricula/extracurricula. According to early schools-within-schools advocates

---

[23] Conant's 1959 *The American High School Today: A First Report to Interested Citizens* is widely considered the genesis of the large school movement.

[24] The 1997 article by Lee and Smith in *Educational Evaluation and Policy Analysis* offers an overview of the school size debate. A study on school size I conducted with Johnson and Elder using Add Health data was published in *Social Science Quarterly* in 2004.

[25] *Schools-Within-Schools: Possibilities and Pitfalls of High School Reform* (Lee & Ready, 2007).

like Raywid,[26] the purpose of such a reorganization is to realize those important economies of scale while also providing a more intimate, personal schooling environment for teenagers. Although the research is not conclusive, it suggests that this schools-within-schools approach has benefits for students, especially for their social and psychological adjustment and especially in traditionally disadvantaged demographic populations (e.g., poor youth, racial/ethnic minorities). I think that the not-fitting-in pathway (especially as it relates to social stigma) is one area in which the schools-within-schools approach will have a positive impact and, through that, promote academic achievement. If impersonal settings create social divisions and allow marginalization to happen and stigma to fester, then perhaps having a well-defined, stable home base within a large school might reduce the likelihood that a gay/lesbian or obese or poor student is stigmatized and/or provide more resources to help him or her cope in positive ways.

Curriculum

Research on the so-called Catholic school effect – the tendency for achievement levels to be higher overall and less unequal across demographic groups in Catholic schools than in public schools and non-Catholic private schools – has emphasized the importance of a common curriculum.[27] Basically, Catholic schools typically have one set of coursework that all students must follow, with little discretion for substituting one class for another or for dropping out of one subject they do not like or find difficult. Eliminating choice eliminates the potential for nonacademic factors (e.g., family background, prejudice) to affect the coursework trajectories of students, which reduces achievement disparities related to these factors. In other words, without

---

[26] See Raywid's 1985 essay in *Review of Educational Research.*

[27] Two books – *Catholic Schools and the Common Good* by Bryk, Lee, and Holland (1993) and *Public and Private Schools* by Coleman and Hoffer (1987) – are still the best sources for reading about the Catholic school effect.

choice, some students cannot make worse (or better) choices about their education than others, which means that their opportunities to learn and achieve are more equal. This "No Bad Choice" philosophy is most often referenced in discussions about disparities in math/science course taking and achievement related to poverty and race because it is basically a back-end way of promoting equality of opportunity in a very important curricular pathway in the new economy.

The logic of this "No Bad Choice" idea might also extend to social risks in high school. After all, evidence from the Add Health and Lamar samples suggests that socially marginalized teenagers took lower-level classes than their peers and were more likely to drop out of math and science. A common curriculum – even if only partially implemented – could conceivably reduce such coursework disparities. We cannot easily influence socially marginalized teenagers' academic achievement or attendance patterns, but we can take steps like this to ensure that their social struggles do not prohibit their accumulation of the course credits that they will one day need to go to college. This is one small, but important, defense against short-term protective actions that are highly problematic in the long term and cannot be easily undone once done in the increasingly cumulative context of secondary education.

Although I think that these organizational reforms related to school size and curricular assignment are relevant to academic risks posed by social struggles in high school, including the not-fitting-in pathway, I cannot say for sure because they were not designed with such social – as opposed to academic – phenomena in mind. The ongoing evaluations of schools-within-schools reorganizations and common curriculum implementations, then, should assess the degree to which students at risk for social marginalization or other social problems – because they are obese, for example – perform better in both social and academic terms relative to their counterparts in other school organizational types.

School as a Focal Point

Thus far, I have focused on schools in this discussion of action because schools have long been a major, and widely accepted, site of policy intervention targeting young people in the United States. Because they organize so many teenagers for such long periods of time and because they have many features that are externally manipulable and because they are, for the most part, under the direct control of the state, schools are the primary entry point when we want to "fix" something about American youth. This is especially true here because, after all, the not-fitting-in pathway is a school-based phenomenon directly relevant to the educational missions of schools. Yet, schools are not the only setting of teenage life, nor the only venue for action in adolescent-specific societal or public health problems. Thus, I view schools as a starting point in efforts to do something about the not-fitting-in pathway in particular and the problematic link between informal and formal education more generally. In the next chapter, I go beyond schools to include other relevant contexts of and actors in adolescent development.

10

Looking to Parents and Other Adults

Despite how much time teenagers spend in high school and how important their school peers are on a daily basis, parents still loom large during the high school years and retain a great deal of power to intervene in their teenagers' lives, especially during times of crisis (Smetana, 2008; Steinberg, 2001; Steinberg & Morris, 2000; Eccles, 1994). Moreover, they retain primary roles as managers of teenagers' journeys through contemporary high school curricula, which, according to Epstein (2005), is precisely why one of the major sections of No Child Left Behind concerns parental involvement in education. Similarly, recall that the Lamar teenagers highlighted the role of nonparental mentors in their lives and explicitly linked such mentors to their understanding of resilience in the face of social problems at high school.

Yet, as I mentioned when discussing the policy dilemma in the last chapter, parenting is not a common, accepted, or easy focus of policy intervention for reasons that are political, cultural, legal, ethnical, and practical, although this is less true for nonfamilial mentoring (Granger, 2008; Spencer, 2006). As a result, my motivation is not just to view the not-fitting-in pathway through the lens of educational policy and intervention but also to discuss this pathway in terms of what parents and other adults with teenagers in high school need to understand and what they can do. In doing so, I follow the lead of Coleman, Schneider, and other social capital researchers interested in education and educational disparities by prioritizing the power of information, understanding that parents, teachers, and other adults need to understand what is going on before they can do something.[1]

CREATING A SOURCE OF INFORMATION

Schools often have a very good idea of what is going on academically in their schools and, at any rate, are forced to collect hard data. Indeed, the whole point of the standardized testing emphasis in No Child Left Behind and other performance benchmarks on the state and district levels is to provide a dynamic, comprehensive picture of what students in a high school are learning and to gauge the rate of success in the school. Parents are major beneficiaries of this information. At least in theory, it enables them to know more about what the school is doing in terms of its educational mission and how well it is serving its students, which is information that can be used to help them decide where to send their teenagers to school and what to demand of the schools to which they do send their teenagers.

What is going on *socially* in schools – what is valued and what is devalued, who is integrated and who is marginalized – is much less clear. Certainly, little hard data exist on this subject, which leaves parents at a major disadvantage in deciding what school is right for their teenagers in social, as opposed to academic, terms. I think that, in following the No Child Left Behind goal of empowering parents to help teenagers educationally, this needs to change.

Without social data, rankings of high school quality lose their meaning, and the notion that parents can and should find the best school match for their teenagers is undercut. As Eccles's pioneering work on middle schools has demonstrated, schools with excellent curricula can still provide an inadequate academic setting for young people if the social, relational, and emotional context is not

---

[1] See *Parents, Their Children, and Schools*, a 1993 edited volume by Schneider and Coleman.

developmentally appropriate. The same logic applies to high school. To illustrate why, I use the hypothetical example of a high school in Texas called Cardinal Hill.

A large public school, Cardinal Hill serves an extremely upscale portion of a large city, has some of the most highly qualified, best-paid teachers in the state who teach the most advanced curricula, and is almost always mentioned in discussions of effective education. Indeed, it regularly appears in the annual "best of" education issue put out by *Newsweek*. Not surprisingly, then, on almost any statistic about *formal* indictors of school or student performance, Cardinal Hill ranks quite high. Consequently, it is widely considered to be a "good" high school. Yet, considering the informal side of education, one cannot be so sanguine about whether Cardinal Hill is a good high school. The student body is characterized by, among other more positive things, rampant materialism, extraordinary senses of privilege and entitlement, cut-throat social warfare, a focus on partying as a form of achievement, festering body image issues, and the punishment of even the slightest hint of difference.

With this in mind, the possibility that most Cardinal Hill students might graduate with incredible opportunities for educational attainment and earning money but real problems with self-image, relating to other people, and getting through life has to be taken into account. What also needs to be considered is the potential for quirky or "weird" teenagers to do worse academically in this high school than at a resource-poorer high school because their social problems are too big a distraction. In other words, the bottom line of Cardinal Hill may be praiseworthy but, at the same time, obscures real risks and real failures. What is at issue here is not *school* failure, at least in conventional terms. Academically, Cardinal Hill is doing its job. It is exemplary, and improving its performance rate would likely be quite difficult. The real issues are twofold. First, on the school level, Cardinal Hill is simultaneously producing a public good in educational and socioeconomic terms while creating public health problems (e.g., substance use, eating disorders, depression). Second, on the level of individual students (rather than on the school level), Cardinal Hill is likely, despite its many academic advantages and resources, interfering with the abilities of at least some teenagers to fulfill their educational potential.

This is not a question of school reconstitution or about which school is meeting the academic needs of the largest number of students. Instead, it is a question of collateral damage that could go along with a school's academic productivity. This is also a question about which school provides the best setting for *any one teenager* to pursue an education given his or her own traits, characteristics, interests, and proclivities. One can extrapolate out, however, to see how these school and individual levels come together. Consider another public school, a solid, stable school with fewer academic resources than Cardinal Hill but more such resources than most other schools, a school with good but not great performance rates. In such a school, the academic risks associated with something like the not-fitting-in pathway would likely do more to dilute the absolute academic standing of the school. With more teenagers on the margins of good or bad performance, social issues would have a broader effect, not just keeping the school from having a perfect testing or graduation rate (as at Cardinal Hill) but making a difference in whether the school was considered academically good or mediocre. In this case, having full information about the informal education in the school would affect the perceptions of parents and other adults about the school in general, not just the parents of certain teenagers and not just perceptions about the social setting the school provides.

My point is that conventional considerations about what makes a high school good, what makes it the right one for a teenager, look very different when teenagers' views about the power of informal processes in high school are excluded from the equation.[2] The school is, after all,

---

[2] In *The Good High School* (1983), Sara Lawrence Lightfoot used case studies of urban, suburban, and elite/private high schools from across the country to demonstrate how the social and academic sides of high schools can work together or undermine each other.

just a building with people in it in their eyes, and that stance is not to be dismissed so readily by adults. If all good things go together or all bad things go together, then whether we take the adult, formal-focused viewpoint, the teenage, informal-focused viewpoint, or both does not really matter. If, however, there is a discrepancy between the formal, educational side of a high school and the informal, social side of high school, then the general labels of school quality and parental decisions about schooling based on these labels become much more complex. We have to develop a sliding scale with which we figure out how much of the academic resources of a school we are willing to give up or do without to gain social resources or avoid social risks.

In other words, parents, other adults, and teenagers themselves need to understand what their tipping points are. The value of giving these actors the opportunity to identify what their tipping points might be is why the need for data on both formal and informal indicators is great. We have plenty of data on the formal side, but, unfortunately, we have little access to such data on the informal side.

In an ideal world, my suggestion would be a two-stage survey of teenagers that high schools conduct every 4 years. In the first stage of the survey, the entire student body completes anonymous questionnaires that collect basic information on the social and emotional well-being of teenagers in the high school: drinking, depression, feelings of connectedness, perceptions of teachers, truancy, and so on. In the second stage, a smaller subset of teenagers (maybe one grade) completes what are called sociometric questionnaires, in which they are asked to list their friends and acquaintances. These sociometric data then lend themselves to mapping out the social networks of peer relations in that subset of the high school. With such a map, the density of social relations (e.g., how much everyone is connected to everyone else) can be assessed, the degree to which small cliques are disconnected from each other or come together in larger PLUs can be known, and the number of isolates (e.g., teenagers connected to no one) can be counted. High schools can then disaggregate the collected data by demographic groups but also by other social groups, such as obesity or other ones highlighted in this book. This enterprise will allow the same kind of assessments of school *health/safety* as the No Child Left Behind data and other data sources collected by the U.S. Department of Education allow for school *performance.*

Of course, we do not live in an ideal world, and the obstacles to this ambitious data collection enterprise are numerous. The biggest obstacle to such an effort is cost. Are costs prohibitive, and, even if not, who would be on the hook for putting up the money? A second major obstacle is what, in policy and public health circles, is often referred to as stakeholder opposition. In this case, stakeholder opposition would most likely take the form of reluctance on the part of school personnel to use school time for such data collection activities, especially when schools are already feeling overburdened by No Child Left Behind.

These obstacles are significant, but, I argue, they can be addressed *if* we place a priority on getting this done. Once designed and tested, the surveys can be quite brief, reused from year to year, and administered in short periods of time at widely spaced intervals (again, my suggestion would be every 4 years). Schools can partner with social and behavioral scientists to conduct these studies. Many scientists will agree to forego payment for their services in exchange for access to the data for their own research. This model was widely used when Head Start was ordered by the government to have all of its thousands of programs conduct rigorous evaluations of their operations and impact (Raver et al., 2008).

Obviously, this model still entails some expenditure of scarce resources, but such a voluntary expenditure would be worthwhile within reason. It recognizes the different ways that high schools can be good or bad, which is an important component of transparency as parents select schools for teenagers and the state rewards and penalizes schools for performance. It demonstrates to teenagers and parents that high schools take seriously the social and emotional well-being of their students. And, not the least, it provides data that may prove useful to high schools' efforts to boost college-going rates and meet important academic benchmarks.

Parents' roles in the linked developmental and educational trajectories of their teenagers, of course, extend well beyond knowing how to assess the multidimensional quality of high schools. They tend to focus less on the school and more on the teenager himself or herself. Recognizing this, I attempted to draw on the results of my work with Add Health and in Lamar as well as the rich interdisciplinary literatures from which this work arose, to lay out five sequential points for parents to consider. Importantly, these five points apply also to teachers, counselors, and other adults with teenagers in their lives.

Know the Risks

Simply being aware of who might be at risk is important. When a teenager has personal characteristics that might lead to social marginalization or stigmatization in high school, parents need to be vigilant. Although I have considered only obesity and same-sex attraction here, the list of potentially stigmatized groups in American high schools is far longer. It also is quite frequently school, community, and group specific. For example, obesity appears to come with far weaker social penalties in African American neighborhoods than in white ones. As another example, poverty, which I did not explicitly study here, is less likely to be stigmatized in an urban, low-income high school than in other high schools. Thus, parents are then left to be the experts about what is valued and devalued in their own teenagers' high social locations and surrounding parts and the concomitant social risks facing their own teenagers. Parents should be especially vigilant during the years in which both their daughters and sons are transitioning into high school and, in general, over girls struggling with weight or body image issues and/or who have confided in them that they are same-sex attracted. The key in doing so is not to reify any stigma they face but instead to be aware of what risks such stigma, if experienced, may pose.

Know the Symptoms

Parents know that risks have been activated when teenagers present symptoms. If teenagers suffer from physical health maladies, they typically show certain symptoms that prompt parents to arrange medical intervention or special care. The same basic protocol applies when teenagers have social and emotional problems that also require some intervention. Some of these symptoms are admittedly hard to detect. Substance use is an example. No matter how much adults think that they can sense or see when teenagers are drinking or smoking pot, these behaviors are often quite invisible to adults. Teenagers have been hiding them with a lot of success for many years in the United States, and they know how to do it. Other symptoms, however, are more readily apparent. Depression has a well-defined set of symptoms (e.g., loss of appetite, sleeplessness) that parents can see. They can Google the Center for Epidemiologic Studies–Depression Scale as a starting point. Furthermore, academic disengagement, in the form of truancy and grades, often gets reported home from schools. When these symptoms appear, parents need to follow up. When a root cause can be determined or is at least hinted, action is required. Parents should not wait or expect it to pass because, even if it does, some consequences may already be taking effect.

Know the Mechanisms

Symptoms are at the surface, so parents and other adults need to go deeper to uncover the mechanisms by which risks translate into symptomatology. Like policy makers, parents are often powerless to change the peer cultures of their teenagers' high schools, short of moving so that their teenagers can attend a new high school, which is often a complete impossibility for many parents. They have far more power to help teenagers deal with what is going on in these high school peer cultures and to prevent their teenagers from setting into motion the chains of problematic events that I have described in this book. What triggers these chains of events is what parents must understand. Identity is the key – how teenagers incorporate what happens at school, along with what happens in the family and in other settings, into their senses of who they are. When the social context cannot be changed, as it often cannot, then supporting positive identity work is the next line of defense.

Know What Supports Resilience

Resilience happens when positive identity development is supported during difficult or trying social circumstances in high school. Parents can offer this support in several ways. They can simply be there for teenagers and make clear that support is always available. What is especially important is providing appropriately positive feedback that can counter negative feedback coming out of high schools or other sources. In addition, giving a sense of acceptance of who teenagers are can ensure that their identity work does not have to involve yet another "actual/ought" discrepancy. To fall back on attachment terminology, parents should continue to be a secure base for teenagers, so that they can take risks and face challenges in the world knowing that their parents will not turn on them.

Another way to offer support is to participate and guide teenagers in their niche selection, helping them to figure out what their talents and skills and interests might be and then actively working to provide opportunities for them to facilitate and engage in these talents, skills, and interests. Parents can help teenagers identify what their domain of achievement is, whatever it is. Similarly, instead of trying to control the media that they consume, parents can teach them to critically appraise the media so that their identities are immune to the mixed messages that they receive. Finding a media activity group is one way of doing so. Another way to offer support is to develop teenagers' future orientation, their sense that high school is temporary and only one stage in a very long life. Parents can keep teenagers focused on the future by discussing post–high school plans with them, be they related to work or college, and arranging activities and trips (e.g., visiting workplaces, reading college guides) to keep these future plans immediate. Many schools, including Lamar, now offer programs (e.g., AVID)[3] specifically to get teenagers thinking about what happens after high school, especially teenagers from more disadvantaged backgrounds whose parents may not have solid information about future opportunities but recognize the need to get such information.

The point is to protect teenagers' identities from discrepancies or spoiling, even if their high school conditions are just right for either or both. For an individual teenager, any kind of protection – full, halfway – matters.

Know That Demands Can Be Made to the School

Parents, especially those from more disadvantaged segments of the population, often misunderstand what role they can play in school. They have the right to demand changes in high schools. Indeed, as the work of Lareau has made clear, loud, complaining parents are often the major driving force when schools do make changes.[4] Now that all schools receiving federal money are mandated to have community advisory councils populated by parents, parents have an explicit venue for taking action.

[3] AVID stands for Advancement Via Individual Determination; see http://www.pac.dodea.edu/edservices/EducationPrograms/AVID.htm.
[4] See *Home Advantage* by Lareau.

Thus, parents should view all of the recommendations about educational policy that I made in the previous chapter as not just a list of steps that high schools can take to protect teenagers from social risks but also a list of demands that they themselves can make at their teenagers' high schools. If the extracurriculum gets cut or services get curtailed, then parents need to voice their complaints. If the high school can be doing something that it is not, then parents need to ask why not. Because numbers matter, parents who band together can make stronger calls for change. Effective buzzwords – e.g., making schools safe, holding schools accountable – will drive home the point by tying parents' concerns to major policy agendas and their related funding streams.

11

In Search of Theory and Action

Several years ago, the filmmaker Michael Moore released an Oscar-winning documentary about the 1999 Columbine High School massacre called *Bowling for Columbine*. For me, as a developmentalist studying educational policy issues with a focus on peer relations, one of the more thought-provoking parts of this documentary involved an interview with the creator of the television series *South Park*, Matt Stone, who grew up in Littleton, the affluent Denver suburb in which Columbine was located. Reflecting on his own high school days, Stone discussed his wish that the two boys who had perpetrated the massacre could have just known *during* high school what they would likely have discovered *after* high school, what most adults have discovered – that all of those seemingly momentous social struggles and identity crises that go on in high school are temporary, that teenagers eventually grow up, get past all of that stuff, and look back on the things that bothered them, that hurt, and see that none of it matters. His words spoke to me, in part, because I had thought the exact same thing back in April 1999 as I watched the horrific footage from Colorado on the television news. "You just had to wait two years or so," I thought, "and everything that seems so bad now wouldn't seem so bad anymore."

Yet, those boys took their deadly action before they had the chance to get over what was happening to them. Of course, most teenagers' social ups and downs in high school are not so dramatic, and, *thankfully*, their coping mechanisms or emotional responses to what goes on in the informal education of high school are not so extreme or bloody.

The general idea, however, is similar; namely, that even temporary situations and circumstances can have long-lasting consequences if they set in motion a chain of events that is difficult to reverse. Thus, high schools and the teenagers attending them might be better served if the "this too shall pass" response of adults to the social currents of high school is replaced by greater focus on helping teenagers navigate these currents until they do pass.

In my view, the fact that not fitting in socially at high school can spur identity issues and socioemotional coping mechanisms that disrupt academic progress and interfere with college going is a clear example of how short-term, even transient, developmental issues can have cascading implications for the life course. In part, this cascade and its long-term implications reflect the raised stakes of educational actions and decision making resulting from the connection between the curricular diversification of American schools and the restructuring of the global economy. As such, it represents a contemporary twist on what is an old developmental story, one that drives home the point that I and many other psychologists, sociologists, and educational researchers before me have made about the need to think about the informal education in high schools as an academic issue and, more specifically, as a target of educational policy and school reform. By making this point, I am not minimizing that the social, emotional, and psychological risks of not fitting in – risks rooted in the interpersonal contexts of high school but embedded in larger demographic, structural, and technological changes in society – matter regardless of how they affect academic considerations and/or college going. These are developmental problems that deserve attention. My argument is that *one reason* that they deserve our attention is because they do have implications for the formal education of high schools, an argument rooted in my awareness that stressing the implications of the informal on the formal is crucial to moving developmental problems into the policy spotlight.

On a personal note, I should acknowledge that, like probably just about everyone, my "gut" response to these issues is to look back on my own high school years. I imagine that this journey was like what I believe is probably the norm – pretty good overall but some definite bumps along the way. Years and miles removed from walking the halls of my high school, I tend to have the same view as many adults. I remember good times, and I tend to minimize the bad times – the times when the social mix of my high school put me in the position of doubting who I was while I was also trying to learn Trig, read Faulkner and Morrison, and bring home the grades that my parents and teachers expected of me – as something of a rite of passage, something that made me stronger. That I did go onto college and beyond would seem to suggest that this reaction is valid, that, ultimately, the social struggles that I faced from time to time in high school did not matter in the long run. Yet, in all honesty, I do not know how my life would have been better or worse in some ways if I had not had those experiences in high school. I will never really know, and no adult will ever be able to answer that question in any other way.

Yet, when we look *prospectively* at teenagers' lives as they unfold, instead of *retrospectively* once they have unfolded, we can provide a more solid answer to this question. The work I have presented here as well as other studies by social and behavioral scientists does suggest that, yes, social struggles in high school can matter in the long run even if the struggles themselves fade over time. Our lives and the systems in which we live our lives are too sequential, too cumulative. In a distillation of how the life course paradigm captures developmental process,[1] one thing leads to another, one experience sets the stage for the next.

Again, in this book, I used college going as the crucible in which to see this life course process in action. In doing so, I anticipated

---

[1] See Elder's presidential address to the Society for Research in Child Development, printed in *Child Development* in 1998.

some criticism for seemingly holding up college going as the be-all and end-all of modern life. Even in the modern economic climate, going to college is not the answer for everyone, and it is certainly not feasible for many regardless of whether it is the answer or not. Young people, their parents, and their mentors need to make those assessments and choices for themselves. The real problem with the not-fitting-in pathway and other formal risks associated with informal education is that they skew those assessments and take away those choices from some teenagers and their loved ones and counselors. Such developmental phenomena put teenagers in the position, once high school is over, in which some options – such as going to college – have been foreclosed years before when they did not even know that it was happening. As with so many policy-relevant scientific topics, what is at issue are probabilities, not absolutes or certainties, but they still matter a great deal.

Whether high school is a blessing or curse for any one teenager, then, it can be a blessing or a curse that keeps on giving long after high school is over. The informal education that occurs in high school filters out across life the same way that the formal education does (Kingston, Hubbard, Lapp, Schroeder, & Wilson, 2003; Rosenbaum, 2001; Csikszentmihalyi & Schneider, 2000). This is something for adults – from parents to policy makers – to remember and to respect. It is a key to helping any one teenager fulfill his or her potential and relevant to improving schools in the United States overall at a time when our educational system is no longer the leader of the world it once was.

And, to be fair, teenagers are not mindless conformists, the unthinking followers that they are often made out to be in developmental research. Like adults, they use the tools they have to work their way through things the best they can. They have a drive to chart the best perceived course through waters that can sometimes get quite rough. That mixture of personal agency and responsibility on one hand with social needs and exchanges on the other is why some teenagers rise from great hardship to do amazing things in life but also why other teenagers turn to violence or self-abuse. Our role is to try to tilt the balance from one side to the other in large and small ways.

Intervention – action – is needed. Such action should take the form of *reactive* steps to help teenagers deal with social problems in high school so that those social problems do not morph into emotional, academic, and behavioral problems. At the same time, it should take the form of *proactive* steps to decrease the likelihood that these social problems will arise in high school for any teenager in the first place.

When intervention is not helping, we must recognize that, understand why, and change course. Consider the money spent on sex education, substance use reduction, and drop-out prevention in high schools. Those well-intentioned efforts may be doomed to fail or at least underachieve if too little thought is given to what kinds of behaviors and what kinds of people are valued and devalued in the peer cultures of those high schools (Hampden-Thompson, Warkentien, & Daniel, 2009; Fields, 2008; Holleran-Steiker, 2008).

A fundamental element of this process is the need to rethink what a good school is and what a proper education entails. Is it measured by academic benchmarks or teenagers' feelings of belonging and acceptance, test scores or friendships? When *Newsweek* comes out with its annual ranking of the best high schools in the nation every year, it is often met with a storm of criticism for relying on some single academic indicator like AP testing rates. Yet, the alternatives suggested by critics typically replace this single indicator with some mixture of multiple academic indicators. No, or at least very little, consideration is given to the social and emotional well-being of teenagers in the school. The truth is somewhere in between, and even if the *Newsweek* rankings do not reflect that balance, the adults who run high schools and send their teenagers to high schools should. One potentially valuable role of developmental researchers is to make a convincing scientific case for why they should.

WORKS CITED

Adelman, C. (1999). *Answers in the toolbox: Academic intensity, attendance patterns, and bachelor's degree attainment.* U.S. Department of Education, Office of Educational Research and Improvement. Washington, DC: U.S. Government Printing Press.

   (2006). *The toolbox revisited: Paths to degree completion from high school through college.* Washington, DC: U.S. Department of Education.

Adler, P., & Adler, P. (1998). *Peer power: Preadolescent culture and identity.* New Brunswick, NJ: Rutgers University Press.

Advancement Via Individual Determination. (2009). www.pac.dodea.edu/edservices/EducationPrograms/AVID.htm.

Ainsworth-Darnell, J., & Downey, D. (1998). Assessing racial/ethnic differences in school performance. *American Sociological Review, 63,* 536–553.

Akerlof, G. E., & Kranton, R. A. (2002). Identity and schooling: Some lessons for the economics of education. *Journal of Economic Literature, 40,* 1167–1201.

Allen, J. P., Porter, M. R., McFarland, C. F., Marsh, P., & McElhaney, K. B. (2005). The two faces of adolescents' success with peers: Adolescent popularity, social adaptation, and deviant behavior. *Child Development, 76,* 747–760.

American Association of University Women. (1992). *How schools shortchange girls.* Washington, DC: AAUW.

Anderson, P. S., & Butcher, K. F. (2006). Childhood obesity: Trends and potential causes. *The Future of Children, 16,* 19–45.

Aseltine, R. H., & Gore, S. L. (2000). The variable effect of stress on alcohol use from adolescence to early adulthood. *Substance Use and Misuse, 35,* 643–668.

Attewell, P., & Domina, T. (2008). Raising the bar: Curricular intensity and academic performance. *Educational Evaluation and Policy Analysis, 30*, 51–71.

Bae, Y., Chow, S., Geddes, C., Sable, J., & Snyder, T. (2000). *Trends in gender equity for girls and women* (NCES 2000–030). Washington, DC: U.S. Department of Education.

Bandura, A. (1997). *Self-efficacy: The exercise of control.* New York: Freeman.
(2000). Social cognitive theory: An agentic perspective. *Annual Review of Psychology, 52*, 1–26.

Barber, B. K., & Olsen, J. A. (2004). Assessing the transitions to middle and high school. *Journal of Adolescent Research, 19*(1), 3–30.

Barber, B. L., Eccles, J. S., & Stone, M. R. (2001). Whatever happened to the jock, the brain, and the princess? Young adult pathways linked to adolescent activity involvement and social identity. *Journal of Adolescent Research, 16*, 429–455.

Baumeister, R. (1998). The self. In J. Howard & P. Callero (Eds.), *Handbook of social psychology, 4th edition* (pp. 780–739). Cambridge: Cambridge University Press.

Bearman, P. S., & Bruckner, H. (2001). Promising the future: Virginity pledges and first intercourse. *American Journal of Sociology, 106*, 859–912.

Bearman, P. S., & Moody, J. (2004). Adolescent suicidality. *American Journal of Public Health, 94*, 89–95.

Benner, A. D., & Graham, S. (2007). Navigating the transition to multi-ethnic urban high schools: Changing ethnic congruence and adolescents' school-related affect. *Journal of Research on Adolescence, 17*, 207–220.

Berlin, L., Zeanah, C., & Lieberman, A. (2008). Prevention and intervention programs for supporting early attachment security. In J. Cassidy & P. R. Shaver (Eds.), *Handbook of attachment* (pp. 745–761). New York: Guilford.

Bernhardt, A., Morris, M., Handcock, M. S., & Scott, M. A. (2001). *Divergent paths: Economic mobility in the new American labor market.* New York: Russell Sage.

Blau, P. M., & Dudley, O. (1967). *The American occupational structure.* New York: Wiley.

Bos, H. M. W., Sandfort, T. G. M., de Bruyn, E. H., & Hakvoort, E. (2008). Same sex attraction, social relationships, psychosocial functioning, and school performance in early adolescence. *Developmental Psychology, 44*, 59–68.

Brown, B., Eicher, S., & Petrie, S. (1986). The importance of peer group ("crowd") affiliation in adolescence. *Journal of Adolescent Research, 9*, 73–96.

Brown, B., Green, N., & Harper, R. (Eds.). (2002). *Wireless world: Social and interactional aspects of the mobile age.* London: Springer.

Brown, B. B., & Klute, C. (2003). Friendships, cliques, and crowds. In G. Adams & M. D. Berzonsky (Eds.), *Blackwell handbook of adolescence* (pp. 330–348). Malden, MA: Blackwell.

Brumberg, J. J. (1997). *The body project: An intimate history of American girls.* New York: Random House.

Bryk, A. S., Lee, V. E., & Holland, P. B. (1993). *Catholic schools and the common good.* Cambridge, MA: Harvard University Press.

Buchmann, B., DiPrete, T. A., & McDaniel, A. (2008). Gender inequalities in education. *Annual Review of Sociology, 34,* 319–337.

Burke, P. J. (2004). Identities and social structure: The 2003 Cooley-Mead Award address. *Social Psychology Quarterly, 67,* 5–15.

Burns, B. J., Costello, E. J., Angold, A., Tweed, D., Stangl, D. K., Farmer, E. M. Z., & Erkanli, A. (1995). Children's mental health service use across service sectors. *Health Affairs, 14,* 147–159.

Cairns, R. B., & Cairns, B. D. (1994). *Lifelines and risks: Pathways of youth in our time.* New York: Cambridge University Press.

Call, K. T., & Mortimer, J. T. (2001). *Arenas of comfort in adolescence: A study of adjustment in context.* Mahwah, NJ: Erlbaum.

Canning, H., & Mayer, J. (1966). Obesity: Its possible effect on college acceptance. *New England Journal of Medicine, 275,* 1172–1174.

Carr, D., & Friedman, M. A. (2005). Is obesity stigmatizing? Body weight, perceived discrimination, and psychological well-being in the United States. *Journal of Health and Social Behavior, 46,* 244–259.

Carter, P. (2006). *Keepin' it real: School success beyond black and white.* New York: Oxford University Press.

Cast, A., & Burke, P. (2002). A theory of self-esteem. *Social Forces, 80,* 1041–1068.

Cast, A., Stets, J. E., & Burke, P. J. (1999). Does the self conform to views of others? *Social Psychology Quarterly, 62,* 68–82.

Ceci, S. J., & Papierno, P. B. (2005). The rhetoric and reality of gap closing: When the "have nots" gain but the "haves" gain even more. *American Psychologist, 60,* 149–160.

Centers for Disease Control and Prevention. (2002). Body mass index. www.cdc.gov/nccdphp/dnpa/bmi.

Cohen, E. G., & Lotan, R. A. (1997). *Working for equity in heterogeneous classrooms: Sociological theory in practice.* New York: Teachers College Press.

Coleman, J. (1961). *The adolescent society: The social life of the teenager and its impact on education.* New York: Free Press.

Coleman, J. S. (1990). *Foundations of social theory*. Cambridge, MA: Harvard University Press.

Coleman, J. S., & Hoffer, T. (1987). *Public and private schools: The impact of communities*. New York: Basic Books.

Collins, W. A., Welsh, D. P., & Furman, W. (2009). Adolescent romantic relationships. *Annual Review of Psychology, 60,* 631–652.

Conant, J. B. (1959). *The American high school today: A first report to interested citizens*. New York: McGraw-Hill.

Cooley, C. H. (1983) [1902]. *Human nature and the social order*. New Brunswick, NJ: Transaction.

Correll, S. J. (2001). Gender and the career choice process: The role of biased self-assessments. *American Journal of Sociology, 106,* 1691–1730.

Corsaro, W. A. (1992). Interpretive reproduction in children's peer cultures. *Social Psychology Quarterly, 55,* 160–177.

Crandall, C. (1994). Prejudice against fat people: Ideology and self-interest. *Journal of Personality and Social Psychology, 66,* 882–894.

Cremin, L. A. (1957). *The republic and the school: Horace Mann on the education of free men*. New York: Teachers College Press.

(1980). *American education: The national experience, 1783–1876*. New York: Harper & Row.

Crocker, J., & Major, B. (1989). Social stigma and self-esteem: The self-protective properties of stigma. *Psychological Review, 96,* 608–630.

Crosnoe, R. (2002). Academic and health-related trajectories in adolescence: The intersection of gender and athletics. *Journal of Health and Social Behavior, 43,* 317–335.

(2006). The connection between academic failure and adolescent drinking in secondary school. *Sociology of Education, 79,* 44–60.

(2007). Gender, education, and the experience of obesity. *Sociology of Education, 80,* 241–260.

Crosnoe, R., & Elder, G. H., Jr. (2004). Family dynamics, supportive relationships, and educational resilience during adolescence. *Journal of Family Issues, 25,* 571–602.

Crosnoe, R., Frank, K., & Mueller, A. S. (2008). Gender, body size, and social relations in American high schools. *Social Forces, 86,* 1189–1216.

Crosnoe, R., & Huston, A. C. (2007). Socioeconomic status, schooling, and the developmental trajectories of adolescents. *Developmental Psychology, 43,* 1097–1110.

Crosnoe, R., Johnson, M. K., & Elder, G. H., Jr. (2004a). Intergenerational bonding in school: The behavioral and contextual correlates of student-teacher relationships. *Sociology of Education, 77,* 60–81.

(2004b). School size and the interpersonal side of education: An examination of race/ethnicity and organizational context. *Social Science Quarterly, 85,* 1259–1274.

Crosnoe, R., & Muller, C. (2006). Family socioeconomic status, peers, and the path to college. Paper presented at the annual meeting of the American Sociological Association, Montreal, Canada.

Crosnoe, R., Muller, C., & Frank, K. (2004). Peer context and the consequences of adolescent drinking. *Social Problems, 51,* 288–304.

Crosnoe, R., & Needham, B. (2004). Holism, contextual variability, and the study of friendships in adolescent development. *Child Development, 75,* 264–279.

Crosnoe, R., & Riegle-Crumb, C. (2007). A life course model of education and early alcohol use. *Journal of Health and Social Behavior, 48,* 267–282.

Crosnoe, R., Riegle-Crumb, C., Field, S., Frank, K., & Muller, C. (2008). Peer contexts of girls' and boys' academic experiences. *Child Development, 79,* 139–155.

Crosnoe, R., Riegle-Crumb, C., & Muller, C. (2007). Gender, self-perception, and the experience of learning disability and failure. *Social Problems, 54,* 113–133.

Csikszentmihalyi, M., & Schneider, B. (2000). *Becoming adult: How teenagers prepare for the world of work.* New York: Basic Books.

Dahl, R. E., & Spear, L. P. (2004). Adolescent brain development: Vulnerabilities and opportunities. *Annals of the New York Academy of Science, 1021,* 1–22.

Dance, T. L. (2002). *Tough fronts: The impact of street culture on schooling.* New York: Routledge.

de Tocqueville, A. (2003) [1863]. *Democracy in America.* New York: Penguin.

Demo, D. H., & Acock, A. C. (1996). Family structure, family process, and adolescent well-being. *Journal of Research on Adolescence, 6,* 457–488.

Dornbusch, S. M. (1989). The sociology of adolescence. *Annual Review of Sociology, 15,* 233–259.

Dornbusch, S., Glasgow, K., & Lin, I. (1996). The social structure of schooling. *Annual Review of Psychology, 47,* 401–429.

Dornbusch, S. M., Herman, M., & Morley, J. B. (1996). Adolescent domains of achievement In G. Adams, R. Montemayor, & T. P. Gullotta (Eds.), *Psychosocial development during adolescence* (pp. 181–231). Thousand Oaks, CA: Sage.

Dworkin, A. G. (2005). The No Child Left Behind Act: Accountability, high-stakes testing, and roles for sociologists. *Sociology of Education, 78,* 170–174.

Eccles, J. S. (1994). School and family effects on the ontogeny of children's interests, self-perceptions, and activity choices. In R. A. Dienstbler (Ed.), *Developmental perspectives on motivation: Volume 40 of the Nebraska Symposium on Motivation* (pp. 145–208). Lincoln: University of Nebraska Press.

Eccles, J. S., & Barber, B. (1999). Student council, volunteering, basketball, or marching band: What kind of extracurricular involvement matters? *Journal of Adolescent Research, 14*, 10–43.

Eccles, J. S., Lord, S., Roeser, R. W., Barber, B. L., & Hernandez-Jozefowicz, D. M. (1997). The association of school transitions in early adolescence with developmental trajectories through high school. In J. Schulenberg, J. L. Maggs, & K. Hurrelmann (Eds.), *Health risks and developmental transitions during adolescence* (pp. 283–320). Cambridge: Cambridge University Press.

Eccles, J. S., & Wigfield, A. (2002). Motivational beliefs, values, and goals. *Annual Review of Psychology, 53*, 109–132.

Eckert, P. (1989). *Jocks and burnouts: Social identity in the high school.* New York: Teachers College Press.

Eder, D., Evans, C., & Parker, S. (1995). *School talk: Gender and adolescent culture.* New Brunswick, NJ: Rutgers University Press.

Elder, G. H., Jr. (1974). *Children of the Great Depression: Social change in life experience.* Boulder, CO: Westview.

(1998). The life course as developmental theory. *Child Development, 69*, 1–12.

Elkind, D. (1967). Egocentrism in adolescence. *Child Development, 38*, 1025–1034.

Entwisle, D., Alexander, K. L., & Olson, L. S. (1997). *Children, schools and inequality.* Boulder, CO: Westview.

Epstein, J. L. (2005). Attainable goals? The spirit and letter of the No Child Left Behind Act on parental involvement. *Sociology of Education, 78*, 179–182.

Erikson, E. (1968). *Identity: Youth and crisis.* New York: Norton.

Ewell, F., Smith, S., Karmel, M. P., & Hart, D. (1996). The sense of self and its development: A framework for understanding eating disorders. In L. Smolak, M. P. Levine, & R. Striegel-Moor (Eds.), *The developmental psychopathology of eating disorders: Implications for research, prevention, and treatment* (pp. 107–133). Mahwah, NJ: Erlbaum.

Festinger, L. (1954). A theory of social comparison processes. *Human Relations, 7*, 117–140.

Fields, J. (2008). *Risky lessons: Sex education and social inequality.* New Brunswick, NJ: Rutgers University Press.

Fine, G. A. (1987). *With the boys: Little League baseball and preadolescent culture.* Chicago: University of Chicago Press.

Fischer, C. S., & Hout, M. (2006). *Century of difference: How America changed in the last one hundred years.* New York: Russell Sage.

Frank, K. A., Muller, C., Schiller, K. S., Riegle-Crumb, C., Mueller, A. S., Crosnoe, R., & Pearson, J. (2008). The social dynamics of mathematics course-taking in high school. *American Journal of Sociology, 113,* 1645–1696.

Frank, K. Sykes, G., Anagnostopoulos, D., Cannata, M., Chard, L., Krouse, A., & McCrory, R. (2008). Does NBPTS certification affect the number of colleagues a teacher helps with instructional matters? *Educational Evaluation and Policy Analysis, 30,* 3–30.

Fuller, B. (2007). *Standardized childhood: The political and cultural struggle over early education.* Palo Alto, CA: Stanford University Press.

Furstenberg, F. F. (2000). The sociology of adolescence and youth in the 1990s: A critical commentary. *Journal of Marriage and Family, 62,* 896–910.

(2007). Should government promote marriage? *Journal of Policy Analysis and Management, 26*(4), 956–960.

Furstenberg, F., Cook, T., Eccles, J., Elder, G. H., Jr., & Sameroff, A. (1999). *Managing to make it: Urban families and adolescent success.* Chicago: University of Chicago Press.

Gamoran, A. (2007). *Standards-based reform and the poverty gap: Lessons for No Child Left Behind.* Washington, DC: Brookings Institution.

Gamoran, A., & Hannigan, E. C. (2000). Algebra for everyone? Benefits of college-preparatory mathematics for students with diverse abilities in early secondary school. *Educational Evaluation and Policy Analysis, 22,* 241–254.

Gardner, S. (1993). Key issues in developing school linked, integrated services. *Education and Urban Society, 25,* 141–152.

Garmezy, N. (1985). Stress-resistant children: The search for protective factors. In J. E. Stevenson (Ed.), *Recent research in developmental psychopathology. Journal of Child Psychology and Psychiatry book supplement No. 4* (pp. 213–233). Oxford: Pergamon.

Gay Straight Alliance. (2009). www.gaystraightalliance.org.

Ge, X., Lorenz, F. O., Conger, R. D., Elder, G. H., & Simons, R. L. (1994). Trajectories of stressful life events and depressive symptoms during adolescence. *Developmental Psychology, 30,* 467–483.

Gecas, V., & Burke, P. J. (1995). Self and identity. In K. Cook, G. A. Fine, & J. S. House (Eds.), *Sociological perspectives on social psychology* (pp. 41–67). Needham Heights, MA: Allyn and Bacon.

Genesee, F., Lindholm-Leary, K. J., Saunders, W., & Christian, D. (2006). *Educating English language learners.* New York: Cambridge University Press.

Gibbs, W. W. (2005). Obesity: An overblown epidemic? *Scientific American, 292*(6), 70–77.

Gilligan, C. (1982). *In a different voice: Psychological theory and women's development.* Cambridge, MA: Harvard University Press.

Giordano, P. C. (2003). Relationships in adolescence. *Annual Review of Sociology, 29,* 257–281.

Giordano, P. C., Longmore, M. A., & Manning, W. D. (2006). Gender and the meanings of adolescent romantic relationships: A focus on boys. *American Sociological Review, 71,* 260–287.

Goffman, E. (1963). *Stigma: Notes on the management of spoiled identity.* Englewood Cliffs, NJ: Prentice Hall.

Goldin, C., & Katz, L. F. (2008). *The race between education and technology.* Cambridge, MA: Harvard University Press.

Goldsmith, P. A. (2004). Schools' racial mix, students' optimism, and the black-white and Latino-white achievement gaps. *Sociology of Education, 77,* 121–147.

Granger, R. C. (2008). After-school programs and academics: Implications for policy, practice, and research. *SRCD Social Policy Report, 22*(2), 3–20.

Greenberg, B. S., Brown, J. D., & Buerkel-Rothfuss, N. L. (Eds.). (1992). *Media, sex and the adolescent.* Cresskill, NJ: Hampton Press.

Greenfield, P., & Yan, Z. (2006). Children, adolescents, and the Internet: A new field of inquiry in developmental psychology. *Developmental Psychology, 3,* 391–394.

Grotevant, H. D. (1998). Adolescent development in family contexts. In W. Damon (Ed.), *Handbook of child psychology* (pp. 1097–1147). New York: Wiley.

Guldi, M., Page, M. E., & Stevens, A. H. (2006). *Family background and children's transitions to adulthood over time.* MacArthur Network on Transitions to Adulthood Working Paper Series. www.transad.pop.upenn.edu/publications/wp.html.

Halpern, C. T., Udry, J. R., Campbell, B., & Suchindran, C. (1998). Effects of body fat on weight concerns, dating, and sexual activity: A longitudinal analysis of black and white adolescent girls. *Developmental Psychology, 35,* 721–736.

Hampden-Thompson, G., Warkentien, S., & Daniel, B. (2009). *Course credit accrual and dropping out of high school, by student characteristics* (NCES 2009–035). Washington, DC: U.S. Department of Education.

Harris, J. R. (1998). *The nurture assumption: Why children turn out the way that they do.* New York: Free Press.

Harris, K. M. (2008). *The National Longitudinal Study of Adolescent Health, Waves I & II, 1994–1996; Wave III, 2001–2002.* Chapel Hill, NC: Carolina Population Center, University of North Carolina at Chapel Hill.

Harris, K. M., Duncan, G. J., & Boisjoly, J. (2002). Evaluating the role of "nothing to lose" attitudes on risky behavior in adolescence. *Social Forces, 80,* 1005–1039.

Harrison, K. (2001). Ourselves, our bodies: Thin-ideal, media, self-discrepancies, and eating disorder symptomatology in adolescents. *Journal of Social and Clinical Psychology, 20,* 289–323.

Hartup, W. (1993). Adolescents and their friends. *New Directions in Child Development, 60,* 3–22.

Hartup, W., & Stevens, N. (1997). Friendships and adaptation in the life course. *Psychological Bulletin, 121,* 355–370.

Heckman, J. (2006). Skill formation and the economics of investing in disadvantaged children. *Science, 312*(5782), 1900–1902.

Hegerty, P. (2009). Toward an LGBT-informed paradigm of children who break gender norms. *Developmental Psychology, 45,* 895–900.

Hess, F. M. (Ed.). (2008). *The future of educational entrepreneurship: Possibilities for school reform.* Cambridge, MA: Harvard Education Press.

Higgins, E. T. (1989). Self-discrepancy theory: What patterns of self-beliefs cause people to suffer? *Advances in Experimental Social Psychology, 22,* 93–136.

Hirschman, C. (2001). The educational enrollment of immigrant youth: A test of the segmented-assimilation hypothesis. *Demography, 38,* 317–336.

Holleran-Steiker, L. K. (2008). Making drug and alcohol prevention relevant: Adapting evidence-based curricula to unique adolescent cultures. *Family & Community Health, 31,* S52–S60.

Howard, J. (1995). Social cognition. In K. Cook, G. A. Fine, & J. S. House (Eds.), *Sociological perspectives on social psychology* (pp. 90–117). Needham Heights, MA: Allyn and Bacon.

Hoxby, C. (2004). *College choices: The economics of where to go, when to go, and how to pay for it.* Chicago: University of Chicago Press.

Hussong, A. M., Hicks, R. E., Levy, S. A., & Curran, P. J. (2001). Specifying the relations between affect and heavy alcohol use among young adults. *Journal of Abnormal Psychology, 110,* 449–461.

Huston, A. C. (2005). Connecting the science of child development to public policy. *SRCD Social Policy Report, 19*(4), 3–18.

(2008). From research to policy and back. *Child Development, 79,* 1–12.

Hyde, J. S., & Kling, K. C. (2001). Women, motivation, and achievement. *Psychology of Women Quarterly, 25,* 364–378.

Ingersoll, R. M. (2005). The problem of underqualified teachers: A sociological perspective. *Sociology of Education, 78*, 175–178.

Jessor, R., Van Den Bos, J., Vanderryn, J., Costa, F. M., & Turbin, M. S. (1995). Protective factors in adolescent problem behavior: Moderator effects and developmental change. *Developmental Psychology, 31*, 923–933.

Johnson, M. K., Crosnoe, R., & Elder, G. H., Jr. (2001). Students' attachment and academic engagement: The role of ethnicity. *Sociology of Education, 74*, 318–340.

Joyner, K., & Udry, J. R. (2000). You don't bring me anything but down: Adolescent romance and depression. *Journal of Health and Social Behavior, 41*, 369–391.

Kahlenberg, R. (2001). *All together now: Creating middle class schools through public choice.* Washington, DC: Brookings Institution.

Karen, D. (2005). No child left behind? Sociology ignored! *Sociology of Education, 78*, 165–182.

Katz, L., & Autor, D. (1999). Changes in the wage structure and earnings inequality. In O. Ashenfelter & D. Card (Eds.), *The handbook of labor economics, Vol. 3a* (pp. 1462–1558). Amsterdam: North-Holland.

Kearney, M. C. (2006). *Girls make media.* New York: Routledge.

Kingston, P. W., Hubbard, R., Lapp, B., Schroeder, P., & Wilson, J. (2003). Why education matters. *Sociology of Education, 76*, 53–70.

Kinney, D. (1999). From "headbangers" to "hippies": Delineating adolescents' active attempts to form an alternative peer culture. *New Directions for Child and Adolescent Development, 84*, 21–35.

Kirst, M. (1994). Equity for children: Linking education and children's services. *Educational Policy, 8*, 583–590.

Kozol, J. (1991). *Savage inequalities.* New York: Crown.

Kreager, D. A. (2008). Guarded borders: Interracial teen dating and difficulties with peers. *Social Forces, 87*, 887–910.

La Greca, A. M., & Lopez, N. (1998). Social anxiety among adolescents: Linkages with peer relations and friendships. *Journal of Abnormal Child Psychology, 26*, 83–94.

Labaree, D. (1988). *The making of an American high school: The credentials market and the Central High School of Philadelphia, 1838–1939.* New Haven, CT: Yale University Press.

Labaree, D. F. (1997). Public goods, private goods: The American struggle over educational goals. *American Educational Research Journal, 34*, 39–81.

Lareau, A. (1989). *Home advantage: Social class and parental intervention in elementary education.* London: Falmer.

Larson, R. W., Richards, M. H., Moneta, G., Holmbeck, G., & Duckett, E. (1996). Changes in adolescents' daily interactions with their families from ages 10 to 18: Disengagement and transformation. *Developmental Psychology, 32,* 744–754.

Lawrence, R. G., & Birkland, T. A. (2004). Guns, Hollywood, and school safety: Defining the school-shooting problem across public arenas. *Social Science Quarterly, 85,* 1193–1207.

Leadbeater, B., Blatt, S., & Quinlan, D. (1995). Gender-linked vulnerabilities to depressive symptoms, stress, and problem behaviors in adolescents. *Journal of Research on Adolescence, 5,* 1–29.

Lee, V. E., & Ready, D. D. (2007). *Schools-within-schools: Possibilities and pitfalls of high school reform.* New York: Teachers College Press.

Lee, V. E., & Smith, J. B. (1997). High school size: Which works best and for whom? *Educational Evaluation and Policy Analysis, 19,* 205–227.

Lee, V. E., Smith, J., & Croninger, R. (1997). How high school organization influences the equitable distribution of learning in mathematics and science. *Sociology of Education, 70,* 128–150.

Lightfoot, S. L. (1983). *The good high school: Portraits of character and culture.* New York: Basic Books.

Link, B. G., & Phelan, J. C. (2001). Conceptualizing stigma. *Annual Review of Sociology, 27,* 363–385.

Lucas, S. R. (1999). *Tracking inequality: Stratification in American high schools.* New York: Teachers College Press.

Ma, X. (2001). Participation in advanced mathematics: Do expectation and influence of students, peers, teachers, and parents matter? *Contemporary Educational Psychology, 26,* 132–146.

Mahoney, J. L., Larson, R. W., & Eccles, J. S. (Eds.). (2005). *Organized activities as contexts of development: Extracurricular activities, after-school and community programs.* New York: Routledge.

Markus, H., & Nurius, P. (1986). Possible selves. *American Psychologist, 41,* 954–969.

Markus, H. R., Uchida, Y., Omoregie, H., Townsend, S. S. M., & Kitayama, S. (2006). Going for the gold: Models of agency in Japanese and American contexts. *Psychological Science, 17,* 103–112.

Marsh, H. (1987). The big fish little pond effect on academic self-concept. *Journal of Educational Psychology, 79,* 280–295.

Marsh, H., & Hau, K. T. (2003). Big-fish-little-pond effect on academic self-concept. A cross-cultural (26 country) test of the negative effects of academically selective schools. *American Psychologist, 58,* 364–376.

Marsh, H., Trautwein, U., Ludtke, O., Koller, O., & Baumert, J. (2005). Academic self-concept, interest, grades, and standardized test scores: Reciprocal effects models of causal ordering. *Child Development, 76,* 397–416.

Masten, A. S., & Coatsworth, J. D. (1998). The development of competence in favorable and unfavorable environments: Lessons from research on successful children. *American Psychologist, 53,* 205–220.

McCartney, K., Burchinal, M., & Bub, K. (Eds.). (2006). Best practices in quantitative methods for developmentalists. *Monographs of the Society for Research in Child Development, 71*(3).

McFarland, D. A. (2001). Student resistance: How the formal and informal organization of classrooms facilitate everyday forms of student defiance. *American Journal of Sociology, 107,* 612–678.

McFarland, D. A., & Pals, H. (2005). Motives and contexts of identity change: A case for network effects. *Social Psychology Quarterly, 68,* 289–315.

McLoyd, V. (1990). The impact of economic hardship on black families and children: Psychological distress, parenting, and socioemotional development. *Child Development, 61,* 311–346.

McNeely, C., Nonnemaker, J., & Blum, R. (2002). Promoting student connectedness to school: Evidence from the National Longitudinal Study of Adolescent Health. *Journal of School Health, 72,* 138–146.

Meier, S., Kohn, A., Darling-Hammond, L., Sizer, T., & Wood, G. (2004). *Many children left behind: How the No Child Left Behind Act is damaging our children and our schools.* Boston: Beacon.

Merton, R. K. (1957). *Social theory and social structure.* New York: Free Press.

Mickelson, R. (2001). Subverting Swann: Tracking as second generation segregation in Charlotte, NC. *American Educational Research Journal, 38,* 215–252.

Miller, K., Sabo, D., Farrell, M., Barnes, G., & Melnick, M. (1994). Athletic participation and sexual behavior in adolescents: The different worlds of boys and girls. *Journal of Health and Social Behavior, 39,* 108–123.

Millstein, S. G. (1988). *The potential of school-linked centers to promote adolescent health and development.* Washington, DC: Carnegie.

Milner, M. (2004). *Freaks, geeks, and cool kids: American teenagers, schools, and the culture of consumption.* New York: Routledge.

Mirowsky, J., & Ross, C. E. (2003). *Social causes of psychological distress, 2nd edition.* New York: Aldine de Gruyter.

Modell, J. (1989). *Into one's own: From youth to adulthood in the United States, 1920–1975.* Berkeley: University of California Press.

Moody, J. (2001). Race, school integration, and friendship segregation in America. *American Journal of Sociology, 107,* 679–716.

Morgan, S. L. (2005). *On the edge of commitment: Educational attainment and race in the United States.* Stanford, CA: Stanford University Press.

Mosteller, F. (1995). The Tennessee study of class size in the early school grades. *The Future of Children, 5,* 113–127.

Muller, C. (2001). Adolescent Health and Academic Achievement Study. Population Research Center, University of Texas at Austin. www.prc. utexas.edu/ahaa/index.html.

National Academy of Sciences. (2007). *Rising above the gathering storm: Energizing and employing America for a brighter economic future.* Washington, DC: National Academies Press.

National Center for Education Statistics. (2007). Overview of public elementary and secondary students, staff, schools, school districts, revenues, and expenditures. http://nces.ed.gov/pubs2007/overview04/.

National Coalition of LGBT Health. (2009). Healthy People 2010: Companion document for lesbian, gay, bisexual, and transgender health. http://www. nalgap.org/PDF/Resources/HP2010CDLGBTHealth.pdf

National Commission on Excellence in Education. (1983). *A nation at risk: The imperative for educational reform.* Washington, DC: U.S. Department of Education.

National Institute of Diabetes and Digestive and Kidney Diseases. (2009). Statistics related to overweight and obesity. http://win.niddk.nih.gov/ statistics/.

Nichols, J. D., & White, J. (2001). Impact of peer networks on achievement of high school algebra students. *Journal of Educational Research, 94*, 267–273.

Ogbu, J. (1991). Low performance as an adaptation: The case of blacks in Stockton, California. In M. A. Gibson & J. Ogbu (Eds.), *Minority status and schooling* (pp. 249–285). New York: Grand.

Parke, R. D., & O' Neil, R. (1999). Social relationships across contexts: Family-peer linkages. In W. A. Collins & B. Laursen (Eds.), *Minnesota Symposium on Child Psychology, Vol. 30* (pp. 211–239). Hillsdale, NJ: Erlbaum.

Pfiefer, J. H., Brown, C. S., & Juvonen, J. (2007). Teaching tolerance in schools: Lessons learned since Brown v. Board of Education about the development and reduction of children's prejudice. *SRCD Social Policy Report, 21*(2), 3–17.

Piaget, J. (1955). *The child's construction of reality.* London: Routledge.

Pinhey, T. R., Rubinstein, D. H., & Colfax, R. S. (1997). Overweight and unhappiness: The reflected self-appraisal hypothesis reconsidered. *Social Science Quarterly, 78*, 747–755.

Pipher, M. (1994). *Reviving Ophelia: Saving the selves of adolescent girls.* New York: Ballantine.

Plank, S. (2000). *Finding one's place: Teaching styles and peer relations in diverse classrooms.* New York: Teachers College Press.

Plank, S. B., & Jordan, W. J. (2001). Effects of information, guidance, and actions on postsecondary destinations: A study of talent loss. *American Educational Research Journal, 38*, 947–979.

Powell, A. G., Farrar, E., & Cohen, D. K. (1985). *The shopping mall high school: Winners and losers in the educational marketplace.* Boston: Houghton Mifflin.

Prinstein, M. J., & La Greca, A. M. (2002). Peer crowd affiliation and internalizing distress in adolescence: A longitudinal follow-back study. *Journal of Research on Adolescence, 12,* 325–351.

Puhl, R., & Brownell, K. D. (2001). Bias, discrimination, and obesity. *Obesity Research, 9,* 788–805.

Radloff, L. S., & Locke, B. S. (1986). The community mental health assessment survey and the CES-D scale. In M. M. Weissman, J. K. Meyers, & C. E. Ross (Eds.), *Community surveys of psychiatric disorders* (pp. 177–189). New Brunswick, NJ: Rutgers University Press.

Radziwon, C. D. (2003). The effects of peers' beliefs on 8th-grade students' identification with school. *Journal of Research in Childhood Education, 17,* 236–249.

Raver, C. C., Jones, S. M., Li-Grining, C., Metzger, M., Smallwood, K., & Sardin, L. (2008). Improving preschool classroom processes: Preliminary findings from a randomized trial implemented in Head Start settings. *Early Childhood Research Quarterly, 23,* 10–26.

Raywid, M A. (1985). Family choice arrangements in public schools: A review of the literature. *Review of Educational Research, 55*(4), 435–467.

Resnick, M. D., Bearman, P. S., Blum, R. W., Bauman, K. E., Harris, K. M., Jones, J., Tabor, J., Beuhring, T., Sieving, R. E., Shew, M., Ireland, M., Bearinger, L. H., & Udry, J. R. (1997). Protecting adolescents from harm: Findings from the National Longitudinal Study of Adolescent Health. *Journal of the American Medical Association, 278,* 823–832.

Riegle-Crumb, C. (2006). The path through math: Course sequences and academic performance at the intersection of race/ethnicity and gender. *American Journal of Education, 113,* 101–122.

Riegle-Crumb, C., Farkas, G., & Muller, C. (2006). The role of gender and friendship in advanced course-taking. *Sociology of Education, 79,* 206–228.

Riegle-Crumb, C., Muller, C., Frank, K., & Schiller, K. (2005). National Longitudinal Study of Adolescent Health: Wave III education data codebook. Carolina Population Center, University of North Carolina at Chapel Hill. http://www.laits.utexas.edu/ahaa/docs/Weights_2005_Riegle-Crumb.pdf.

Roeser, R., & Eccles, J. S. (2000). Schooling and mental health. In A. J. Sameroff, M. Lewis, &S. Miller (Eds.), *Handbook of developmental psychopathology* (pp. 135–156). Dordrecht, Netherlands: Kluwer.

Rosenbaum, J. (2001). *Beyond college for all: Career paths for the forgotten half.* New York: Russell Sage.

Rosewater, A. (2009). *Learning to play and playing to learn: Organized sports and educational outcomes.* Oakland, CA: Team Up For Youth.

Ross, C. E. (1994). Overweight and depression. *Journal of Health and Social Behavior, 33,* 63–78.

Rudolph, K. D., & Conley, C. S. (2005). The socioemotional costs and benefits of social-evaluative concerns: Do girls care too much? *Journal of Personality, 73,* 115–138.

Russell, S. T., & Joyner, K. (2001). Adolescent sexual orientation and suicide risk: Evidence from a national study. *American Journal of Public Health, 91,* 1276–1281.

Russell, S. T., McGuire, J. K., Lee, S.-A., Larriva, J. C., Laub, C., & California Safe Schools Coalition. (2008). Adolescent perceptions of school safety for students with lesbian, gay, bisexual, and transgender parents. *Journal of Gay and Lesbian Issues in Education, 5,* 11–27.

Russell, S. T., & Sigler-Andrews, N. (2003). Adolescent sexuality and positive youth development. In D. Perkins, L. Borden, J. Keith, & F. A. Villarruel (Eds.), *Positive youth development: Beacons, challenges, and opportunities* (pp. 146–161). Thousand Oaks, CA: Sage.

Rutter, M., Maughan, B., Mortimer, P., & Ouston, J. (1979). *Fifteen thousand hours: Secondary schools and their effects on children.* Cambridge, MA: Harvard University Press.

Ryan, A. M. (2001). The peer group as a context for the development of young adolescent motivation and achievement. *Child Development, 72,* 1135–1150.

Sameroff, A. (1983). Developmental systems: Context and evolution. In P. Mussen (Ed.), *Handbook of child psychology, Vol. 1* (pp. 237–294). New York: Wiley.

Savin-Williams, R. C., & Cohen, K. M. (1996). *The lives of lesbians, gays, and bisexuals: Children to adults.* Fort Worth, TX: Harcourt Brace.

Sawhill, I., Weaver, K., Haskins, R., & Kane, A. (Eds.). (2002). *Welfare reform and beyond.* Washington, DC: Bookings Institution.

Scaramella, L. V., Conger, R. D., & Simons, R. L. (1999). Parental protective influences and gender-specific increases in adolescent internalizing and externalizing problems. *Journal of Research on Adolescence, 9,* 111–142.

Schiller, K., & Hunt, D. (2003). Accumulated disadvantages: Racial and social class differences in high school mathematics course trajectories. Paper presented at the American Education Research Association annual meeting, Chicago.

Schmidt, W. H., McKnight, C. C., Houang, R. T., Wang, H. C., Wiley, D. T., Cogan, L. S., & Wolfe, R. G. (2001). *Why schools matter: A cross-national comparison of curriculum and learning.* San Francisco: Jossey-Bass.

Schneider, B. (2007). *Forming a college-going community in U.S. schools.* Seattle: Bill and Melinda Gates Foundation.

Schneider, B., & Coleman, J. S. (Eds.). (1993). *Parents, their children, and schools.* Boulder, CO: Westview.

Schneider, B., & Stevenson, D. (1999). *The ambitious generation: America's teenagers, motivated but directionless.* New Haven, CT: Yale University Press.

Schneider, B., Swanson, C. B., & Riegle-Crumb, C. (1999). Opportunities for learning: Course sequences and positional advantages. *Social Psychology of Education, 2,* 25–53.

Schofield, J. W. (1995). Review of research on school desegregation's impact on elementary and secondary students. In J. A. Banks (Ed.), *Handbook of research on multicultural education* (pp. 597–616). New York: Macmillan.

Schuman, H. (1995). Attitudes, beliefs, and behaviors. In K. Cook, G. A. Fine, & J. S. House (Eds.), *Sociological perspectives on social psychology* (pp. 68–89). Needham Heights, MA: Allyn and Bacon.

Sedikides, C. (1993). Assessment, enhancement, and verification determinants of the self-evaluation process. *Journal of Personality and Social Psychology, 65,* 317–338.

Shettle, C., Roey, S., Mordica, J., Perkins, R., Nord, C., Teodorovic, J., Brown, J., Lyons, M., Averett, C., & Kastberg, D. (2007). *The nation's report card: America's high school graduates* (NCES 2007–467). Washington, DC: U.S. Department of Education, National Center for Education Statistics.

Smetana, J. (2008). It's 10 o'clock: Do you know where your children are? Recent advances in understanding parental monitoring and adolescents' information management. *Child Development Perspectives, 2,* 19–25.

Spencer, R. (2006). Understanding the mentoring process between adolescents and adults. *Youth & Society, 37,* 287–315.

Stanton-Salazar, R. D. (2001). *Manufacturing hope and despair: The school and kin support networks of U.S.-Mexican youth.* New York: Teachers College Press.

Steinberg, L. D. (2001). We know some things: Parent-adolescent relationships in retrospect and prospect. *Journal of Research on Adolescence, 11,* 1–20.

  (2008). A social neuroscience perspective on adolescent risk-taking. *Developmental Review, 28,* 78–106.

Steinberg, L. D., Brown, B. B., & Dornbusch, S. M. (1996). *Beyond the classroom: Why school reform has failed and what parents need to do.* New York: Simon & Schuster.

Steinberg, L. D., Dornbusch, S. M., & Brown, B. B. (1992). Ethnic differences in adolescent achievement: An ecological perspective. *American Psychologist, 47,* 723–729.

Steinberg, L. D., & Morris, A. S. (2001). Adolescent development. *Annual Review of Psychology, 52,* 83–100.

Stevenson, D. L., Schiller, K. S., & Schneider, B. (1994). Sequences of opportunities for learning. *Sociology of Education, 67,* 184–198.

Stone, M. R., Barber, B. L., & Eccles, J. S. (2008). We knew them when: Sixth grade characteristics that predict adolescent high school social identities. *Journal of Early Adolescence, 8,* 304–328.

Stryker, S. (1987). Identity theory: Developments and extensions. In K. Yardley & T. Holmes (Eds.), *Self and identity: Psychosocial perspectives* (pp. 89–104). New York: Wiley.

Sutherland, E. (1947). *Principles of criminology.* Philadelphia: Lippincott.

Swann, W. B., Jr., Stein-Seroussi, A., & Giesler, B. (1992). Why people self-verify. *Journal of Personality and Social Psychology, 62,* 392–401.

Taylor, C. (1989). *Sources of the self: The making of the modern identity.* Cambridge, MA: Harvard University Press.

Taylor, S. E. (1998). The social being in social psychology. In D. T. Gilbert, S. T. Fiske, & G. Lindzey (Eds.), *The handbook of social psychology, Vol. 1* (pp. 58–95). Boston: McGraw-Hill.

Thies, K. M. (1999). Identifying the educational implications of chronic illness in school children. *Journal of School Health, 69,* 392–397.

Thomas, W. I., & Thomas, D. S. (1928). *The child in America: Behavior problems and programs.* New York: Knopf.

Turner, S., & Bound, J. (2006). *Cohort crowding: How resources affect collegiate attainment.* National Bureau of Economic Research Working Paper Series 12424.

Tyson, K., Darity, W., & Castellino, D. R. (2005). It's not a "black thing": Understanding the burden of acting white and other dilemmas of high achievement. *American Sociological Review, 70,* 582–605.

U.S. Department of Education. (2001). The No Child Left Behind Act of 2001. www.ed.gov/policy/elsec/leg/esea02/index.html.

Vreeman, R., & Carroll, A. (2007). A systematic review of school-based interventions to prevent bullying. *Archives of Pediatric and Adolescent Medicine, 161,* 78–88.

Watt, T. T. (2003). Are small schools and private schools better for adolescents' emotional adjustment? *Sociology of Education, 76,* 344–367.

Way, N., & Chu, J. (Eds.). (2003). *Adolescent boys.* New York: New York University Press.

Weinstein, R. (2002). *Reaching higher: The power of expectations in schooling.* Cambridge, MA: Harvard University Press.

Wells, A. S., Holme, J. J., Revilla, A. T., & Atanda, A. K. (2008). *Both sides now: The story of desegregation's graduates.* Berkeley: University of California Press.

Werner, E. E., & Smith, R. S. (1992). *Overcoming the odds: High risk children from birth to adulthood.* Ithaca, NY: Cornell University Press.

Wiseman, R. (2002). *Queen bees and wannabes: Helping your daughter survive cliques, gossip, boyfriends, and other realities of adolescence.* New York: Three Rivers.

Xie, H. (2005). Social aggression: Challenges and opportunities. *Social Development, 14,* 550–554.

Yeung, K. T., & Martin, J. L. (2003). The Looking Glass Self: An empirical test and elaboration. *Social Forces, 81,* 843–879.

Zhou, M. (1997). Growing up American: The challenge confronting immigrant children and children of immigrants. *Annual Review of Sociology, 23,* 63–95.

INDEX

Add Health, 13, 18–19, 48, 54–5, 66,
  68, 74, 86–7, 91, 93–5, 97–8,
  106, 109, 111, 115, 121, 123, 126,
  129–30, 142, 173, 187–8, 191–2,
  196, 204, 212–13, 219, 226, 228,
  236
Adler, Patricia, 41
Adolescent Society, The, 8, 40,
  See Coleman, James
Akerlof, George, 6, 46, 136
alcohol use, 54–5, 60, 104, 106, 109, 127,
  169, 192, 194, 196, 237
American Association of University
  Women report, 208

Barber, Bonnie, 5, 43–4, 46, 136
Bernhardt, Annette, 72
Beyond the Classroom. See Steinberg,
  Laurence
Body Project, The. See Brumberg, Joan
  Jacob
Bos, Henny, 117, 121
Brown, B. Bradford, 6, 43, 76, 133, 204
Brumberg, Joan Jacob, 62
Buchmann, Claudia, 208
Burke, Peter, 140

Carter, Prudence, 41
Catholic school effect, 227
Centers for Disease Control and
  Prevention, 121

Century of Difference. See Hout,
  Michael
cliques and crowds, 36, 42, 46, 52, 56, 77,
  83, 133–4, 136–7, 144, 147, 169,
  177, 204, 234
Coleman, James, 4–5, 8–9, 40–1, 45, 49,
  62, 75–7, 230, 250
Columbine High School, 9, 45, 220, 241
confounds, 92–5
coursework, academic, 4, 9, 47, 54, 67–8,
  90, 99, 211, 227–8

Differential Association Theory, 51, 58
disengagement, 105–7, 141–2, 194, 237
Divergent Paths. See Bernhardt, Annette
Dornbusch, Sanford, 6, 37, 43, 76
drinking. *See* alcohol use

Eccles, Jacquelynne, 5, 43–4, 46, 84, 204,
  211, 218, 231
Eckert, Penny, 43
Eder, Donna, 41–3
Elder, Glen H., Jr., 66
Elkind, David, 211
English language learners, 7, 214
Erikson, Erik, 138
extracurricular activities, 188, 193–4,
  197, 219, 252

Facebook, 23, 26, 33, 36, 71, 152
Fischer, Claude, 72–3

formal processes of schooling, 37–9,
  45–6, 63, 77–9, 84
Frank, Kenneth, 42, 55, 57, 136, 205
Freaks, Geeks, and Cool Kids. See Milner,
  Murray

Gamoran, Adam, 67, 211
gay. *See* lesbian/gay
gay-straight alliances, 222
genetics, 55, 94–5, 174
Gilligan, Carol, 208
Giordano, Peg, 42, 133–4
Goffman, Erving, 115–17, 140, 166
Goldin, Claudia, 72
Good High School, The. See Lightfoot,
  Sara Lawrence

Harris, Judith Rich, 49
Hegerty, Peter, 120, 216
homosexuality. *See* lesbian/gay
Hout, Michael, 72–3, 253

identity development, 142, 158–70
identity discrepancy, 20, 131, 139–42,
  158, 165–6, 168, 175, 183
identity, spoiled, 140, 165–7, 171,
  213, 254
immigration, 14, 20, 39, 51, 64, 66, 94,
  112, 215
individuation, 48, 211
informal processes of schooling, 38–9,
  45–7, 63, 77, 79, 233
information processing, 131–7, 143–57
integration, racial, 39, 78–9, 134
internalization, 51, 53, 57–8, 104, 106–7,
  141–2, 168, 203, 262
Into One's Own. See Modell, John

Johnson, Monica, 66, 213

Katz, Lawrence, 72, 254
Kearney, Mary Celeste, 224
Keeping It Real. See Carter, Prudence
Kinney, David, 43, 136
Kozol, Jonathan, 212

La Greca, Annette, 43
Lee, Valerie, 67, 226
lesbian/gay, 14, 19, 114, 117–21, 126–8,
  130, 140, 145, 189, 192–4, 196,
  207, 209, 215, 222, 236
Lightfoot, Sara Lawrence, 212
Looking Glass Self, 56, 104, 138, 164
Lucas, Sam, 68

Many Children Left Behind. See Meier,
  Deborah
marijuana, 107, 109–12, 124, 126, 192,
  196, 237
Marsh, Herbert, 84
McFarland, Daniel, 43, 136
Meier, Deborah, 219
mentors, 11, 79, 181–2, 186, 225, 230, 244
Merton, Robert, 105
Milner, Murray, 41–3, 136
Modell, John, 62
Morgan, Stephen, 68
Muller, Chandra, 14, 55, 57, 68, 97
multicultural education, 220, 223
MySpace, 23, 36, 71, 152

Nation at Risk, A, 3, 67
National Institutes of Health, 118–19
Newsweek, 45, 153, 232, 245
No Child Left Behind, 3, 7, 45, 68–9, 78,
  214, 216, 219, 230–1, 235
Nurture Assumption, The. See Harris,
  Judith Rich

obesity, 12, 14, 19, 74, 114, 116–22,
  124–6, 128, 130, 140, 145, 148,
  150–1, 153, 155, 163, 167, 189,
  192–3, 196, 207, 209, 215–16,
  221, 223, 227, 235–6, 250

parents, 11, 14, 16, 21–2, 40–1, 48–9,
  51, 59, 61, 64, 68, 77, 79, 88, 94,
  144–5, 155–7, 160, 166, 172,
  179–80, 182, 188, 191, 193–4,
  196, 211, 225, 230–1, 233–40,
  243–4

Peer Power. See Adler, Patricia
Piaget, Jean, 102, 132
PLUs, 133, 136–7, 143, 146–9, 151, 168, 172, 177–8, 218, 234
pot. *See* marijuana
poverty, 153, 214, 228, 236
Prinstein, Mitchell, 43
protective factors, 174–99

Race between Education and Technology, The. See Goldin, Claudia
race/ethnicity, 6, 15, 20, 39–40, 51, 55, 65–6, 68, 74, 79, 88–9, 94, 106, 112, 123, 160, 181, 185, 212–13, 216, 218, 227
religion, 185, 189
resilience, 174–99
returns to higher education, 13, 72, 75, 114
Reviving Ophelia, 208
Rising Above the Gathering Storm, 3, 67
risk amplification, 191–4, 196–7
Rudolph, Karen, 211
Russell, Stephen, 121
Rutter, Michael, 5, 45

same-sex attraction. *See* lesbian/gay
Savage Inequalities. See Kozol, Jonathan
Schneider, Barbara, 67, 97, 211, 230
school size, 226, 228
School Talk. See Eder, Donna
schools within schools movement, 226–8

self-enhancement, 168, 172
self-esteem, 79, 168, 223
self-medication, 104, 106–7, 142, 169, 197
self-verification, 141–2, 168–9, 172
services, health, 217
services, school-linked, 3, 7, 216–17, 225, 235, 240
skipping school. *See* truancy
social class, 6, 14–16, 20, 24, 51, 55, 69, 159, 170–3, 212–15, 218
social comparison, 153–7
social feedback, 143–53
socioeconomic status, 10, 15, 40, 43, 47, 55, 69, 84, 91, 94, 106, 112, 118, 123, 174, 212–13, 215, 232, 251
sports, 20, 44, 66, 103, 137, 184–5, 188–9, 194, 218–19
Stanton-Salazar, Ricardo, 68
Steinberg, Laurence, 6, 43, 49, 76–7, 204
stigma, 114
Sutherland, Edwin. *See* Differential Association Theory

Thomas, W. I., 12, 157
transitions, 40, 48, 64, 72, 211, 220, 236
truancy, 106–7, 109–12, 124, 126, 192–3, 196, 234, 237

U.S. Census, 14, 64, 72, 92–3
U.S. Department of Education, 97, 235

Who I Am Project, 17–18, 143, 158–64, 177, 181–3, 185